Also available at all good book stores

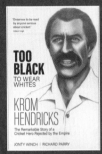

9781785318252

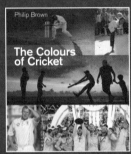

9781785319952

9781785318191

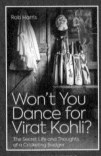

9781785317798

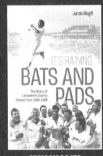

9781801500678

9781785319860

9781785318405

9781785317644

9781785316630

LAKER
& LOCK

LAKER & LOCK

The Odd Couple

CHRISTOPHER SANDFORD

First published by Pitch Publishing, 2022

Pitch Publishing
9 Donnington Park,
85 Birdham Road,
Chichester,
West Sussex,
PO20 7AJ
www.pitchpublishing.co.uk
info@pitchpublishing.co.uk

A CIP catalogue record is available for this book
from the British Library.

ISBN 978 1 80150 086 9

Typesetting and origination by Pitch Publishing
Printed and bound in India by Replika Press Pvt. Ltd.

Contents

To Adam

Acknowledgements

I OWE a debt a gratitude to many individuals who contributed to the shaping of this book. Most of them did so by kindly answering my questions about Jim Laker and Tony Lock, or by providing material on those great cricketers and their time. One or two others helped the cause more inadvertently, such as the gloriously feckless public officials of Washington state, where I mostly live, whose accordion-style cycle of lockdowns and other restraints at least provided an opportunity to write another book while waiting on our rulers' caprices, refurbished as these individuals now are into a sort of sanitary dictatorship devoted to the religion of health. Nonetheless, it goes without saying that neither our political masters, nor any of the names listed below, can be blamed for the shortcomings of the text (some of whose statistics have been rounded up or down for clarity's sake). They are mine alone.

For archive material, input or advice I should thank, professionally: AbeBooks; Jon Alexander; Alibris; *America*; Dennis Amiss; Arundel Wealth; Mike Atherton; Callum Berrill; Jack Birkenshaw; Bookfinder; Emma and Geoff Boycott; Simon Brand; the *Brazen Head*; Mike Brearley; the British Library; the British Newspaper Library; Jane Camillin; Central Lutheran; Church of St Mary le Ghyll; Emily Clark; Common Ground; CricketArchive; the *Cricketer International*; the Cricket Society;

the Cricket Society of Scotland; Sophie Cross; the *Daily Mail*; the Davenport Hotel; the late Ted Dexter; Emerald Downs; Essex CCC; Keith Fletcher; the General Register Office; Paul Godsland; the late Tom Graveney; Grumbles; Stephen Hall; Nigel Hancock; *Hedgehog Review*; the History Press; Robin Hobbs; Richard Holdridge; Jane Jamieson; Rob Kelly; Imran Khan; Leicestershire CCC; Barbara Levy; Limpsfield Church of England School; Limpsfield Parish Council; the Rev Sheena McMain; Christine McMorris; Malvern College; Mandalay Bay, Las Vegas; the MCC; the late Keith Miller; the Mitchell Library, Glasgow; *Modern Age*; the late Richard Morgan; the National Archives; National Gallery; Northamptonshire CCC; *The Oldie*; Peter and Jill Parfitt; Jim Parks; Pat Pocock; Nigel Popplewell; Sir Oliver Popplewell; Kevin Powell; Derek Pringle; the Radleian Society; Tim Reidy; Renton Public Library; Neil Robinson; Rebecca Romney; Sandy Cove Inn, Oregon; Seaside Library, Oregon; Seattle CC; Seattle Mariners; Robert Simonson; *The Spectator*; Micky Stewart; Andrew Stuart; Raman Subba Row; Surrey CCC; Surrey History Centre; Jon Surtees; Sussex CCC; Roger Tolchard; Derek Turner; Gavin Turner; University of Washington; Daniel Vernon; Vital Records; Western Australia Cricket Association; *Wisden Cricket Monthly*; and Simon Wright.

And personally: the Rev. Maynard Atik; Pete Barnes; the late Richie Benaud; Alison Bent; Rob Boddie; Creed Bratton; Robert and Hilary Bruce; Jon Burke; John Bush; Lincoln Callaghan; Don Carson; Steve Cropper; Celia Culpan; the late Deb Das; Chris Davies; Monty Dennison; Chris Difford; the Dowdall family; Barbara and the late John Dungee; Jon Filby; Lisa Fischer; Steve Fossen; Malcolm Galfe; Tony Gill; James Graham; Freddy Gray; Jeff and Rita Griffin; Steve and Jo Hackett; Duncan Hamilton; Alastair Hignell; Charles Hillman; Alex Holmes; Jo Jacobius; Mick Jagger; Julian James; Robin B. James; Jo Johnson; Lincoln

Kamell; Aslam Khan; Carol Lamb; Terry Lambert; Belinda Lawson; Eugene Lemcio; Todd Linse; the Lorimer family; Nick Lowe; Robert Dean Lurie; Les McBride; Dan McCarthy; the late Charles McIntosh; Dennis McNally; the Macris; Lee Mattson; Jim Meyersahm; Jerry Miller; Sheila Mohn; Yvette Montague; the Morgans; Harry Mount; Colleen and the late John Murray; Greg Nowak; the late Chuck Ogmund; Phil Oppenheim; Valya Page; Robin and Lucinda Parish; Owen Paterson; Bill Payne; Peter Perchard; Marlys and the late Chris Pickrell; Roman Polanski; Robert and Jewell Prins; the Prins family; Ailsa Rushbrooke; Rupert Rushbrooke; Debbie Saks; the late Sefton Sandford; Sue Sandford; Peter Scaramanga; Danny Seraphine; Silver Platters; Fred and Cindy Smith; the Smith family; Debbie Standish; the Stanley family; David Starkey; the late Thaddeus Stuart; Jack Surendranath; Belinda and Ian Taylor; Matt Thacker; Huw Turberville; the late Ben and Mary Tyvand; William Underhill; Derek Underwood; Diana Villar; Ross Viner; Lisbeth Vogl; Phil Walker; the late Charlie Watts; Alan and Rogena White; Debbie Wild; the Willis Fleming family; the late Aaron Wolf; Heng and Lang Woon; the Zombies.

My deepest thanks, as always, to Karen and Nicholas Sandford.

C.S.
2022

Let them loiter in pleasure, or toilfully spin
— I gather them in, I gather them in.

Park Benjamin, *The Old Sexton*

Ashes to ashes, dust to dust. If Laker
doesn't get you, Lockie must.

Popular refrain of
English cricket grounds in 1956

1

The Copper and the Delinquent

FOR ONCE the sun was shining in an otherwise dismally wet season at the Kennington Oval on the morning of Wednesday, 16 May 1956 as the opening pair of Ian Johnson's touring Australian side went out to bat against Surrey. Irrespective of who should win or lose it, the three-day match seemed to be set for a run feast. The captains had thumbed the wicket in a listless sort of way before they tossed, but Johnson didn't hesitate to bat when he won. Earlier in the week the tourists had scored 547/8 declared against a strong Nottinghamshire attack at Trent Bridge. At one stage in the match, Colin McDonald, on his way to a score of 195, had unleashed a stinging cover drive that had hit the pavilion fence and bounced back almost to the bowler's hand. On its ferocious passage from the bat, Nottinghamshire's substitute fielder Jack Kelly had rashly put one of his hands in the way of the ball and was so bruised by the encounter he played no more cricket for a month.

Surrey had chosen to rest their stalwart medium-pacer Alec Bedser, down with gastric trouble, for the Australian match. Broad-shouldered, huge-handed and consistently accurate, Bedser had returned figures of 7-41 and 7-28 for his county in a fixture earlier in the week against Glamorgan. His absence was keenly felt that bright spring morning at The Oval. As Keith Miller strode through the ground's Hobbs Gates shortly before ten o'clock, he remembered looking down to see a newspaper hoarding proclaiming 'ODDS ON AUSSIES', and, on a neighbouring stall, 'STERLING CRISIS: LATEST' – 'two of the classic headlines of the England of that time', he later remarked, and perhaps both still as pertinent today as they were nearly 70 years ago.

Apart from the overall balance of power between the two teams that morning, it has to be said that Surrey's 34-year-old Jim Laker was an unlikely candidate as the destroyer of the highly regarded opposition batsmen. A somewhat lugubrious figure at the best of times, Laker had arrived at the ground after a sleepless night helping to nurse both of his infant daughters through a bad case of the flu. After inspecting the wicket he'd gone on to announce that his arthritic spinning finger was giving him particular gyp that day, and that on the whole he would prefer not to play. Not for the first time in their long association, his captain, 38-year-old Stuart Surridge, had had to talk him round. In the event Surridge threw Laker the ball after just 50 minutes' play, at which point the tourists' score stood at 60 without loss. He kept bowling unchanged for the next four and a half hours, at the end of which the visitors were all out for 259 and his own analysis read 46-18-88-10. It was only the second time in cricket history that an English bowler had taken all ten Australian wickets in an innings, and the last occasion, also at The Oval, had come in 1878.

Even in the midst of the rapidly unfolding drama, with crowds racing in to the ground to see possible history in the making, Laker contained his excitement. *The Times*'s correspondent left an enduring picture of the off-spinner's essentially stoical approach to his craft. 'He came on to bowl, broad of beam and red-faced, and he continued to the end, completely unemotional, his shoulders hunched. Always he hitched up his trousers, always he licked his fingers. His run-up never varied, his legs hardly bending at the knees, his strides short.' Laker was briefly troubled by Miller during the afternoon session, but even then he failed to be rattled. 'I wasn't unduly worried since Keith tended not to linger on these occasions.' Surrey gained a lead of 88 on the first innings, due in part to Laker's score of 43, including two fours and a six in one over bowled by the Australian captain.

The tourists came out to bat a second time. They managed just 107 all out. Laker contented himself with 2-42, while his 26-year-old slow bowling partner, the left-handed Tony Lock, took 7-49. Critics often remarked on the striking difference between Surrey's so-called spin twins, in attitude as well as technique. 'As soon as Lock began to bowl straighter and to a fuller length,' E.W. Swanton wrote in the *Daily Telegraph*, 'he had the Australians in continual distress. There was venomous spin, a stark Spofforthian hostility, and threatening fielding to his own bowling.'

Keith Miller once said that facing Laker and Lock had been like interacting with a well-groomed Crufts champion at one end and a rabid pit bull at the other. Miller also remembered that at one stage at The Oval he'd been taking guard against Laker while Stuart Surridge was 'bollocking Lock as they stood there in the leg trap, telling him to bowl tighter the next over, and after about the third flying fuck-you of the exchange I pulled back from the wicket and told the umpire I wasn't going to bat with that sort of language ringing in my ears'. And this was a former Aussie Rules football player and wartime bomber pilot. Perhaps it was all just an astute bit of man-motivation on Surridge's part.

Surrey duly won the match by ten wickets, becoming the first county to beat an Australian touring side since C.B. Fry's Hampshire in 1912. No one invaded the pitch, nor showed any particular emotion at the result. In due course Surrey's president Lord Tedder presented Laker with a cheque for £50 and the match ball. The *News Chronicle* in turn signed him up for a series of instructional articles, and the manufacturers of the sports drink Lucozade splashed his face on advertising posters up and down the country, over the slogan, 'Sunny Jim takes 10 wickets for 88 runs. How's that for sustained energy?' In his quiet way, Laker admitted he was 'quite pleased' by it all.

Lock was not. For his own efforts against Australia he collected only his standard match fee of £17, or roughly £160 in today's money. There were no ghosted newspaper articles, and no advertisers came calling to solicit his services. More to the point, Lock was vocally unhappy to again take what seemed to him a subordinate role to Laker, and particularly so when the press came to compare their first-innings returns against Australia: no wickets for 100 and all ten for 88 respectively. At one stage in the proceedings, Lock had been wheeling away from the less desirable Vauxhall End to Keith Miller, and Miller hit him high and hard straight to Surrey's all-rounder Dennis Cox at deep extra cover. The score at that point was about 230/9, and Laker had taken all nine. Cox later admitted that he'd taken a moment to assess the situation as the ball hung in the air above him, and then decided to drop the catch in as subtle a way as possible. Lock was not amused.

'There were strong words spoken in the dressing room,' Cox admitted, still wincing at the memory many years later. 'To say Lockie was disgruntled would be a major understatement. The man's competitiveness ran off the chart. I saw him with Jim on many occasions when they had what appeared to be a perfectly normal and amiable conversation. After Laker left, Tony would say to me, in effect, "I certainly set that bugger straight," or, "I let him have it."'

It seemed to both Cox and others that whenever Lock so much as pulled on a pair of whites and went out to play either for Surrey or England, knowing that Laker was in the same team and that 'Sunny Jim' would as likely as not be the centre of attention, his attitude went beyond mere insecurity and touched what Cox called 'almost straitjacket heights'. In the course of a long dinner in May 1989, Lock genially informed me, 'Jim and I sometimes competed with each other as much as with the other buggers [the opposition],' but that on the whole this had been a 'bloody good thing' for both them and their team. Other contemporary reports tend to support this view.

Certainly 1956 was another highly successful year for Surrey, who had already won the County Championship the last four seasons running. By a happy coincidence, it also happened to be Jim Laker's benefit year. The county's programme had got off to a brisk start in late-April Cambridge, where they quickly disposed of the university side. The 20-year-old Ted Dexter was making his first-class debut for the students, and was bowled for nought early on the first morning, possibly contributing to the poor impression Laker had of him for much of the next ten years. Surrey then went down to Lord's and fell to a strong MCC side, drew at home to Derbyshire, somehow lost away against lowly Northants, but then recovered to beat Glamorgan, the tourists, and Leicestershire in quick succession. Following that they surprisingly lost to Nottinghamshire, Lock taking figures of 8-81 and 5-63, but Surridge showed his mettle as a captain when he promptly called his team together and told them, 'There's one column in the championship table that means everything. Far better to have 100 points in it and a few defeats thrown in than 90 points from the same number of matches and an unbeaten record.' Lock interpreted this remark as a mandate to 'always attack the fucking batsman', a credo of which he needed little further persuasion.

Surrey then went on to not so much beat as annihilate Gloucestershire, whom they bowled out on their own field for 52. In their first nine matches of the season, Laker and Lock had taken 43 and 48 wickets respectively, or roughly five each per match. Just by way of comparison, Somerset's highly regarded left-arm spinner Jack Leach took a total of 17 wickets in his ten first-class matches in the 2021 home season, and a further 27 in six overseas Tests against Sri Lanka and India, for an overall success rate about half that of his two England predecessors.

June 1956 ushered in the rain, and England began a five-Test series with Australia to which we'll return later. Over the next ten weeks Surrey played 17 more three-day County Championship matches. They won 13 of them, lost two and drew two. In the middle of June the county hosted Yorkshire at The Oval in Laker's testimonial match. It rained torrentially on the first day, and neither side's batsmen loitered for long after that. Laker took six wickets in the match and Lock nine. They both faced a gauntlet of admiring schoolboys when arriving at the Hobbs Gates for each day's play. Surrey had batsmen of the calibre of Peter May, Bernie Constable and 25-year-old Ken Barrington at their disposal that season; Peter Loader and Alec Bedser were in charge of the seam bowling; and in Arthur McIntyre they enjoyed the services of a classically neat wicketkeeper and a controlled cyclone with the bat. Some critics thought Surrey's strongest card was their never-say-die captain, but Lock didn't agree. With his lifelong tendency to see himself as a victim of authority, he frequently thought Surridge guilty of bullying him. 'I'll miss him more in the field than as a skipper,' Lock wrote by way of a tribute on Surridge's retirement. 'Apparently his theory was that Jim Laker as a bowler responded to the kid-glove treatment whereas I needed the "hammer". He thought I bowled better when angry. I can't say I agree.'

Surridge himself confirmed at least some of this suspicion when he later said:

> If you wanted Tony to go you had to give him a few swear-words. But with Jim, one harsh word and he was finished.

I swore at him only once and he couldn't bowl for an hour. Couldn't bowl. Had no idea what was going on. With Jim you had to encourage him – 'Come on, Jim. Get it going.' He wasn't so much angry that I had sworn as upset. He just couldn't stand that sort of approach at all.

In April 1956 the Brylcreem company, latterly popularised by Denis Compton, had announced it would award a silver cup and a cheque for £100 for the best bowling performance by an Englishman that season. Laker must have thought the prize was all but resting safely in his pocket after his haul against the Australians, but then just three weeks later Nottinghamshire's 28-year-old off-spinner Ken Smales went on to take all ten Gloucestershire wickets for 66 in a match at Stroud. Following that Lock in turn found himself bowling for Surrey against Kent on a damp wicket at Blackheath. Laker was again resting his spinning finger that game, which was played on a pitch *The Times* described as 'offering the bounce of a capricious trampoline'. Lock helped himself to a return of 6-29 in the first innings, and 10-54 in the second. That might have seemed to settle the issue with Brylcreem – not a natural patron, it has to be said, for the balding left-armer – but just 19 days later Laker went out to bowl for his country in the fourth Test at Old Trafford. His second innings analysis read 51.2-23-53-10. It was the fourth all-ten return by an English spinner in just over two months, and it meant that he'd won the sponsor's money by the margin of a single run. Shortly afterwards, Lock wrote, 'Naturally, I was disappointed by my own lack of success at Manchester, but Jim's triumph, and England's great win made amends … As we walked off our captain Peter May came alongside me and said, "Well bowled, Tony. Forget the scorebook. You played your part, too."'

Could this be the moment for some gracious word of thanks on Lock's part, one victorious England cricketer to another, or even for a becoming acknowledgement that Laker had been the better bowler on the day?

Not quite. 'Drop dead,' Lock informed his captain.

* * *

Laker was unable to overcome his suspicion, particularly ingrained in him after his wartime service in the army, that no matter his achievements on the field he would always remain one of cricket's other ranks, essentially there to take orders from his social superiors. Such individuals would never accept him as an equal, still less see him in the light in which he saw himself. Laker referred to Errol Holmes, his first captain at Surrey, as 'the biggest snob I ever met'. Holmes, a former Royal Artillery officer, had a receding chin, a bluff leadership style, an upper-class accent so fruity his men could barely understand his commands, and a travelling wardrobe when playing in away matches that included both a black and a white dinner-jacket. Holmes wore a Harlequin cap while in the field, and tended not to actively encourage a spirit of folksy egalitarianism, preferring to take decisions by unilateral fiat rather than a democratic show of hands. Later in life, Laker's wife Lilly confirmed that her husband 'didn't like being told what to do'. Like Lock, his basic distrust of authority figures strengthened one of his characteristics, recognised by those who came across him even in his early days, his self-sufficiency and preference for his own company. He was essentially a rebel of the right, and in some ways the classic loner.

Laker was a hard man to get to know, then, and one who didn't always forgive and forget. Over the years he acquired an impressive list of fellow cricketers for whom he didn't much care. There was his sometime Test captain Len Hutton, for instance. 'He "flapped" on the field [and] made wrong decisions under pressure,' Laker wrote, or Hutton's successor in office Peter May, whom he described as 'aloof and distant' with an aversion to the press that was largely his own doing for having once written a 'tactless and ill-timed series of articles that brought him a lot of grief'. And those were just the players whom Laker at least admired for their peerless batting skills. There were several others who drew his ire for their technical shortcomings as much as their personal foibles. 'Brian Close, I am afraid, has gone as far as he is going,' Laker wrote in 1959, proving himself an only modestly gifted predictor of events in view of the fact that Close went on to be a highly successful if controversial captain of England, and was still turning out for his county nearly 20 years later. Or there was Denis Compton, whom Laker provoked almost to the point of a libel action when he wrote, 'I did not consider [him] to be specially bright.' Of his England bowling colleague Johnny Wardle he said, 'He is a selfish player, a man who gives his captain an immense amount of trouble' – a classic case of projection on Laker's part, some critics felt.

The above list is far from exhaustive. In fact when coming to assess the number of times Laker went into print to rubbish his colleagues, a biographer finds himself somewhat spoilt for choice. Of Colin Cowdrey, he wrote, 'I don't think much of his captaincy – it can sometimes be a puzzle, [and] the same is also true of his batsmanship.' Even this was mild compared to his assessment of Ted Dexter, whom he variously thought a 'festival cricketer', of 'nowhere near the necessary class' and, perhaps most damning of all, 'the poor man's Trevor Bailey'. Bailey was very much the sort of man Laker admired – classless, tough, hungry for the fight, but happy to share a convivial drink with his opponents at the close of play.

Just as Laker's bowling was famously thrifty and precise, so something similar applied to his manner. After a particularly thrilling passage of play, he might express his sense of glee with the words, 'Enjoyed that.' He was a traditionalist, as opposed to a narrowly ideological conservative, often remarking on the declining standards of behaviour in cricket and elsewhere. Appearing as a player-coach in New Zealand when he was still just 29 years old, Laker was appalled by the dress code of some of his junior colleagues, calling the parade of casual trousers and gaudy shirts an 'extraordinary display of colour', and harrumphing, 'There is no excuse for not wearing the correct clothes when [they] come to work.' He rated 'temperament' as the single greatest ingredient of success, defining it as equal parts 'steady nerves, 100 per cent concentration, and raw courage'. He wasn't embarrassed in later life to speak of his admiration for Margaret Thatcher. Whatever one thinks of the results, both individuals emphasised the merits of private enterprise, sound fiscal policy at both the family and national level, and the primacy of personal responsibility over reliance on the state. Both were a strange mixture of parts, steeped in tradition but allergic to the sclerotic English class system. In Laker's case, at least, a cold exterior belied a man given to warm and lasting friendships with those earning his trust.

That Laker was a cricketer of the highest rank the following pages will, perhaps, again demonstrate. He saw his primary role on the field as to do a job rather than to entertain either the crowd or himself. Playing cricket was a perfectly proper and dignified profession – or at least it should be, he always informed anyone who asked – and he acted accordingly. John Arlott said of him, 'He [was] never a demonstrative player.' But he was a studious one. 'Laker always strolled back to his mark at his characteristically constabulary gait,' Arlott wrote, 'look[ing] up to the sky as he turned and then jogging the approach he used artfully to vary, constantly changing the number of steps [to] defeat the batsman's timing.' He never went into a war dance of fury when things went wrong, and similarly restrained himself when things went right. There's a photograph of Laker walking off the field at Old

Trafford just after having set a bowling world record unlikely ever to be beaten; he wears his usual studded boots, baggy whites, and a slightly bored expression; he looks calm, mildly embarrassed, and thoroughly English. Later that night Laker stopped off for a drink in a pub where the other customers stood around the bar watching a replay of his triumph on the television news. He didn't say anything to draw attention to himself, and no one recognised him, which was how he liked it.

For all that, Laker was fiercely competitive. Some of his descriptions of opposition players were almost flattering compared to his reaction to team-mates. Over the years he thought Tony Lock to be 'full of potential', 'excessively plain-spoken', a 'bit of a character' – not necessarily a good thing in Laker parlance – and 'his own worst enemy … when things weren't going well I saw him, too often, try to bowl faster and faster – and drop shorter and shorter. To [the] batsmen, it was the bowling equivalent of a blank cheque.'

Later, in his post-retirement career, when he became something of a writer, Laker would often favour the ironical or satirical approach. His puckish side came out when, in his first autobiography, he displayed two photographs of Lock and himself taken in 1948 and 1958 respectively. Lock's hair has noticeably receded in the second photo, while Laker looks exactly the same. The caption reads, 'Who changes more in ten years?' In fact they had little in common but their ability as cricketers. Between them they appeared in 1,104 first-class matches and captured a total of 4,788 wickets. 'I would take a lot of convincing,' Laker remarked towards the end of his life, 'that as a bowling combination, we ever had any serious rival.'

* * *

Perhaps the best way to approach the career of that sometimes infuriating, always compelling and infinitely combative character

Tony Lock is to ask the question: What is it about English slow left-arm bowlers? Cricket never seems boring when they're around. Considering they represent one of the game's most refined arts it's curious how often they seem to be of the scrappy, belligerent type as personalities. A former well-known English cricketer who later went into the psychology field once told me that it was as if such men were weighed down by what he thought might be an inferiority complex. 'Maybe it's the classic case of a fast bowler's mind being trapped inside a slow bowler's body,' he speculated.

Yorkshire and England's inimitable Hedley Verity, for one, is rightly remembered today as being among cricket's great Renaissance Men, and ultimately as a fallen war hero, but the second he put on whites friend and foe alike quickly came to appreciate that Verity's qualities also included a ruthlessness bordering on sadism. A generation later, Yorkshire's Johnny Wardle, after battling stoically through recurrent injuries to capture 1,846 first-class wickets over the previous dozen years, brought off the rare double of getting himself both sacked by his county and disinvited from an England tour of Australia for having put his name to a particularly tart series of articles in the *Daily Mail*. Nowadays he'd be a highly marketable commodity, with his own ghosted newspaper column and a bestselling memoir under a title like *Sex, Lies and Surgical Tape* or *Original Spin*; but in the late 1950s he was a pariah.

Then there was Kent and England's Derek Underwood, an extremely affable soul of whom I once wrote, 'The archetypal "nice guy", he hates most of his opponents while on the field.' Underwood promptly rang me to complain. 'It should have been "all his opponents",' he said. Phil Edmonds's career, in turn, was punctuated by various – to put it no stronger – misunderstandings with authority in general and the Middlesex captain Mike Brearley in particular. Around 1976 and 1977, Edmonds would revel in the name 'Margaret' – leader of the opposition – in his county's dressing room. Coming up fast behind him at Lord's was a certain Phil Tufnell, nowadays a national treasure but 30 years ago a staple figure of the tabloid press, including the famous story involving his girlfriend, their love child, and a brick to the head that reportedly made the chairman of selectors' gin slop from its glass.

More recently there's been Mudhsuden Singh 'Monty' Panesar, an exemplary servant of English cricket, if not one without his occasional lapses, for instance the time when he chose to urinate on a doorman following his eviction from a Brighton nightclub, or more broadly speaking his decision, however arrived at, to play for no fewer than three first-class counties in just over four years. Meanwhile, the prodigiously talented Surrey and England left-armer Zafar Ansari elected to retire from competitive cricket at the age of 25, shortly after making his Test debut, in order to work for a legal charity supporting young people with immigration, housing or school issues – an entirely laudable career move on his part, if one that seems to further enhance the typical left-arm spinner's reputation for independence of thought. We've already touched on the excellent Jack Leach, the indomitable batting hero of England's Headingley Test win against Australia in 2019, and by all accounts one of those sporting eccentrics, not infrequently hailing from the West Country, whom the British seem to take to themselves.

For volatility, aggression and sheer bloody-minded front, however, none of the above could hold a candle to Tony Lock. Nor for determination: like Johnny Wardle, Lock often needed to strap himself up like a mummy even to get on the field, and there are numerous accounts of him spinning his fingers raw, the blood dripping down his forearm in his delivery stride. Tom Graveney, who played with and against Lock for 20 years, called him 'the angriest bowler in cricket history'. He 'hated' batsmen and, until the arrival of Phil Edmonds, was the only spinner known regularly to employ the bouncer. To Neville Cardus, Lock was 'a fellow of total antagonism, ready to get you out of the way, back to the pavilion almost before you knew where you were … If he didn't happen to be bowling when you were taking your first ball, as likely as anything he'd catch you out at close short leg, a pickpocket of a catch, bare-faced daylight robbery.' Rarely content merely to take the half-chances, Lock would add flourishes – a somersault, possibly, or a cartwheel or two – for good effect. Perhaps he really did have an inferiority complex, or perhaps he was what we would now call bipolar.

Lock's Surrey team-mate Ken Barrington said of him, 'Tony could be the nicest guy in the world, loved kids and animals – nothing was too much trouble, he'd give you the shirt off his back – or he could be leaping around like a nutcase. A flying headbutt in the dressing room counted as a friendly "hello" by his standards.' Either way, it's agreed Lock was a peerless left-arm bowler, arguably the greatest ever to represent England, and at all times much more than merely Jim Laker's foil.

Part of the contrast with Laker was physical. 'Uncle Jim', as his younger colleagues knew him, was suitably avuncular-looking, solid and neatly dressed, with a good head of crinkly hair. Lock was wiry, folically challenged, and with something of the air of a malign scarecrow. Cardus once described him bowling at The Oval while still only in his mid-20s with the sun 'gleaming off his balding brow', making him look 'decidedly evil – almost a torturer of the opposition'. Others thought he had more than a dash of schoolboy impishness about him, as if he'd just run away from ringing some grown-up's doorbell. Never too fastidious about his appearance, Lock often made do with a baggy white cricket shirt, sleeves habitually rolled down, greying old trousers, and a pair of out-sized Chaplinesque boots, the soles all but detached from the uppers, flapping rhythmically on the grass as he ran in to bowl. For much of his career he seemed to survive largely on a diet of cigarettes and heavily sugared black coffee, and Ken Barrington fondly remembered the 'slipstream of stale fag smoke' that followed in Lock's wake. He left school at 16, unqualified, and apart from two years' National Service made a living out of cricket for the rest of his life, eventually describing himself as an 'international consultant' in the sport, and coming to be a popular children's coach in his adopted home of Australia until his involvement with his young pupils came to an abrupt end. It would be fair to say that Lock was no rocket scientist, but that he possessed a certain native shrewdness. He was also earthy, gruff, and kissed up to no one, including the average English cricket committee as it was constituted in the 1950s. Like Laker he was essentially a loner, but capable of deep and lasting loyalty to those he trusted.

'I don't think Tony did a day's work in his life,' Peter May once told me. 'For about 20 years all he did was bowl his heart out all day, field like a tiger, score runs, chivvy the side along and generally do everything in his power to undermine the opposition. In other words, all he did was enjoy himself doing the things he loved. Tony was born to play cricket. You could never see him sitting in an office or taking orders from on high. I was his captain and I tried once or twice. It was like talking to a wall. As a rule I found it best just to turn him loose on the opposition and let him get on with it. You almost felt sorry for the poor batsman when Tony came running in to him, teeth bared, muttering away at him under his breath.'

People who had played with or against Lock still marvelled at his hostility years later. It consumed him. Perhaps the most obvious example of it – apart from his bowling – was the way he fielded. Lock favoured the backward short leg position, crouching there almost indecently near the batsman's hip pocket, but failing that anything close to the action was fine by him. It wasn't only that he had the reflexes of a highly caffeinated panther, he was utterly fearless with it. In the Headingley Test against the West Indies in July 1957 he caught the left-handed Garry Sobers in the first innings after Sobers played an authentic leg glance off the seamer Peter Loader and the fielder made about three yards to catch the ball one-handed – *right*-handed – a bare two inches off the ground. No one else in the side would have considered it a chance.

In the second innings, the same batsman smashed the bowler off the back foot for a shot that seemed destined to pierce the gap between deep point and cover for four. 'Sobers made off down the pitch, never suspecting that Lock would cut off the ball,' *The Times* reported. In fact he not only cut it off, he swept it up and in one fluid motion snapped it back 20 yards to break the wicket and beat Sobers's suddenly despairing lunge to the finish line. It proved to be one of the key moments in a rapidly accelerating West Indies collapse, and for some time afterwards the visitors' batsmen competed with each other to be the first to shout 'No!' whenever the ball came anywhere within Lock's sphere of influence. It was like playing against a team with at least 12 men in the field, Sobers once ruefully noted of the match, which the tourists duly lost by an innings. 'Whatever happened to British fair play?' he asked.

Six years later, again at Leeds, the same batsman had just posted a chanceless century against an England attack spearheaded by Fred Trueman and Derek Shackleton when Lock came on to bowl. To again quote *The Times*, 'Sobers promptly struck a straight drive as good as any in the day. Lock, throwing himself to his left, held the ball one-handed as he fell, before emerging to whirl both the ball and himself in the air and thence to begin a sort of Cossack dance of ecstasy. The batsman was transfixed, as though disbelieving what he saw … Many in the crowd must have shared his sentiments.'

Whether you were actually in the middle with Lock, or merely watching him from the comparative safety of the stand, you soon got used to the sight of the truly spectacular catch or the seemingly impossible run-out followed by that familiar split second of shocked silence before the crowd started applauding and the unhappy batsman recovered himself to plod his weary way home to the pavilion. Perhaps the spirit of competition just ran in the family. One day when Lock was just 12 he was picked to represent his local village side in Surrey against a Services XI, and his own father, who was on the other team, clean-bowled him second ball. No quarter was ever given, and none was asked. Lock senior once watched his wife and his son play a Sunday afternoon game of tennis and in between sets he sidled up to mutter to Tony, 'Your mother has a weak backhand. Use it.'

So when the moment came Lock had no trouble in convincing himself that as a first-class cricketer he was really involved not so much in a friendly sporting contest as he was in a death struggle that pitted him against not only the other side but quite often his colleagues and team-mates as well. We'll return to his unique rivalry in this context with Jim Laker. Perhaps Lock's next most obvious antagonist was Johnny Wardle, with whom he often competed for the England selectors' affections. The two left-armers did not greatly care for each other. Lock found himself bowling for Surrey against Yorkshire one hot afternoon in July 1957 in Wardle's benefit match at Bradford. There was a full house, and as usual in these encounters between the northern and southern counties, a certain edge had crept in to the proceedings. In due course, Peter May, Surrey's captain, in keeping with cherished cricketing tradition, told Lock to give the beneficiary one off the mark. Lock was not happy, but after some further debate on the subject he duly floated one down outside Wardle's off stump, which the batsman gratefully clipped for a single. Under other circumstances, that might have satisfied honour to all parties' satisfaction. But Wardle had a puckish side to him, too, and after quickly completing the run he turned at the crease and loudly called his partner for a second. This was taking charity altogether too far for Lock's taste, and seeing what was happening he took off like a gazelle into the covers, scooped up the ball and turned, ready to fire it back in at the stumps, just as he did with Sobers in that month's Test at Leeds. But before he did so he looked up and saw Wardle now leaning on his bat at the non-striker's end, convulsed with mirth at having discomfited his spin-bowling rival. The crowd lapped it up, too, and there was a lot of laughter. It may have proved counter-productive, however, because in the end Lock had figures of 4-43 in the first innings and 4-44 in the second, with Bradford's *Telegraph & Argus* newspaper reporting, 'He sent it down with undisguised venom, at genuine medium pace. It was like watching an executioner.'

Laker caught some of the essential Lock duality when he wrote of him in 1959:

> How shall I remember him? The fiery, determined Lock, putting every ounce of himself into his bowling between my own overs? Or the schoolmasterly Lock, whom I once listened to coaching in the nets at The Oval, 'Come *forward* … with your leg and pad together …'

That was another point of contrast. Laker rarely if ever practised, let alone deigned to pass on any advice, and as a rule had to be forced to turn his arm over in the nets. Like most English cricketers of the day, he basically trained on a regime of cheese sandwiches and cigarettes. Reporting back from their winter lay-off, the players tended to just turn up, sign in with their county secretary, and then drift down the corridor for a cup of tea and a natter in the dressing room. Laker took the game seriously, but he seems to have played it with the clear conviction that there might ultimately be more to life than propelling a hard red leather ball at a man holding a lump of wood in his hands. Even as he was more or less single-handedly winning the Ashes, Laker's England team-mates widely suspected him of being guilty of subversive activities such as reading books or forming his own opinions on the political issues of the day. 'Jim would stay up late quietly arguing his case. He was always boning up about philosophy and history, while the rest of us settled for a beer and a shag,' Godfrey Evans reminisced of the 1958/59 MCC tour of Australia. Lock, by contrast, was more narrowly focused. The first line of his only book (Laker wrote at least five of them) reads, 'As long as I can remember, cricket has meant everything to me.'

In their older age, both men tended to be more charitable to one another. Laker said of Lock's protracted Indian summer as captain of Leicestershire, 'Tony's enthusiasm was infectious, and he led by example … He imbued the side with the belief that they were as good as any other and taught them never to give up hope. It was an astonishing performance.'

Lock's matching tribute to Laker was both fulsome and contained an air of faint bemusement:

> He never said whether he was pleased or sorry about his bowling. The odd slight grin, or shrug of the shoulders, would be the only indication that he had any opinion at all about what had just happened. I was different.

He was; and like most men of character he had strong prejudices, perhaps even more so than Laker. Errol Holmes cast a superbly languid eye over both young players when they joined the Surrey staff in 1946. Laker, he informed his committee, was already a 'finished cricketer [and] good trier, if a little unpolished – a thorough Yorkshireman', while Lock was 'very young and very pleased with himself, full of wind, but has possibilities'. Laker as a rule saw the wisdom in Kipling's lines about taking triumph and disaster in one's stride, while Lock appeared to be on some permanent audition for the sort of film role made popular around that time by Jerry Lewis at his most antic: loud, brash and slightly exhausting. Whether bowling or catching, his manner in the field often appeared to be artificial and over-emphatic, as though he really were acting a part, his gestures theatrical, his movements jerky and awkward. When appealing for a dismissal, Richie Benaud wrote, 'Laker was apologetic, Lock a demander.' Peter May added, 'Jim remained serene, and sometimes just a little too detached from the proceedings for his own good,' while 'Tony was a high-maintenance character,' and at times 'like a child who wanted your constant attention as captain and got huffy if you didn't respond'. In a crisis, where Laker's nerves were steady, Lock was at the mercy of his. Ken Barrington said, 'Jim remained calm if the umpire happened to turn him down. Tony behaved like a lit firework.' Lock was also a pioneer of the sort of syncopated war dance that typically accompanies each fall of wicket in modern-day cricket – colleagues knew that unless they took swift evasive action they could expect to be roped in for a full-bodied communal hug by the successful bowler, if not more than that, and that his fist-pumping antics on these occasions as a whole were often even more impressive than the actual dismissal they celebrated.

* * *

How should we assess the value of a great bowler? Crunching the numbers of their wickets is one obvious method, but it's not the whole story. Simple accountancy doesn't capture the worth of the true bowling artist. That's down to the intimidating effect his mere presence on the field has on the batsmen.

Stuart Surridge commented on the happy coincidence of having both Laker and Lock simultaneously at his disposal in the all-conquering Surrey sides of the 1950s, when he said, 'If a batsman wanted to get away from Jim, as they generally did, then they had Tony to deal with at the other end. They got no respite. As their captain I was also in the position of knowing that if one of them got a hatful of wickets in the first innings the other one would be bloody sure to try and top it in the second.' Surridge also fondly remembered that Laker and Lock had always competed to be the first to pass the 100-wicket mark for the season. Lock himself acknowledged this symbiotic aspect of the relationship when in his 1957 autobiography, after blithely picking himself for his own fantasy World XI, he wrote, 'To bowl spinners alongside me, there is only one man – Jim Laker. Further comment on his bowling skill is superfluous. From my point of view, it's great to have him at the other end.'

Laker in turn readily appreciated the merits of having a bowling partner who could be expected at all times to tie down, stifle and generally harass the batsman. He once took Lock aside during their early days together at The Oval. 'We discussed things, and I told him he ought to bowl quicker,' Laker recalled. 'I spent the better part of two weeks in the nets' – a singular occurrence in itself – 'showing him how to spin the ball, explaining that he had to get his fingers round it and really turn it.' It was an act of kindness, if not one wholly untainted by self-interest. Surridge said, 'Jim chipped away at the batsman, often happy enough just to contain him. Tony's constant belief [was] that he was going to take a wicket with every ball. I lost track of the number of times a man got out to one of them because he was frustrated by the other one, and did something stupid as a result.'

Surridge conceded that having two world-class spinners operating in tandem on the uncovered – and frequently underprepared – Oval wickets of the 1950s 'didn't exactly harm' Surrey's prospects during the club's unparalleled run of County Championship-winning seasons. It's widely agreed that Surrey's groundsman Bert Lock (no relation, although he might as well have been) worked miracles in transforming the ground from the unused but fully equipped wartime internment camp it remained until November 1945, with barbed wire strung across the playing area, into an arena fit for top-class cricket, with a marked receptiveness to spin, just six months later. Laker and Lock weren't only wonderfully skilful professionals, then, but were also supremely lucky to do most of their work at The Oval under the playing regulations of the immediate post-war years. As Neville Cardus wrote, 'Laker, in particular, was clever to begin playing cricket and bowling off-spin after the alteration of the lbw rule dangerously penalised batsmen who had brought to a fine art the use of pads to brilliant off-breaks pitching on the stumps and cutting back like a knife.'

With all this flair and success on his native field, Laker himself used to frequently make the point that he was just as effective when bowling away as he was at home, and the statistics partly bear him out. While he took 687 first-class wickets at The Oval at around 17.30 apiece, his average (if also his number of dismissals) was significantly lower at the likes of Worcester, Old Trafford and Hove, to give just three geographically far-flung examples.

While Lock was figuratively and quite often literally at the batsman's throat, Laker was more contained on the field and more laconic, even sphinx-like, off it. 'Jim learned to conceal his feelings with that deadpan expression which became second nature to him,' Surridge said. Lock summed it up this way: 'Jim and I were not always the greatest of friends, or for that matter friends at all, for he was a very hard man to get to know, very deep and quiet.' Apart from their peerless bowling, they had little personally in common.

Laker was more than seven years older, a product of the industrial north and a notably difficult childhood. Lock was a country boy with the twin advantages of a cricket-loving father with access to the idyllic ground at Oxted in Surrey, and the early patronage of Sir Henry 'Shrimp' Leveson Gower, the county club's president throughout the 1930s. Neither man was especially generous when it came to sharing the credit for his achievements, and they had few words of real warmth to say about each other in their various books. In later life Lock went on to live happily in Australia, which he described approvingly as a 'raw, untamed country' of the sort where it's somehow difficult to imagine the more fastidious Laker wishing to settle. Surridge said, 'Tony was tense and truculent, and frequently highly vocal with it,' and added, 'The mere idea of Jim showing emotion was absurd.' But despite Laker's trademark inscrutability, hot fires evidently smouldered just below the surface. His bridge-burning post-retirement autobiography eschewed the usual leisurely stroll through past matches and instead offered an energetically sustained rant against Peter May and others of the 'traditional Oxbridge elite', the results of which shattered the prevailing tone of sepulchral calm in the committee rooms of Lord's and The Oval with much the same force as a well-aimed hand grenade.

Laker is probably the more familiar of the pair, simply because his achievements in 1956 at Old Trafford are inextricably bound up with first impressions: many children of the 1960s, whether cricketers or not, would have grown up hearing of his name, and even people who would never think of attending a Test match are vaguely aware that he did something special. Lock himself was painfully alive to this imbalance in their popular stature, and he sometimes took it in his stride and sometimes didn't. People who knew him best refer to his self-sufficiency, determination, irritability and capacity for ingratitude, qualities common to many great public performers. More than Laker, he was fanatically devoted to the craft of being a professional cricketer. In a further contrast, as a rule Lock considered himself supremely lucky just to be getting paid for doing what he loved best. The domestic game was going through one of its cyclical crises in the late 1950s, with many first-class cricketers and their county committees calling for fewer matches of the full two-innings variety and an extended mid-season break in the interests of the players' fitness and enthusiasm. Lock was having none of it. 'I am not convinced that cricket six days a week is too much,' he wrote in 1957. 'People in other walks of life have to work just as hard for six days as we do, without complaining about feeling stale. If they did, they would soon be reminded by the boss on which side their bread was buttered.'

The other pertinent themes in Laker and Lock's lives were their mutual aversion to the neo-feudalism of English cricket in the days before the abolition of 'gentleman' and 'player' status; their ability to both exasperate and inspire their team-mates; their capacity for intense friendships and undying hatreds; their innate conservatism, at least as it might strike us today, in Laker's case grounded in a childhood filled with the last vestiges of a Victorian way of life – pea-soup fogs, bowls and pitchers for bathing, and potted meat covered with a thick coat of yellow animal lard – and memories of actual survivors, too. He grew up in the Bradford of J.B. Priestley, to a soundtrack of clattering trams and the thought-annihilating thunder of factory presses blasting day and night, where Lord Hawke in his 1880s Cambridge blazer, like some comic but also faintly sinister Gilbert and Sullivan grandee, was still the hands-on Yorkshire club president, famously telling his county's AGM in 1925, 'Pray God, no professional cricketer shall ever captain England.'

Perhaps it would simply be fair to note that there was something of a generation gap between Laker and Lock, not only in their age but also their fundamental outlook on life. In January 1950, just as both men were finding their feet as professional cricketers, a classic police drama called *The Blue Lamp* presented two British archetypes of the new decade in the film's lead roles. One was the solid and stoutly conventional London copper George Dixon, of later Dock Green fame, played by 54-year-old Jack Warner. Superbly pragmatic and efficient, he dealt briskly with the day's issues and then went back home again to his pipe and slippers in the modest suburban lodgings he shared with his dutiful wife. He was dry, stoic, and gently humorous, and while you could safely count on him for a sympathetic hearing of your problems in life, you probably made a mistake if you sought him out solely for a therapeutic natter about your feelings of low self-esteem or alienation. Born in 1922, Laker was squarely in the Dixon tradition.

By contrast, *The Blue Lamp*'s other chief protagonist, the brooding hoodlum Tom Riley – as portrayed by 28-year-old Dirk Bogarde – seemed to herald the coming plague of rock and roll, with its preferred working environment of smoky cellars and richly aromatic espresso coffee bars, and a clientele who increasingly shunned the old Utility uniform of baggy grey flannels and sensible lace-up shoes for an ensemble of black, gold-threaded 'Teddy Boy' jackets and elastic-sided, crepe-soled boots of suspiciously continental design. By and large, this generation was impatient to dispense with the privations of war and the conventions of army life, both of which loomed large in the national consciousness of the early 1950s. Of course, neither the young nor the old of that era were the abstractions they're sometimes presented as by historians. They were made of flesh and blood like us, and with comparable feelings of love and hatred, resolve and doubt, with fears like us, too, even if what occasioned those fears was different. It would be a stretch to claim that Tom Riley and his real-life counterparts were part of some broader, cohesive revolution underway against the Britain of *It's That Man Again*, with its grinding conformity and interminable queues at the local butcher's shop. In short, Jack Warner and Dirk Bogarde may not always have been the stock personality types they sometimes appear to be in *The Blue Lamp*. But in so far as the older of the two men could be said to evoke the dour, self-effacing, commonsensical British male ideal of the 1940s, and the younger of the two anticipated the ornate, self-obsessed age of the 1960s, you could make a case for saying they double for Jim Laker and Tony Lock respectively.

* * *

On Wednesday, 1 August 1956 the touring Australians arrived at The Oval to play Surrey for the second time in just nine weeks. By then they must have been heartily sick of the sight of Laker, who had already taken 51 wickets in the course of his five previous meetings with them that summer. It was raining at the scheduled start of play, as it would do with depressing frequency that month. Despite the weather, the ramshackle but in its way lovely old ground with its gasometer backdrop was full to the rafters. Laker himself appeared prominently on the back pages of the morning newspapers being sold at the gate. The front pages were dominated by the developing crisis in the Middle East. Five days earlier, just as England and Australia were settling in for the fourth Test at Old Trafford, the Egyptian president Gamal Nasser had seen fit to nationalise the Suez Canal Company, not only in breach of the 1888 Treaty of Constantinople, but also, of more practical concern, posing a serious threat to Britain's oil supplies. As at Munich in 1938, if on a smaller scale, it was a case of whether Britain should make a foreign dictator's transgressions a *casus belli*, or seek to negotiate instead. Fuel rationing soon returned, and was seemingly accepted without a murmur of complaint, although it might conceivably have resulted in some marginal increase in the hatred for politicians.

Anthony Eden's Conservative government eventually chose the more belligerent of the two options. Unfortunately, the hoped-for American support in the matter never materialised. In fact President Eisenhower's ire with the British was sufficient for Eden to remember having picked up the hotline in Downing Street one morning to hear a flow of soldierly language at the other end so furious that he had felt it best to hold the instrument away from his ear. It was all a 'regrettable lapse' in the 'special relationship', the PM was forced to admit, as the roof fell in on the Atlantic alliance, Britain hurriedly withdrew her troops, and the Soviet Union threatened to launch retaliatory nuclear strikes on western Europe.

It's worth dwelling on the tragicomic humbling of the British establishment at Suez for a moment, if only because it marked the moment when the Anglo-American balance of power came to assume its modern tone, with London essentially acting as a branch office of its Washington headquarters. As Elvis Presley appeared on British television screens for the first time that same month, John Osborne's socially eviscerating play *Look Back in Anger* gave rise overnight to the kitchen sink school of public expression, and the retailer Tesco opened the nation's first self-service supermarket in St Albans, it's arguable that what we now call 'modern' Britain – or even 'the 1960s' – really began in the wet late summer of 1956.

In the event they never got on the field for the first day's scheduled play at The Oval. On the second day the Australians managed 143 all out, Laker taking four of the wickets and Lock just one. Surrey did marginally better, declaring at 181/9. When Laker came in to bat with the score on 86/6, the visitors' fast left-arm bowler Alan Davidson generously announced that he would give him one off the mark. Laker duly swung at the first ball, which was slow but straight, and was clean bowled. Lock in turn threw the bat for a brisk 39, and after that the match dissolved into one of those cheerless stop-start affairs punctuated by umpires' inspections and an occasional half-hearted chant from the free seats of 'We want cricket.' The Surrey professionals each received their standard £17 fee for the match, which ended in the inevitable draw.

Under normal circumstances it might seem that midweek county matches played in a damp August, particularly with the Australians still around, would be in the nature of an anticlimax for spectators and players alike. But this conspicuously wasn't the case with Surrey in 1956. They towered above all their domestic competition, and there were often long queues at the Oval gates before the start of each day's play. Admittedly the county's next home match, with Nottinghamshire, could be called only partly successful; Surrey managed just 87 in the first innings, but then pulled themselves together and fought the game out to the last blow for another draw. They then disposed of Essex at Clacton in a little over two days, made equally short work of Middlesex at The Oval, and earned another rain-affected draw – but also 12 bonus points – at home to Sussex. Meanwhile, Laker and Lock were steadily piling up the wickets, and under Surridge's captaincy the atmosphere on the field was generally as keen as in a Test match. 'The skipper threw himself 100 per cent into the team effort,' Lock allowed in print, before adding somewhat cattily, 'Nothing else mattered to him, [and] why would it? As an amateur he had no cares about his personal performance, and no worries about maintaining his form or keeping fit for Test matches, as happens with others of us.'

By the time Surrey went up to play Middlesex again in the middle of August, this time at Lord's, they were in sight of their fifth consecutive County Championship trophy. Their rivals just to the north were among their strongest challengers, along with the likes of Lancashire, Gloucestershire and Northamptonshire.

There was a certain edge to encounters between the two London sides at the best of times, which makes it slightly curious to read in Lock's memoir *For Surrey and England*, 'Even Jim Laker, in his record-breaking season, was once left out when he was fit to play. This was against Middlesex at Lord's. As the home team were breaking all precedent by granting a financial collection to a professional from another county, in recognition of Jim's achievements in his benefit season, England's off-spin hero was not exactly pleased.'

Here some discrepancy exists between Lock's account and those of several other Surrey players who noted that Laker had shown a marked reduction of offensive spirit after taking a certain amount of stick from the visiting batsmen in the recent match against Sussex, and had declared himself unfit for duty the following week as a result. John Murray, the Middlesex wicketkeeper on the day, told me, 'We had a whip-round for Laker in the dressing room, just before the start. You wouldn't normally do that except it was his benefit year, and of course he'd stuffed the Aussies bloody nearly single-handed in the Tests. So we passed the hat. Twenty or 30 quid, it was, which wasn't bad when you consider we were making about a tenner each, 15 if you were lucky, for the full three-day match. Well, the Surrey boys duly turned up at the ground that morning, but no Jim. They said he'd hurt his finger somehow. Very bitter about it, they were. You heard a few harsh words uttered in his direction in those days. Lovely bowler, though.' Surrey won the match at Lord's, where Lock took 12 wickets, and retained the title in the process.

When all the figures were added up, Laker earned about £11,000, tax-free, from his benefit season, which was serious money for an English county cricketer in 1956. He estimated that he added a further £200 from ghosted newspaper articles, and exactly £100 by selling 1,000 signed copies of the Old Trafford

Test scorecard at two bob apiece. Towards the end of the season the Rothman's tobacco office in Sydney offered him a contract worth £3,000 a year for three years to be their roving PR representative in New South Wales, a notable act of magnanimity on their part to Australia's tormentor. Laker thought about it, but turned them down. As we've seen, he then added another £100 when he pipped Lock by a single run, 10-53 against 10-54, for the best English bowling analysis of the year.

Perhaps the Oval pitches were poorly prepared or even doctored in 1956 to give the county's spinners an advantage, but taking the season overall it still seems that the right side ended on top. Laker bowled 959 overs in first-class play, fully 364 of them maidens, and took 132 wickets at 14.43 apiece. Lock sent down 1,058 overs with an even more frugal 437, or well over 40 per cent of them, maidens, finishing with 155 wickets at 12.46, and throwing in 44 often gravity-defying catches. Of course, statistics such as mere dismissals are absurd for such men. You might as well review a book by counting the number of words in it. Later in September, Surrey organised a modest press conference for their victorious team at The Oval, and one of the national correspondents asked Laker, who was sitting there in his customary neat grey flannels and blazer, with a pen sticking out of the breast pocket, what particular qualities a spinner needed to be successful in English conditions.

Without hesitating, Laker said, 'A good sense of humour.' There was an appreciative ripple of laughter. After that the same individual turned to Lock, who was not so much sitting in a wooden chair as sprawling in it almost full-length, legs crossed, the picture of self-contentment, a cigarette dangling between his gnarled spinning fingers. 'Can you tell me,' the journalist enquired, 'what you consider to be your greatest success and your greatest failure this season?'

Lock took a few more leisurely drags of his cigarette, casually flicked some ash on the nearby rug, and exhaled a cloud of smoke before replying. 'Sorry, mate,' he said. 'I don't quite understand your second point.'

It brought the house down.

2

Arms and the Men

JIM LAKER was past his 60th birthday when he first came to know his father, and by then it was posthumously. Long since retired from active cricket, Laker had gone on to become a highly regarded television commentator and occasional public speaker whose dry, almost mournful delivery of a punchline made him a popular turn on the sports club dinner circuit. At the time in question he was still living in south-west London with Lilly, his Austrian-born wife of 30 years, and on occasion their two adult daughters. It was a tight-knit family. When they were growing up in the 1950s and early 1960s the girls had sometimes liked to cut out the Help Wanted columns from the papers and half-jokingly tell their father, then one of the most famous sportsmen in Britain, that he should get a proper job, a remark which delighted him.

One morning in January 1983 Laker opened a letter from the former all-rounder Peter Parfitt, of Middlesex and England, who was then running a large pub with an attached banqueting room in the village of Elslack on the Yorkshire–Lancashire border. About once a month Parfitt put on a sportsman's dinner which typically involved a well-lubricated meal rounded off by a guest speaker such as Alex 'Hurricane' Higgins or Jack Charlton. He and Laker, who was 14 years older, hadn't been particularly friendly on the cricket field. But Parfitt told me he'd 'obviously respected Jim as a great bowler' and more to the point knew him to be a good bet to invite up as a speaker. 'Like me, he had a basic set-piece routine which he used wherever he went, working on the basis that an audience in Leeds wouldn't care if they were hearing the same gags he'd used the week before in Bournemouth or Brighton. Plus there was the added bonus that he was a born Yorkshireman, even if he happened to have defected south, and that always went down well with the locals. I had no trouble selling tickets.'

A day or two after advertising the event, Parfitt received an unusual phone call. The man on the other end of the line was Norman Petty, an occasional cricketer who worked as an accountant in the neighbouring town of Barnoldswick. He said he was greatly looking forward to the evening with Laker, whom he assumed would also be paying a visit to the local cemetery. 'Why would he do that?' asked Parfitt, who had no idea what his caller was referring to. Petty told him it was because Laker's father Charles was buried there. 'No one had ever said anything about it before,' says Parfitt, although of course there was no particular reason why anyone should.

Parfitt digested the information for the next day or two. He knew that Laker's inner life remained a mystery even to his friends. The sort of people who came to hear him speak at dinners often remarked on his simplicity and good manners, and his ability to deliver a pricelessly dry joke. When tragedy struck a friend or colleague, he was a consoling force who always managed to find the right words of sympathy. But people also noticed that he kept his emotional distance, and rarely if ever referred to his early life. So Parfitt wasn't quite sure what to expect when he in turn rang Laker to confirm the arrangements for their night together, before adding, 'Of course, you know your father is buried in our local churchyard?'

There was a lengthy silence on the line before Laker replied. 'I never knew my father,' he said simply. Parfitt remembers having then ended the conversation feeling more than a little embarrassed.

When the day came, Laker gave his usual polished performance for the paying audience, circulating round the room, signing autographs, posing for photos, and then delivering his stock speech in that deep, precise voice and deadpan tone that somehow made the old jokes fresh again. 'It all went off very well,' says Parfitt, himself an accomplished raconteur. 'Jim then spent the night in the spare room above the pub. He came down again in the morning neatly dressed, as always, tweed jacket, biro tucked in the top pocket, shirt and tie, flannels, shoes well shined. I noticed he was carrying a camera. After breakfast I was going to drive him to the station, and before we set off Jim said quietly, "Can you take me to see the grave?"'

An hour later, the two old cricketers were duly threading their way a little warily between the rows of cracked-marble tombs and lopsided headstones scattered around the Norman churchyard of St Mary le Ghyll in Barnoldswick, about a mile over the county border into Lancashire. It was a bright, cold day, the ground covered with a sleet that had frozen in the night so that it seemed as if the ancient church, the bare trees and all the granite stones and crosses had been varnished with ice. Parfitt remembers it as a curious scene. 'Jim eventually found the spot,' he says. 'The sun was shining but there were still a few puffs of mist hovering about, which gave it all a slightly ghostly feeling. Jim stood there for a long time in silence, completely expressionless, sometimes raising the camera for a picture, and then falling back into gloom again. It was bloody cold, I remember, one of those mornings when your breath comes out in little cloudy gusts.'

The principal name on the grave in front of them was that of Charles Henry Laker, who had lived between 1878 and 1931, meaning that Jim would have been nine at the time of his father's death. 'He was buried with two ladies on top of him,' Parfitt remembers. 'They were named Annie Sutcliffe and Elizabeth Halstead, and I gathered that the first was old Charlie's common-law wife and the second was their daughter. I would have liked to ask Jim more about it, but something about his expression didn't encourage it. So we just stood there, Laker at the grave's edge, and me a discreet distance behind him. Completely silent. Not another soul around. After a while Jim turned around, still poker-faced, nodded back to the headstone with the names of his father and the two women on it, and said, "It looks like the old boy was a bit of a lad, then." And that was it. Without another word we walked back together to the car, and I drove him off to the station for his train home to London. I never saw him again.'

* * *

Laker's early life, unlike the later myth, was not one of relentless northern hardship and shoeless poverty. Contrary to the popular impression at the time he became a national celebrity, he was neither especially poor nor particularly unhappy as a young boy. He did, however, enjoy a childhood that was strikingly unconventional, even somewhat scandalous, by the standards of its day. Without descending too far into the briar patch of psychiatry, it might offer a clue as to why he tended to go his own way in later life.

James Charles Laker – initially known as Charlie, but answering to 'Jim' from about his sixth birthday – was born on 9 February 1922 in the family's terraced home at 36 Norwood Road in the agreeably named Frizinghall, on the northern fringes of Bradford. His father, Charles, was a stonemason and bricklayer who was originally from the area around Horsham in West Sussex. Most accounts describe the elder Laker as a charming but rather weak man who failed to realise the potential of his life due to a tendency to 'overdo the Bacchic rites, and an excessive indulgence of the carnal instinct', as one early writer delicately put it. In plain language, he enjoyed a drink and sex. A Sussex friend named Horace Albright remembered Charles as 'a restless man, good looking and quite vain with it, burning with frustrated ambition', an all-round sportsman and 'the best raconteur I ever heard, especially when it came to the saloon-bar sort of jest not fit for mixed company'. Another friend remarked that Charles had enjoyed a passing resemblance to the American film cowboy Tom Mix, and wasn't above signing an autograph in that name, even if it was never quite established why the singing star of *A Ridin' Romeo* and many others like it might have come to be engaged as a jobbing plasterer on the new Horsham town hall annex.

In 1915, Charles – in a reserved occupation, and thus spared wartime conscription – moved north to Bradford. He may have simply been in search of work, although it's thought possible he might equally have welcomed the opportunity to put some 200 miles between himself and one or more of the romantic entanglements he left behind in Sussex. We know that in early 1916 he set up home with a bespectacled 38-year-old infant school teacher named Ellen Kane, and that the couple's daughter, Susie, was born later that year. It's not clear if Ellen and Charles ever formally married, although this might have been problematic in light of the fact that Ellen had never divorced her first husband Henry Kane, a Bradford printer whom she'd met as a young woman in a local dance hall. In any event her second child with Charles, the future Jim Laker, followed six years after her first. It seems that there was soon an upheaval in the family's affairs, because in early 1924 Charles deserted Ellen to live in Barnoldswick with another woman. He died in hospital at Skipton, at the age of 53, after having contracted silicosis, an incurable lung disease caused by breathing in the dust found in manufactured stone. His last recorded words were, 'I'm sorry.' As Jim grew up he was told that he had been only two years old when his father had died, and he seems not to have questioned the matter again until the crisp winter morning nearly 60 years later when he found himself standing at Charles's grave.

Ellen Kane's own story was complicated. One of four children born to a Barnsley railway worker and his young wife, she'd married Henry Kane at the age of 20 and in time had three daughters, Mollie, Margaret and Doreen, with him. Six years into the marriage Henry abandoned the home and was never seen there again. As with Charles Laker's later defection, it's not known what specific event, if any, triggered the crisis. Perhaps the supposedly diffident husband was just mismatched with his enterprising wife. But whatever it was, it was enough for Henry to leave not only the Bradford area but the country. In April 1905 he booked an assisted passage on the Blue Anchor Line's SS *Geelong*, later sunk in a collision, bound for Adelaide. This was the moment Ellen resolved to find work as a teacher, a career she pursued, if never formally qualified, until very nearly the end of her life 40 years later, becoming a formidable and highly respected local figure in the process. Jim was unambiguous about his mother. He credited her for wisdom and courage, and especially for imparting to her five children the belief that they were their own masters. 'She told us – my older sister and I when we were just kids – that we were just as good as anybody else, and never to tug our forelocks to our so-called betters,' he recalled. Laker's most convincing biographer, Alan Hill, describes Ellen as 'Tireless ... mercurial in temperament [with] a particular dislike for rigid rules. She had a strong and entirely personal moral code [which] did not always coincide with that decreed by society.'

As best we can gauge from a handful of surviving anecdotes, Ellen ably managed both home and work and never shirked heavy toil. It's said that around 1925 she personally built the family's first indoor lavatory, and in general had the quiet determination and inner resourcefulness that would reappear in her son. Certainly Jim's young life was centred on his mother. She taught him at the Calverley school five miles up Leeds Old Road in Pudsey, where he may conceivably have rubbed shoulders with a local boy six years older by the name of Len Hutton, and he soon showed reading and writing skills well above those of the other children. Ellen made and mended his clothes for him, enrolled him to act in school pageants, and in later years never missed one of his local football or cricket matches. She also imparted her essential faith in human goodness, along with a matching belief in the value of uncompromising self-reliance, perhaps the foundation of the independent streak Laker would display as an adult.

By all accounts it was a close, mutually protective household, if also an unorthodox one. Ellen was aged 43 when her only son was born. Small, plain-featured and somewhat shrill, which was no more than could be said of many English schoolmistresses of the era, she was also fond of dressing up and regularly changing her hair colour. As a neighbour named Audrey Hirst would recall, not entirely approvingly, as a middle-aged mother Ellen was still capable of attracting wolf whistles as she 'sashayed around' the streets of Bradford. Ellen told her employers that she was a widow, and young Jim was advised never to publicly acknowledge her. When they got to the Calverley school each morning, which they reached on foot, or by hitching a lift on a passing milk float, she was Mrs Kane and he was J.C. Laker. To add a further layer of complexity to the family arrangements, Jim seems to have regarded his three adult half-sisters as his aunts. Away from the school, it was thought that Ellen, Mollie, Margaret and Doreen were siblings, and guardians of the orphans Susie and Jim. One-parent households weren't as in vogue in the 1920s as they are today. Perhaps it's no wonder that in later years Laker tended to be guarded when asked about his childhood. On his first day at the nearby Salt School for Boys, where he started in September 1932, a teacher routinely enquired about his parents' names and address. The ten-year-old was silent for some time. Prodded further, he grunted, 'I've been told by my mother never to tell my business.'

As a rule, then, Laker preferred not to dwell in his later books and press interviews on the subject of his father, except to say that he 'never knew him', since he 'died when I was only one or two years old'. In fact Charles had been alive and living over the brush just 20 miles away from his deserted family's home until past the time of Jim's ninth birthday. 'I think that was a tremendous influence,' Laker's friend and later commentary box colleague Don Mosey reflected. 'I don't think there's any question about that, and not all to the good. It seems to me that his father's disappearance and the way [Laker] grew up, often with as many as five strong-willed northern women around the place, that some of that rubbed off on Jim. He wasn't mean or "warped" or anything of the sort, but I think that kind of separateness, of being different from other kids, rubbed off. And that's where all that sense of being difficult with authority figures and everything else came from.'

Laker nonetheless always spoke warmly of his seven years at senior school, one of those solid, fussily ornamented flint buildings that characterised the model mill-town envisioned by the Yorkshire textiles magnate Sir Titus Salt. In later days its most famous graduate remembered it as a 'thoroughly Victorian' institution, and, strange as it may seem to modern cars, he meant it as a compliment. One end-of-term report described the teenaged Laker as 'a straightforward sort, above-average intelligence, and [with] the voice of a lark'. As well as singing in the choir at St Barnabas Church in nearby Heaton, Jim played competitive tennis and football, and was known to disappear on his bike from breakfast to dinnertime on a Saturday to pedal the 15 miles south, through the evocatively named suburb of Fartown, which he and his friends invariably pronounced in such a way as to maximise its full comic potential, to watch the rugby league side in action at Huddersfield. In time Laker turned out for his school cricket XI and then for Saltaire in the Bradford League, without ever giving notice of any latent genius with the ball.

'I wasn't a budding world beater,' Laker recalled of his first season for Saltaire at the age of 16. The club's yearbook supports this, noting, 'His bowling varied from the studious to the irresponsible.' If anything, Laker was regarded as a batsman who could turn his arm over, third or fourth change, in a crisis. He played 50 matches for the club over the course of three seasons, finishing with 526 runs and 79 wickets 'taken at gentle medium-pace, and not cheaply', according to the annual. His closest friend on and off the games field was a slightly younger school class-mate named Fred Robinson, who described him in staccato terms, 'Very positive. Colourful vocabulary. Very supportive.' This same source would remember Laker in later years as more like a Chinese box. 'If you crossed the outer wall, then you faced another wall, then another, ad infinitum.'

Laker was at least good enough to be invited by a postcard signed by the Yorkshire secretary John Nash to go for coaching at the county's 'Headingley indoor academy' in October 1938. The facility in question turned out to be a porous-roofed shed of military décor tacked on to the rear end of a stand. Pronounced subsidence in the building's concrete floor meant that the artificial turf sloped perceptibly from one side to another, which was at least good practice when it later came to playing at Lord's. But despite the modesty of the place it proved an invaluable higher education. They were all there that month: Yorkshire's veteran batsman and left-arm spinner Maurice Leyland, the sometime England wicketkeeper Arthur Wood, and, aged 22 and 33 respectively, Len

Hutton and Hedley Verity, the former fresh from his record innings of 364 in the summer's final Test against Australia, the latter soon to take an army commission and ultimately to fall in action while fighting in the Allied invasion of Sicily, and both now about to set off for a final pre-war MCC tour of South Africa. It was the quality of insight into the hard realities of cricket Laker took from his hours in the Headingley shed, along with the gruff advice of the county professionals, that prompted him to think bigger. Of 58-year-old Benny Wilson, a prolific all-rounder for Yorkshire at around the turn of the 20th century, he remarked, 'I got to know and respect him as a coach and mentor, and he would needle me about improving my game. A very capable and a very good man, if not one of the world's cosiest personalities.'

Laker was given a Colts trial by Yorkshire in 1939, though apparently 'did nothing with the ball except launch a few optimistic seamers down the leg side'. But according to the *Leeds Mercury*, his batting had a 'phlegmatic, unmoved' quality to it that would have been in keeping with the overall character of Yorkshire cricket in the 1930s. He finished the 1940 season with Saltaire with 257 runs at an average of 32, and just seven wickets at 35 apiece. Alf Burgoyne, the Saltaire secretary for over 50 years, wrote of a match in which Laker scored 57 and Len Hutton 52, 'I know which of 'em I would have picked, and it wasn't Len.'

There were two significant developments for Laker in 1941. Having left school and taken a £2-a-week trainee job with Barclays Bank in Bradford, he decided to follow his friend Fred Robinson's example and volunteer for war service. This commendable gesture came at the height of the 'knock-for-knock' bombing raids, as Hitler referred to the aerial offensive unleashed again Britain from September 1940. When the moment came the recruiters advised Robinson that he was too young and to try again in six months' time, but 18-year-old Laker, billing himself as 'almost 20', was told to report back for duty on Monday. He was euphoric, so far as the word could ever fairly apply to him, to promptly find himself in the Royal Army Ordnance Corps (RAOC), not only a 'more worthwhile job than sitting about on my backside as a junior bank clerk', but also an outfit that at least as this stage of the war served as a nursery for budding sportsmen as much as it did an active fighting unit. 'They issued me with a wool uniform – it weighed about 20 pounds when it was wet – and other than doing some marching around they basically let you play football or cricket all day.'

The second major development in Laker's life that year was his decision to try his arm as a spin bowler. It doesn't detract in any way from the long hours of practice he subsequently put in, both in the army and civilian life, to say that his transformation from a willing if only fitfully effective seamer, with a bucking, plunging run-up, into the eternally patient and neatly harmonised spinner – a role apparently first suggested by Wilson, and reinforced by his RAOC team captain – was more or less an overnight conversion. Laker was a natural. His early efforts were relatively crude by comparison to his performances in the later 1940s, with his almost freakish control and the confidence which came from years of experience. But the elements on which he built them were there from the beginning.

Well-educated and endowed with an incisive mind, Laker was above all else a thinking cricketer. He possessed not only the spinner's classical delivery action, sideways on, eye trained over the left arm, front foot braced, but also the innate intelligence to go with it. Laker could and did imperceptibly vary his speed, for instance, depending on the foibles of the individual batsman or the state of the wicket. Arthur McIntyre, Surrey's wicketkeeper in their County Championship-winning team of the 1950s, summed him up. 'What made Jim so great was that he could turn one ball and create doubt for the man on strike – as well as for me behind the stumps – and then undercut the next one to make it go straight without any change of action … There are strapping great kids around 20 years old who flit in and out of a side, then disappear, and there are others you look at and say, he's not just a cricketer, he's a thinker. Jim was one of those.'

John Arlott believed Laker could even gauge to the millimetre the width of his spin. 'He achieved this by quite a number of methods – by changing the point of his grip so that his spinning finger slipped on the smooth surface of the ball instead of gripping on the seam; by trying to pitch the ball on its flat surface so that it slid on; by varying the point of release; and by checking his follow-through.' Not too many bowlers could aspire to all that. The future England captain Keith Fletcher, who played in the same county side as Laker in the 1960s, adds the detail, 'Jim gave the ball such a snap between thumb and finger as he released it that you could hear it fizz through the air, which I can assure you gives you a nasty sort of feeling if you're the batsman. You can *tell* something's going to happen – you just don't know what.' It's worth repeating that, in addition to these technical gifts, Laker possessed the slow bowler's ideal temperament: he was patient, collected, dogged and a bit stubborn – and as his future county captain Peter May said of him, 'He also enjoyed the priceless gift of silence, which made him stand out in a side where everybody talked far too much.'

Ellen Kane's investment of all her hopes and ambitions in Jim's future success had an obvious effect on his personality. He absorbed her confidence that he would prove to be someone special and achieve great things, regardless of any obstacles placed in his way by bovine authority figures. It was a powerful legacy. But Ellen's immediate hopes for her son didn't include him going off to war at the age of just 19, particularly when he was promptly issued with tropical kit and told to report for embarkation to Egypt. In fact, she made something of a fuss about it.

'Mother was quite distraught, and much to my embarrassment spent half that week pounding the doors of every officer she could find complaining about the injustice of an under-age soldier being dispatched overseas with such haste,' Laker recalled. Ellen probably needn't have worried, because Jim landed, in his own words, 'one of the army's cushiest numbers', a non-combative role that allowed him plenty of time for cricket. It was literally a turning point for him, because the dusty and frayed coconut batting strips of variable bounce he encountered on the playing fields of Cairo proved to be gratifyingly receptive to spin. As a rule, the typical army batsman didn't go to the wicket in Egypt with the luxury of a three- or four-day match stretching before him. This was cricket played in a format roughly 40 years before its time, usually with 50 overs a side and quite often less. Sooner rather than later the batsman had to hit out and take his chances. The wickets fairly demanded to fall to a bowler with the skill and intelligence to exploit the conditions. Laker soon returned figures of 8-30 in a one-day match at the Gezira Sporting Club, and within only a few months he found himself representing an England side against Australia in front of 12,000 servicemen on a park carved out of the ancient botanical gardens on the island of Zamalek just outside Cairo, where pink-billed hummingbirds ringed the outfield and white-coated attendants with ruby sashes and fezzes (a young Welsh trooper named Tommy Cooper was among those present, and got the idea for his later iconic headgear while in Egypt) served refreshing glasses of qasab sugar juice in marquees trimmed by patriotic bunting. 'Not exactly Bradford Park Avenue on a wet Monday,' the bowler wryly noted.

Laker's immediate commanding officer, 33-year-old 2nd Lt. (later Captain) Peter Smith was a trim, crisp-haired figure whose bearing might fairly have been described as military even before he signed up to fight in September 1939. More pertinently, Smith had already played some 300 matches as a professional at Essex, for whom he regularly took 100 wickets a year with a mixture of seam and leg-spin. Busy, suave and big-hearted, with a passing resemblance to the actor David Niven, Smith had nonetheless had to clutch hard at the remnants of his good humour when, on a non-playing Friday afternoon in August 1933, a message flashed on the screen of the Chelmsford cinema where he was sitting asking him to report immediately to the Essex county secretary. The secretary in turn showed Smith a telegram summoning him for international duty against the West Indies in a Test beginning the following morning at The Oval. Curiously, no one seemed to be particularly expecting him when he arrived at the ground. Eventually Smith had asked Bob Wyatt, who was captaining England in the match, whether or not he would be in the final 11, and Wyatt had to admit that he had no idea what he was talking about. The telegram had not come from the MCC. Smith had to wait a further 13 years before another message arrived inviting him to play for England at The Oval. This time it was genuine.

It's worth lingering on Smith and his story for a moment, if only because he made a lasting impression on the young cricketing recruit under his command. The tale of the hoax telegram, in particular, can only have further fuelled the mind of a man who was to become known for his cynically humorous view of human nature, and there was also the obvious attraction of having a CO who happened to be one of England's leading cricketers. The term 'role model' barely existed back then, but the stoical and debonair Smith, twirling the ends of his moustache before smoothly gliding in to bowl, offered an intoxicating vision of adult life as a paid, flannel-clad utopia free from the boredom and drudgery represented by the likes of Barclays Bank in Bradford. Now the fire really began to ignite for Laker, who later described himself as 'smitten' by cricket from about the age of 20.

When it came to actual bowling, Laker was a curious compound, extremely self-confident one moment and a bag of nerves the next. Several witnesses insist that he'd often been physically ill before going out in the field. By now he was fast learning the twin bowling virtues of thrift and penetration, proved himself adaptable to changing conditions, and knuckled down to any criticism provided it was both constructive and well-informed. He took 26 wickets, including one return of 5-10, in the space of four representative matches in September 1942. The following season he turned out for the British army side against New Zealand, and the correspondent for the *Egyptian Gazette* – referring to him a little freely as 'Jack' – praised him for his 'wonderfully rhythmical, rocking delivery', with a wheeling action 'that transfixed the batsman as the fakir does the snake'. Laker spread his fingers so wide and snapped them so hard when releasing the ball that he was already rubbing his skin raw around the knuckles, a significant cross for him in later years, but the returns were there in the scorebook. He took 221 wickets in the 1944 Egyptian season, essentially July to November, at 5.7 apiece, and the *Gazette* ran headlines along the lines of 'Spinner's 7-Wicket Haul Turns Tie', 'Saltaire Cricketer Makes Name for Himself' and, more than once, 'Our Jack Runs Rampant'.

In later years, Laker liked to repeat the story of his once having taken five wickets in an innings during a two-day match against a strong combined Australia and New Zealand side, following which he found himself setting off down a dusty road, heavy cricket gear in each hand, for the five-mile walk back to camp. After a few minutes, a jeep with a regimental flag flying from the bonnet had pulled up and a superbly pukka brigadier with a cut-glass accent had offered the young soldier a lift, which Laker accepted gratefully. As they drove off, the officer asked where Jim had just come from and was told 'Alamein'.

'Tell me, corporal,' the brigadier asked, 'what's the position there now?'

'Well, sir,' said Laker, 'the Aussies were 320/8 at the close, but we missed a few chances.'

According to Laker, there had then been a rapid falling-off in the brigadier's hospitality, as a result of which he was summarily evicted from the jeep. 'The brass in question had not been talking about cricket,' Laker later explained, adding that he, Jim, had given an unorthodox, two-fingered salute as the officer's vehicle sped off.

It's a good story, with an almost theatrical quality to it: as in a stylised Hollywood film, an honest young artisan is abused by his cruel and effete boss, inviting the audience to share the injustice of it all. According to Don Mosey, 'What's most significant in the tale as Jim used to tell it is that it gives us the clearest possible indication of his deep-seated dislike, or contempt, of authority.' It was a theme that would recur throughout Laker's subsequent career. 'As I walked back to base through the desert, I realised that on one side of life there were the guardians of wealth and privilege, and on the other members of an oppressed class who did most of the work,' Laker later wrote. Again, there's a sort of cinematic vividness to the scene. The humble yeoman trudges home on foot as the undeserving toff sweeps past in his chauffeured transport, and the moment is etched in time as, with a sudden insight, the young man grasps the true essence of life. It may even have been true, as Laker always insisted, although it's worth noting that the active fighting around El Alamein had ceased some 18 months before the officer allegedly asked for the lone soldier's assessment of conditions there, and that the Axis forces throughout North Africa had in fact surrendered en masse in May 1943.

* * *

Graham Anthony Richard 'Tony' Lock also had a somewhat unusual upbringing for the time. Among other hardships, his mother Martha died when he was only 11, close to the age Laker lost his estranged father. While such things naturally come as a shock to a child, there's no guarantee of how they might react. Both Laker and Lock essentially grew up in a one-parent household at a time when this still drew comment in the community. But more important than that is the striking contrast in temperament and style between their developing personalities: the flamboyant Lock, displaying a lack of restraint and a freedom of speech that alternated with bouts of despondency to the point that might suggest an undiagnosed case of manic depression, in contrast to the reserved Laker, who rarely if ever lost his cool in public. Once again without wishing to descend too far into the abyss of psychiatry, biographers always seem to recall Sigmund Freud's line on these occasions: the dictum that 'a man who has been the indisputable favourite of his mother retains the feeling of a conqueror' was clearly true in Laker's case. For Lock, life seemingly consisted more of the need for constant self-assertion along with the nagging sense that he was adrift in a hostile world. It's arguable that he had the sort of personality disorder in which the natural development of relationships with others fails to take place, and only the person himself, *his* needs, feelings and thoughts are experienced as real. Such an individual can rarely if ever relax his eternal vigilance around others. Lock could be warmly gregarious, hospitable and friendly; he was also temperamental, sensitive to the least slight, and never forgot a word of criticism. Godfrey Evans once told me that he'd 'thought Tony a very well-meaning guy who was also a bit like a human time bomb. You didn't want to be around him when he went off.'

Lock was born on 5 July 1929 at his family's home at 36 Granville Road in Oxted, which was then part of the timbered village of

Limpsfield on the Surrey–Kent border, where his war veteran father Fred worked as a private chauffeur and was an all-round local sports personality, known for his lively swing bowling. It was an eminently respectable neighbourhood, bordered by neatly trimmed hedges, and with an old-fashioned red Edwardian wall box set on an ivy-clad post just outside the Locks' front gate. The fifth of July was a Friday that year, and the next morning Fred went out to play for his home club against a visiting side from Croydon. One of his opponents later recalled, 'He rushed up to me and excitedly said, "We had a son yesterday, and he's going to play for England!"'

The young Lock grew up in a close but mutually competitive family, with an older brother, Bryan, and a father who, having once been offered terms by Surrey, but not wishing to take the financial risk involved, might conceivably have looked to one or both of his sons to fulfil his frustrated ambitions. In time Bryan abandoned the struggle, but Tony was apparently predestined to be a professional cricketer. At the age of six he was photographed proudly wearing white flannels, pads and gloves, and holding a bat nearly as broad as he was. He also had the patronage of the headmaster of his village school, Leonard Moulding, of whom it was said he had only two immutable demands of his seven to 15-year-old charges: that they graduate with at least the basic facility to read and write, and they play a sport to the absolute pinnacle of their ability.

Lock first turned out for his school XI at the age of ten, and by 13 he was the side's captain. They played on the handsome, tree-lined ground laid out on Limpsfield Common, with a slightly ramshackle scoreboard at one end and a few deckchairs scattered either side of the ancient roller on the other. 'The square was excellent and we were allowed to have the school nets rigged up on the turf close to the match wickets,' Lock recalled. 'We never had the fear of getting a crack on the head from a ball of good length, and we learned to play with a straight bat instead of backing away and aiming hopeful swipes. Mr Moulding would put a white handkerchief on a good length to help accuracy.' These were the sort of time-honoured virtues that sophisticated skills academies around Britain now spend millions of pounds each year trying to instil in their students.

Lock, then, was exposed to organised cricket at a younger age than Laker was. As teenagers, both of them were regarded as all-rounders rather than specialist bowlers. Both in their way were fanatically keen on other sports, both sang in their church choir, and both showed early signs of being self-willed and resistant to authority. Laker was the more academically gifted of the two, Lock tending to fall back in later years more on a native wit than any pretence of intellectual brilliance to express an opinion. One was diffident, the other was well able to look after himself, and showed no lack of confidence in his relationships with his fellow pupils or teachers. Lock was seemingly born to play professional cricket; Laker might never have done so without Hitler's intervention in his life.

Still, their childhoods defy easy contrast between one of unremitting northern graft and another of bucolic Home Counties privilege. Fred Lock insisted that his sons be taught other matters as well as sport, instructing his wife, 'Stint them until they know the value of money. Teach them to rely on themselves. Let them find out what the world is like.' On top of the central tragedy of Martha's death from cancer at the age of 51 there was also the fact that Limpsfield lay uneasily close to the outskirts of London and thus on the path of the nightly German bombing raids. By the summer of 1944, when Tony turned 15, the first of Hitler's V1s, the so-called miracle weapons, began to fall. The local *County Post* newspaper of that June and July gives some of the flavour. 'Flying bombs Night and Day ... Five air-raid warnings ... Parents, Daughter and Cook Killed ... Tragedy of Two Twins.' Of its kind,

Limpsfield followed a classic history among southern English communities: in the 1930s the Depression set in like a chill High Weald fog, and lifted just in time for the Luftwaffe. This was the atmosphere in which the young Lock grew up – in a home shattered by the early death of a parent and subject to the recurrent terrors of war. Somewhere in these formative years, the teenager also developed a noticeable stutter. It came and went over time, but was still pronounced enough for Lock's county cricket colleagues in the 1960s to affectionately know him as 'B-b-bowl', which is how he expressed himself when he particularly wanted an over.

There may have been very little else in the whole history of organised cricket quite like the zeal of Lock when thrown the ball and surveying the unfortunate batsman with a mixture of scorn and pity, muttering all the while, before bounding in with his short, businesslike trot and suddenly whippy action, accompanied by a climactic grunt. In his early teens, still with a headful of sandy hair that flopped around as he ran, he relied on flight rather than spin, or failing that just speared it in low and disconcertingly fast from round the wicket at the right-hander's off stump. While precocious, Lock didn't burst with sudden brilliance on the cricket world. He generally took a wicket or two an innings, and tended not to loiter with the bat. But as a young player no one made more of his natural gifts, or drove himself harder than he did.

It's often been said that Lock should have been a fast bowler (his father had told him he didn't have the build for it), but as it happened he soon found a suitable alternative outlet for his limitless reserves of pent-up aggression in the way he fielded. Tony's natural skill at catching a ball was honed by playing a game called 'Wall' in the school playground. The rules were simple. A boy was stationed in front of the building's back gate in the attitude of a man facing a firing squad, and three or four colleagues, standing about 15 yards away, would then hurl tennis balls at him with all their might.

The idea was to hit the target as hard and as often as you could, or alternatively to hare after the ball should it rebound off the gate. No one fancied their chances playing the game when Lock was involved, because he always fired the ball in at them like a rocket, and with devastating accuracy. But when his own turn came to be the mark he simply shot out a hand and caught everything they threw at him. He was widely known as a tough competitor. After reading the list of entrants for the school sports day's cross-country run in June 1944, another young athlete was seen sprinting home shouting along the way, 'My God! Lock is in the race! We're screwed!'

Lock was also lucky in his mentors, because as well as both his cricket-mad father and headmaster, he soon came to the notice of Henry Leveson Gower (pronounced Looson Gore, and popularly known as 'Shrimp'), a four-year Oxford blue in the 1890s, Test selector, MCC stalwart, and more to the point a long-serving president of Surrey. The great man lived in the next village to Limpsfield, and liked to drive over in his Rolls-Royce (he was also a successful City stockbroker) on a Saturday afternoon to watch the local schoolboys in action. He wrote presciently to the Surrey committee in July 1944, 'The left-arm lad [Lock] is tremendously keen, a bit hot-headed, and may prove a real prospect for the future so long as he keeps his feet on the ground.' As a result Tony was in the Surrey Colts side, playing alongside boys who were two or three years older than he was, just a few days after his 15th birthday. He took 1-10 in his first match and 7-37 in his second. In September the Surrey yearbook said of him, 'G.A.R. Lock (left arm slow), although very young, will be an asset to the side in the future.' He turned out for the Colts in the Victory summer of 1945 and took the wicket of Worcestershire's 26-year-old Charles Palmer, a future England player. Palmer later reminisced, 'He was loud, wore a red cravat in the field, loved bowling, hated the batsman. I marked him down as someone who would likely either go to prison or become a great cricketer.'

The future High Court judge Oliver Popplewell played for the Colts alongside Lock in the summer of 1945. 'He [Lock] was a great competitor, and even then didn't take too many prisoners,' Popplewell told me. 'His father was a great supporter and took Tony to task if he didn't perform up to standard.' No less a figure than the 62-year-old Jack Hobbs – the Master – coached the young Surrey side, which would be roughly akin to having Mozart offer you free piano lessons as a teenager.

'At that time I had no idea of making a living out of cricket,' Lock wrote. Instead, discovering with finality that his scholastic gifts were meagre, he left school at 15 and resigned himself to a career of honest if unrewarding manual toil. He first dug ditches, then delivered milk, and after that took a comparatively well-heeled job as an apprentice to a cabinetmaker in his workshop near the banks of the River Eden at Oxted. He lasted about a week there. 'Part of my work was to smooth down the rough edges of the glass tops of dressing tables with pumice stone,' Lock recalled. 'I was at this job one afternoon, but thinking more about the next day's cricket match. My left hand slipped, ran across the glass and left an ugly scar on the shiny surface. As a cabinetmaker, I had been bowled out.'

The period in Britain from around 1944 to 1950, when Lock was reaching adulthood, was probably the hardest of the 20th century. Even for one of life's incurable optimists, it was an era characterised by icy nights in gaslit rooms, initially to the accompaniment of German rocket attacks, of whale fat and tinned beef, and all the other comically vile ingredients of a serious sacrifice he never forgot. Clothing coupons and food queues long remained a way of life; 14 years of rationing ended only in July 1954, and even then luxury commodities like butter and petrol were hard to come by. Lock later said of the winter of 1945/46, 'Our life was so cold and grey and generally grim you'd sometimes wonder who won the ruddy war.' But he wrote that 40 years after the event. Most of his surviving letters and notes of the time are singularly upbeat, with lines such as, 'Mr Sandham from Surrey asked father if I was fit – said there may be a place there for me.' None of the known correspondence ever talks about austerity or misfortune or making do in a single-parent household, where Fred now worked as a fitfully employed painter and decorator. It's all about cricket.

In June 1946 Andrew Sandham, Hobbs's long-time batting partner and now the Surrey coach, was again in touch. He wanted Lock to come in for a full trial at The Oval. A week later another letter arrived at Granville Road from the county secretary. It offered Lock terms of £3 10s a week (about £45 today) for the rest of the season. Even with this modest stipend, Lock recalled, 'I danced around the house, whooping for joy.' He played his first professional match for the county side beginning on 13 July, against Kent at The Oval. He scored one not out, batting at number 11, and took no wickets. Lock had turned 17 only a week earlier, which meant that he was the youngest player ever to represent Surrey and that he actually made his debut before Laker, who first turned out for the county side just four days later, at the age of 24. The latter's introduction to the first-class game was slightly more auspicious; he took 3-78 and 3-43, and was said to have 'deported himself with distinction' in his team's six-wicket win over Combined Services.

The Tony Lock who reported for duty at The Oval in the late summer of 1946 was a strange mixture of parts: ambitious but unfocused on the field, opinionated and awkward off it. A boisterous exterior belied an adolescent prone to periodic depressions, whose deference to senior players masked a simmering aversion to authority. Lock still lived at home, had a local girlfriend named Audrey Sage – his future wife – but otherwise seems to have preferred his own company. Like many outwardly convivial people, he was probably a bit lonely. It's also worth repeating how young he still was. When the drinks came out in that first Kent match, Lock noticed that his 38-year-old Surrey team-mate Alf Gover, whose benefit year it was, had his own special glass. The teenager innocently asked him what was in it, and Gover invited him to take a sip. 'I did – and spat it out again all over the wicket,' Lock recalled. Gover's 'dynamite-strength' whisky was a rude introduction for the young county debutant, who at that stage of his life had never tasted anything stronger than Ribena.

* * *

By early April 1945 Jim Laker's role in Hitler's downfall was rapidly drawing to a conclusion. Granted a month's leave by the army, he went back to spend it at his mother's new terraced home in Manningham, close to the Bradford City football ground. At 67, Ellen remained, as her son recognised, 'a loner and a law unto herself'. She was still teaching and had recently acquired a high-powered motorbike to get her across town to her latest school at Thornbury. It's been speculated that Ellen was suffering from cancer, but had chosen not to worry anyone about her condition. Towards the end of the month she suggested that Jim take the train down to Eastbourne to spend a few days with his half-sister Doreen. 'Perhaps she had a premonition, because she insisted on accompanying me to the station,' Laker recalled. By the time his train had reached the south coast six hours later his mother had collapsed and died. A neighbour discovered her body lying across the bed the following morning. In her will Ellen left Jim her entire estate, including the house and £900 in the bank, and nothing to her four daughters.

Laker briefly went back to Egypt, got, as the jargon of the day had it, buggered about by the army, and eventually landed a lowly desk job at the War Office in Whitehall. While there he lodged with an RAOC friend at his family home in Waldram Park Road in Forest Hill, south London. Finally demobbed in the spring of 1946, Laker chose to stay put and began appearing with some success for Catford in the Kent Cricket League. In one of his first matches, he took all ten opposition wickets, eight of them bowled, for 21 runs with his 'quite proficient medium-pace off breaks', in the measured words of the club annual. Performing the same role as Henry Leveson Gower with Lock, the Catford president selflessly wrote to recommend his side's new match-winner to the Surrey committee. Laker duly went for a trial that July. He impressed Andrew Sandham, with 42,000 first-class runs behind him, by bowling him between bat and pad in the nets, and was offered a one-year contract at £6 a week, plus match fees in summer, as a result. Since this was more than Barclays were willing to pay him, he accepted the county's terms and settled in London, thus migrating in the opposite direction to his father Charles. One can't help feeling a mistake was made that somehow allowed Laker to slip through Yorkshire's clutches.

Laker's initial experience of county cricket must have been that it was painfully similar to the army. One of the first people he met at The Oval was Leveson Gower, who extended a crushing handshake and addressed the club's latest recruit as 'Fishlock' (a left-handed bat who had made his Surrey debut in 1931), an error neither Laker himself nor anyone else ever corrected. The new boy's cricket coffin was carried upstairs by an ancient retainer and he was shown where he was to change, in a professionals' dressing room furnished by a thin strip of mud-coloured carpet, a few mismatched hard chairs and some splintered lockers for the players' equipment. On matchdays Laker ate his lunch and tea in a long, bare side room with two tables on which were laid plates of white bread and a variety of sweaty pink meats accompanied by a tureen of congealed gravy, the room and food both smelling obscurely of stale cigarette smoke. As Alec Bedser later remarked of the professionals' working environment at The Oval, 'There was a constant haze of equal parts dried sweat and fags around the dressing room, and when Surrey were batting and everyone was crammed in there it got so thick you sometimes bumped into the furniture when you walked around.'

The players' out-of-town travel arrangements and accommodations were not luxurious. They went by third-class rail and often lodged at a seaside bed and breakfast with moulding walls and a thin bed like a derelict park bench. If there was ever a team meeting no one there spoke about 'having a strategy' or 'sharing a vision'. When someone got hurt, the same elderly retainer would show up and train an army surplus sun lamp on the affected spot. The junior Surrey players were known by their surnames and the amateurs answered to 'Mr' or 'Sir'. There was something of a class divide apparent in this relationship, and perhaps it could hardly have been otherwise in light of the fact that almost all the playing staff had recently served at either officer or enlisted level in one branch or another of the armed forces.

Captaining Surrey that first post-war summer was the lean, wavy-haired figure of 32-year-old Major Nigel Harvie Bennett, a superbly urbane character with a languid drawl, but whose cricket fell some way short of the truly proficient. The tale of Bennett's appointment became part of the game's folklore.

According to *Wisden*:

> Alec Bedser called it simply 'the cock-up', and blamed it
> on the general muddle everywhere after the Second World
> War ... Events apparently unfolded like this: When Monty

Garland-Wells, Surrey's chosen skipper for the 1946 season, had to withdraw, the committee decided to offer the leadership to Major Leo Bennett, a well-known and talented club cricketer. While the search was on for Major Leo, Major *Nigel* Bennett popped in to renew his membership after the war. The pavilion clerk took the papers to the secretary, who happened to have the chairman with him: they offered the captaincy to this Major Bennett, who accepted. He soon revealed his inexperience, twice rolling the new ball back along the ground from the covers for overthrows past a gobsmacked Alf Gover ... In a later match, Bennett asked Jim Laker to open the bowling; when Laker pointed out that he was actually an off-spinner, the captain said, 'But you bowl quick too, don't you?'

After his Surrey debut against the Combined Services, Laker played for the county twice more in the second half of the 1946 season. He took 1-26 and 1-22 in the home draw against Hampshire, and showed his nerves when coming in to bowl to the visitors' Rodney Exton. Alf Gover had sent down the previous over and was still pulling his sweater back over his head in his position at short leg when Laker let go. The batsman came forward, got an edge, and the ball lodged between the temporarily blinded fielder's knees. It was a fair catch. 'Was that your slower one, bowler?' Bennett enquired. Laker was wicketless in his final match of the season, but between his legacy from Ellen and his stipend from Surrey he had enough on hand to spend the next six months taking the tram into Wandsworth each weekday morning to practise at the same Alf Gover's indoor school. It proved to be the coldest winter in living memory, and there was no heating of any sort on Gover's premises. Early in the spring Major Bennett resigned his position as Surrey captain, having played a total of 31 first-class matches with a batting average of 16. The 42-year-old Errol Holmes, another major, returned as county captain in 1947, and Bennett moved to the West Country, where he played many years' club cricket for Taunton. He died in 2008, at the age of 95.

As Surrey's captain, Errol Reginald Thorold Holmes, late of Malvern and Oxford University, had a very distinct skill: he polarised people. Typically adorned by a Harlequin cap and white linen cravat, he was recognisably, and proudly, of the old school. Jack Hobbs once said of him that 'he set a fine example in the field' and 'would not tolerate anything shady or underhanded', while the peerless cricket writer Ronald Mason was on ground well beyond that when he wrote of watching Holmes in his pre-war playing days at The Oval: 'At his best he was a beautiful bat, and made all hearts beat in his airy grace and flowing Malvernian style ... God, how I did love that man!' Set against these plaudits, there were also those who thought Holmes, with his piping voice and extended vowels, an anachronistic and even faintly ludicrous figure in the bracing new world of the Attlee government and all that ensued, and perhaps just a touch too keen on maintaining certain *ancien régime* mannerisms, such as his habit of communicating with his batsmen in the middle by telegram, or addressing his professional players while in the field as 'My good man' and avoiding their company entirely at all other times.

Laker was firmly of the second school of opinion on Holmes. 'The man was quite frankly the biggest snob I ever met,' he once remarked. 'He had very dark, cold eyes, a barking accent, and a habit of saying "chop, chop" after every command.' Laker always remembered a particular moment in the 1947 season when only an hour after the close of play one warm Tuesday evening at The Oval the Surrey team had caught the slow train down to Portsmouth, where they were due to play Hampshire in a three-day match starting the next morning. During that hour, Laker, as junior pro, was responsible with the help of the elderly pavilion attendant for carrying all his team-mates' equipment down to the ground's front gate, into a fleet of taxis and up to Waterloo, after which he took his own third-class seat, before unloading the same kit on arrival at the other end, personally escorting the amateurs' baggage to their town centre hotel, and at last making his way on foot to his own dockside lodgings where an unappealing cold collation awaited him on the sideboard.

The next morning, Laker walked the two miles to the United Services ground, came on to bowl first change, and took eight Hampshire wickets for 69 runs. He later recalled, 'Afterwards the captain asked me to go down to the gate and buy him an evening paper, and the great Leveson Gower, who'd come down to watch, passed me in the corridor. "Well bowled, Fishlock," he said. And that was it. All very hierarchical, cricket was in those days, to put it no stronger.' In a later article, Laker characterised it as 'like P.G. Wodehouse without the laughs'.

Judging from the way he moved erratically up and down the order that summer, Laker was still regarded as a batsman who could usefully turn his arm over. He managed to score 33 and 60 for once out against a strong Middlesex attack at Lord's, but by the start of the 1948 season – now as a capped player – the experiment seems to have been abandoned. After that the county yearbook refers to him as 'a solid Number 8 or 9 who [can] add tail-end runs'. Never conceding any legitimacy to authority, Laker in turn regarded his team captain and others like him as incompetents, charlatans and twerps. He was now dangerously impervious to criticism.

At that point Lock was the more easily defined of the pair. He was the first authentic slow left-arm bowler ever to play for Surrey in the county's 100-year history, and as a result was regarded as a sort of exotic and potentially dangerous wild beast in a team full of household – some of them pedigree – cats and dogs, a status he might not have actively disowned. Certainly there was something a bit feral about the way Lock crouched in the field, prehensile hands outstretched, quivering with expectation, and positively menacing about his habit of staring at any umpire rash enough to refuse one of his uniquely full-throated appeals. Once he did a full somersault after bowling and shouted for lbw lying flat on the pitch. By contrast, Laker was more apt merely to enquire conversationally, 'Was that close?' and, if not close enough, to convey his disappointment by almost imperceptibly raising an eyebrow and giving a world-weary tug to his trousers. 'Jim was all on the inside,' Lock himself once observed, admitting that he was 'different' – as anyone seeing him trot back to his mark, veins bulging in his forehead, giving an exhorting clap to his fielders, always bristling with impatience to get at the batsman again, would have recognised.

The two Surrey debutants had first met when reporting for duty at The Oval in July 1946. By coincidence, the long saga of mutual rivalry and perseverance that characterised their relationship as a whole would reach its public climax exactly ten years to the day later. Their first appearance together in the same side came over the late-May Whitsun holiday in 1947, in a second XI match at the Ashley Down ground in Bristol. Laker took four wickets in the Gloucestershire first innings, and Lock took two. It was a curious affair by all accounts. The pitch was described as 'sandy', which was unusual for Bristol in May, and for once Lock dropped his catches in the leg trap. In later years, Laker had the good grace to recall his exasperated comment to the Surrey captain, 'Do the kid a favour and stick him on the boundary. He'll never be a short leg as long as he plays the game.' It may have been a premature verdict even then, because Lock finished that season with 11 catches in the same number of matches, and was on his way to a career total of 830 (third in the all-time list), nearly a quarter of them taken off his own bowling.

It was often said both at Surrey and elsewhere that Laker was the 'more intelligent' of the pair, while Lock was a country lad at heart who gave free rein to his inner teenager well into his adult years. Laker was also stubborn, but not a thruster. He never hated batsmen as such. He only hated their batting. He put great store in moving on. 'Anger is a waste of energy,' Laker once said. 'Steam which is used to blow up with anger would be better used to drive the engine.' Sometimes he varied the metaphor but always to make the same underlying point. Lock was quicker to the boil. Nearly 20 years into the future, a junior player managed to drop a simple chance off his bowling, and those who witnessed the bowler's subsequent fury would long speak of the scene in hushed tones, like old salts recalling a historic hurricane. Even when he was happy, Lock could sometimes seem a bit intimidating, with his high forehead gleaming with sweat and nostrils flared like those of a jittery racehorse. But perhaps he was also more 'real' than Laker. There was never the stamp of omnipotence or infallibility about Lock's cricket. Quite often he followed up the really unplayable ball with a total duffer, or vice-versa. Lock was not born with genius like Laker. He had to work at it, twice completely remodelling his entire delivery action, the second time at an age when lesser men might reasonably have considered retirement, and emerging both times as good a bowler, if not better, than before. Neville Cardus once wrote, 'There is not a man sitting in the Free Seats any day watching him who doesn't feel, "There, but for the grace of God, go I; that's the way I'd play cricket myself if I were good enough."' He was speaking about Bill Edrich, but it also rings true of Lock.

Within his own rules of engagement Laker was perfectly good company, and he thrived on intelligent talk of the sort not always available in the typical professional cricketers' dressing room of the

1940s. Although a conservative in both meanings of the word he wasn't a snob in the sense of rating people solely by social status. As we've seen, he was profoundly unimpressed by rank or privilege, unless these were combined with real talent or distinction. He thought the junior players at Surrey were treated like dogs, and even in later years could still work himself up into a state of fury when recalling the ordeal of carrying his captain's bags around ('Holmes had a ruddy polo mallet at one stage'), among other indignities.

To the much younger Lock, life on the English cricket circuit was all more of an extended schoolboy's adventure. As he saw it, he was being paid, if poorly, to do what he loved, and a certain amount of inconvenience simply went with the territory. Shortly after his Surrey debut, Lock found himself packed on to a Bank Holiday train from Paddington to Penzance, where he was due to play the following morning for his county's second XI against Cornwall. 'Every compartment was jammed to its corridors with people heading west,' Lock remembered. 'With a match in front of us, we felt like resting. Most of the team gave up the idea in the general crush. But it didn't bother me. I clambered on to a luggage rack and in next to no time was fast asleep.' Going out into the field at the picturesque St Clare Ground after a night spent sharing a room in a local pub, he picked up seven cheap wickets in the match, wheeling away, in *The Cornishman*'s apt simile, 'like a well-run train keeping its schedule'.

Laker finished the 1947 season with 79 first-class wickets in 18 matches, and Lock with four off two. The former was rewarded by selection for the MCC winter tour of the West Indies, while the latter now took his turn for 18 months' National Service. Characteristically, Lock saw his hitch with the Royal Artillery as something of a lark – posted to Oswestry in Shropshire, he spent most of the summer of 1948 playing cricket – although thanks to the even limited amount of square-bashing involved it was now that he first experienced the pain in his right knee that nagged him for the rest of his career. Popular with his fellow teenaged recruits, it has to be said he was not otherwise a conspicuous success in the military. One of Lock's party pieces was to take an officer the men particularly disliked, then for hours on end to talk with that man's voice, walk with his walk, and mimic his gestures and mannerisms. The impersonations became so polished that as a gag he once shouted 'Attention!' outside the door of a Nissen hut and then walked in to find his fellow squaddies standing ramrod straight at the ends of their bunks, awaiting a snap inspection. 'The army was good fun, and you got paid too,' he once remarked of his time in uniform.

Oddly enough, while Lock revelled in institutional life in the Shropshire barracks, Laker did not greatly enjoy his winter in the Caribbean under the captaincy of Gubby – later Sir George – Allen, who at the age of 45 was perhaps optimistically listed as one of the tour party's fast bowlers. The group travelled not by today's first-class jet, but in a three-to-a-cabin banana boat which pitched and rolled its way across the Atlantic through a series of December storms. The players' seaborne Christmas dinner was notable only for the large number of vacant seats around the table. Laker acquitted himself well in his first Test, at Barbados, where he took 7-103 and 2-95 in the draw against a West Indies team led by the great George Headley. Brian Chapman wrote in *The Guardian* that this was 'a magnificent Test debut ... The West Indies' Jeffrey Stollmeyer, already out, was standing alongside me when Laker came on. He gasped with astonishment when he saw the break-back off the first ball. So probably did Headley, who had to deal with it. A couple of balls later, trying to pull, he swept the ball down on to his stumps.' The bowler himself was typically unassuming about his performance. 'I was bloody lucky it rained overnight and the wicket cover leaked right on a length for me,' he later wrote.

That early success was probably the high point of Laker's tour. Like most of the visitors, he had been looking forward to escaping ration-bound Britain for a paid three-month break in the sun. The reality was uninspiring. The players' accommodations were basic, the food abundant but often disastrously fresh, Allen was firmly of the Errol Holmes school as captain, and the playing conditions were variable at best. In the third Test at Georgetown, held ten feet below sea level, steam could be seen rising from the pitch. There was a bewildering number of English illnesses and injuries, and an emergency call summoned 31-year-old Len Hutton, who himself emerged from the war with one arm shorter than the other, to make a five-stop, four-day flight from the depths of midwinter Yorkshire. Thirty-six hours after arriving, Hutton went out to open the batting for MCC against British Guiana and scored 138. 'I respected Len, even if he didn't much care for me,' Laker later said of a man who was to play a major part in his future Test career. There was a certain amount of tension in the MCC ranks as a whole: the old guard like Gubby Allen and Billy Griffith rubbed shoulders with a fresh batch of newcomers like Laker and Johnny Wardle, not always comfortably. No one had a clue what Allen's overall strategy was, including Allen himself, save that it involved wearing a white dinner jacket on formal occasions.

In the end the West Indies won the series 2-0. The visitors then agreed to a hastily arranged 14th and final match against a club side at Montego Bay, where they duly recorded their sole victory of the tour. Laker took 36 wickets in all competitions, 18 in the Tests, and though handicapped by strained stomach muscles came out on top of the averages. Crawford White wrote in the *News Chronicle*, 'He moved one more step towards a regular place in England's side.'

Meanwhile, as Lock settled in to a relatively carefree 1948 summer of regimental cricket, the first real test of Laker's nerve at the top level would come with his selection to play three Tests against Don Bradman's Australians, one of which in the eyes of many critics was to put him firmly and for ever beyond the pale.

3

'Dull Cricket is not to be Seen'

DON BRADMAN'S 1948 'Invincibles' didn't acquire their name by chance. Despite his allegedly waning powers, Bradman himself compiled 11 centuries on what proved to be his last tour of England, with 2,428 first-class runs as a whole at an average fractionally below 90. The other batsmen included the likes of Sid Barnes, Arthur Morris, Lindsay Hassett and the teenaged Neil Harvey, all of whom finished with career Test averages well above 40, while the bowling was spearheaded by the smoothly feline Ray Lindwall and that singular force of nature Keith Miller, with the agile and pugnacious Don Tallon behind the stumps. They won four of the five Tests, drawing the other one, and 23 of their 31 first-class matches, many of them by wide margins.

Playing Essex at Southend in the middle of May, Australia were dismissed in a single day for what proved to be the only time in the season. Unfortunately, they also scored 721 runs in the process. The carnage might have been worse but for the fact that Miller deliberately allowed himself to be bowled first ball, either as a protest against Australia's merciless demolition of their hosts or as a means for him to be able to get to the local horse races, depending on whose account you believe. The visitors then dismissed Essex twice on the second and final day, winning the match by the tidy margin of an innings and 451 runs. They were that good, and by the end of the summer all England seemed willing to celebrate their side's crushing series defeat with almost audible church bells and cannon fire. 'We lost not only the Ashes, but the sackcloth as well,' the former Test captain Arthur Gilligan was left to write in conclusion.

So Laker had his work cut out for him when, just four weeks after returning from the Caribbean, he went out to play for Surrey against Australia at a bitingly cold Oval. He did nothing. In fact his first-innings return of 1-137 was the worst analysis of his entire career. A fortnight later, representing MCC against the tourists at Lord's, he at least managed a first-innings haul of 3-127. Laker had no chance to improve his figures on either occasion, because the Australians won both matches without the need to bat a second time. They thumped 11 sixes off him in a day at Lord's, seemingly as part of a deliberate strategy to hit him out of the series. 'I didn't know how to stop them thrashing me,' Laker himself was forced to admit, after watching Miller deposit him over the Lord's leg side boundary for nine sixes in a session. 'I became flustered, dropped my guard and was wide open to punishment.'

England's captain Norman Yardley won the toss in the first Test at Trent Bridge and elected to bat on a green wicket with rain in the air, a decision that could be counted only a partial success by the time his side was dismissed for 165 in just two sessions. Laker, ninth man in, top-scored with 63. Yardley wasn't impressed, striking a familiar imperious note by telling the returning batsman, 'I can't understand why you didn't stay there and make a century.' The Australians replied with 509.

Here's how John Arlott described the early part of the tourists' innings:

> Laker sauntered up to the wicket and bowled. He was pushed away firmly for a single in his first over. In the next

he achieved a maiden with a casual air. In his third over he stunned the crowd by bowling to Morris a ball which the batsman pulled on to his wicket while ostensibly playing it to leg. Regaining consciousness, the watchers cheered, and Australia were 73 for one wicket.

Regrettably, that probably marked the high point of England's fortunes in the Test, which they lost with time to spare. Laker took four Australian wickets, including Miller for a duck, at a cost of 138 runs. 'Not good enough,' Yardley remarked of his bowler in the evening press, characteristically blunt in his appraisal. Laker nonetheless got a letter from the MCC inviting him to play in the second Test at Lord's, but there was no entrance pass to the ground in the envelope. Still lodging in Forest Hill, he took the tram and tube to the team hotel at Paddington, then had to talk his way past the gate attendants when reporting for play at ten the next morning. He was bowling to the Australians before lunch. Bradman actually looked to be in trouble in his first over, shuffling around like he'd never played off spin before, and at the end of it he paid the bowler the compliment of calling up the wicket, 'Well done, Jim.' So Laker gave him the same treatment in the next over, only this time Bradman hit him straight back over the top and they had to fetch the ball from under a bench at the back of the Nursery Ground. England lost by 409 runs. Laker's 2-128 in the match was thought deficient, not least by him, and he was one of four players, including Hutton, dropped for the next Test. Miller later recalled that the Australians had 'literally punched the air' when listening to their opponents' names being read out by the BBC, as sonorously as at a state funeral, on their hotel radio.

England at least managed to draw the third Test at Old Trafford, where it rained for a day and a half and 135,000 spectators paid at the turnstiles. That same week Laker ran through the Kent card at

Blackheath with second-innings figures of 6-60, and then, almost immediately playing the same team at The Oval, suffered surely cricket's bitterest fate for a batsman, running himself out for 99 going for what would have been his maiden century. He was back again for the fourth Test at Headingley, along with three other England changes. The selectors' obvious perplexity about how to handle the Australians can only have buoyed the tourists' spirits. Anyway, the Aussies won again, and in the inquest that followed there seemed to emerge a line of thought which was to have a profound effect on Laker's fortunes for the next decade. Not to put too fine a point on it, some of his critics, several of them well positioned in cricket's committee rooms, came to believe that he'd lost his bottle.

The match facts are that England batted first and scored 496, with centuries by Washbrook and Edrich. The Australians replied with 458, Laker 3-113, and the second time around England declared at 365/8. As a result the tourists needed to make 404 runs to win, in about five and a half hours, on a turning wicket, and Godfrey Evans, even then a keen student of the odds, as well as being probably England's finest ever wicketkeeper, once told me that it was a case of '10-1 on a home win, and almost anything you liked against the Aussies'.

Instead, that fifth day at Leeds proved to be one of those agonies of national sporting humiliation which the English seem to do better than most other countries. Bradman came in with the score at 57-1 after 73 minutes. Laker, who had already been bowling for close to an hour, posted four men around the bat on the leg side. Bradman immediately clipped him for four to long-off, against the spin. The next ball the batsman played an almost posthumous late cut for three. Australia were still behind the clock, but as Evans later said in those two or three minutes something palpably changed in the dynamics of the match. Suddenly Compton was bowling his somewhat eccentric left-arm spin, and when that proved insufficiently potent Hutton was called on to have a go. In Neville Cardus's words, 'He delivered five innocent, amiable full pitches from which Bradman and Morris flicked five fours with lazy strokes over the grassy outfield.'

Laker was soon back in action again. He swung his arms, did one or two preliminary calisthenics, touched his toes, handed his sweater to the umpire, measured out his six-pace run, swung his arms again, and at last came in to bowl. Bradman promptly hit him back through long-off for four. Australia were 288/2 at tea, which was a subdued affair in the England dining room. Bradman had just been dropped twice in the slips, and Evans of all people had made the cardinal keeper's mistake of anticipating the boundary instead of the ball and comprehensively fumbled the ensuing stumping chance. 'Around then it began to dawn on me that it wasn't going to be our day,' he recalled, still a bit rueful about it 40 years later.

Laker, it has to be said, was not at his best, with 93 runs coming off 32 second-innings overs without a wicket. Neil Harvey made the winning shot for Australia with 15 minutes to spare. It was in some ways the mirror opposite result to the famous finish of the match between the same two teams at Headingley in 1981. From being certain to win, the dominant side somehow managed to lose. Admittedly the England selectors hadn't helped the cause by failing to pick a second specialist spinner, and the home fielding on the fifth day was sadly defective, possibly because some of the players had already mentally packed up their gear and gone home. As for Laker, his stock plummeted. He'd played poorly at Leeds, but if merely doing that damned a player, he should have had plenty of company on the way down. Instead, he rode alone. From late July 1948, it was increasingly muttered in both county dressing rooms and in Test selecting circles that, put bluntly, he didn't have the stomach for the fight.

Something of a lifelong injustice collector, Laker complained of another distasteful scene when he then went up to play at Leveson Gower's invitation in that year's Scarborough Festival. 'There were eight amateurs in our side, and when lunchtime arrived on the first day they put on their blazers and set off for the president's marquee,' he wrote. Laker and his two fellow professionals assumed that it would be in order to join their colleagues for lunch. 'However, we were told in no uncertain terms by Shrimp that we were not welcome with the nobs. Views were exchanged as a result.' Whatever was said, it was sufficient to ensure that Laker was never invited to play at Scarborough again.

The men at Lord's didn't entirely wash their hands of him – Laker was back for England just over a year later – but from then on there was always that quality of remoteness in their relations that sometimes haunts a player. Laker's reputation now preceded him. Tom Graveney was 21 and just breaking in to county cricket for Gloucestershire that summer of 1948, and he remembered that his older county colleagues like Charles Barnett and Jack Crapp had 'told me to go after Jim, because if you attacked him he folded' – all of which may have been true, but the first time they actually met, in a championship match that August at Cheltenham, Graveney was gracious enough to recall, 'Laker bowled me one that was on a length, perfectly flighted, and in that same split second that I went for the drive and comprehensively missed it the keeper whipped the bails off. "Thanks a lot," I told Charlie and Jack back in the dressing room.'

* * *

While Laker was learning some of the harsh realities of the competitive and class-ridden nature of English cricket, Lock continued to enjoy his paid holiday in the services. He had only fond memories of the whole experience in his autobiography: 'It was all good fun, and educational, too, while from a professional cricketer's point of view I was fortunate that I had only one season away from the first-class game.' He represented the army against the navy at Lord's, and turned out for the Combined Services against both Glamorgan, the eventual county champions, where he took 6-43, and Worcestershire, with figures of 5-59. It was clear to most of his army colleagues that he was going places fast. The plain-spoken Alan Shirreff, later successively of Hampshire, Kent and Somerset, was Lock's captain in the Services side and found his young team-mate to be 'like the skipper of someone's yacht, loud, breezy, and with a hearty manner ... He wasn't without charm, but there was an attitude there that seemed forced', making him wonder whether it was because 'Tony was basically uneducated, and saw everyone as a potential threat to his wellbeing. As a personality, he was very much of the have a go persuasion, not the forward defensive type.'

Shirreff soon discovered this to be literally true of Lock's cricket, too, when in the Worcester match he sent his star bowler in as night watchman. The Services' score then stood at 1-1, following on 152 behind, and they had to see out another 20 minutes in poor light. 'Just stay there,' Shirreff told his outgoing batsman. The bowler, Geoff Darks, right-arm fast, came in off a long run. The first ball he bowled to Lock was one of his quickest, just short of a length on the leg stump. Lock came out to meet the ball, when it suddenly jumped – and so did Lock, giving a lusty upward swipe with his bat that pretty well completed a full circle in its execution, and sent the ball skidding first bounce over the long-leg rope. The bowler nearly decapitated him with his second ball and to the third one, on a length, Lock launched another rustic heave, missed it in the semi-dark and was clean bowled. 'You stupid cunt,' Shirreff informed him in the dressing room.

This extreme dislike of taking orders, hardly the ideal talent for a teenaged army recruit, followed Lock throughout his playing career, and to some extent right up to the end of his life. As we've seen, a second psychological handicap in those early days was his tendency to swing between the manic and the depressive, with a fondness for antic behaviour and schoolboyish pranks (pressing a hot tablespoon on a colleague's bare flesh was among his party tricks) matched by brief but intense moments of introspection. One or two of those who knew Lock only in the former state tended to write him off as 'a loud-mouthed, dubious and sadly provincial oik', to quote Errol Holmes, but set against this Jack Hobbs thought that he had 'steel', and that his manner was 'quiet and unemotional – a man without nerves'.

Perhaps Hobbs was being generous, because most of those who played either with or against Lock remembered him for his highly strung nature. It was a constant struggle to contain his emotions. If Lock was happy, as he generally was, he let you know it; if he wasn't, he could darken a room simply by entering it. He was also physically courageous. After suffering further knee problems in the army he was sent to hospital to have his cartilage removed. The surgeon who performed the procedure told him that he had been crippled almost beyond repair, and that at the very least he could never hope to run or even walk freely again without discomfort. This would have been a depressing enough prognosis for any 19-year-old to absorb, let alone one with his heart set on playing professional sport. Lock thanked the doctor for his opinion, left the army with a medical discharge in March 1949, and only a little over a month later was back playing full-time cricket again, continuing to score runs, take wickets, and above all to bring off hundreds of impeccable flying catches at regular intervals over the next 22 years.

* * *

It would obviously be a stretch to claim, as some have, that his hammering by the 1948 Australians 'destroyed' Jim Laker, particularly in light of his performance against the same opponents eight years later. But clearly the whole affair left its mark. Richie Benaud summed up the general perception when he wrote, 'That match at Leeds stayed with Jim for a long time and, though he [played] for England soon afterwards, he wasn't able to command a regular place in the Test side until 1956 … When he did so he was simply too good on the pitches of that year for the Australian batsmen.' These would have been especially sweet words of vindication for Laker, a man with an unfailing memory for an insult or injury, however many years might pass from the original grievance.

In the meantime, overlooked for the 1948/49 MCC tour of South Africa, Laker worked diligently on his action at Alf Gover's school, as usual carrying his bulky cricket bag up on the tram each morning, and back again in the evening. He emerged as a bowler who, in Benaud's words, 'made you play every delivery, [with] a command of length, spin and flight that left no doubt in any but the England selectors' minds that he was already a great master of his craft'. A more important consequence of the Leeds Test of 1948, however, was that it taught Laker an invaluable lesson in patience, as well as in the vagaries of Test cricket. As Bradman himself wrote to him, 'If Godfrey Evans had been a little more alert, I would have been a spectator for most of the Headingley match, and you would have been the cause of it.'

* * *

Laker and Lock were reunited in a Surrey side under the gentleman captain Michael Barton which went on to a respectable fifth place in the championship table, a harbinger of the county's unparalleled run of success in the 1950s. In 1949 they had two or three recognisably great players, several others who were on the way up, and a potent secret weapon in their groundsman Bert Lock. As a rule, the pitches at The Oval of this period tended to start off lushly grassed and then to steadily acquire a reddish-brown patina like that of the faded, geometric criss-cross pattern liberally mixed with cigarette ash ground in to the worn strip of carpet in the professionals' dressing room. Bert Lock's treatment of The Oval playing area was not entirely coincidental with the arrival on the scene of two world-class spinners. Micky Stewart, who came in to the Surrey side a year or two later, recalls, 'The pitches at The Oval were as flat as a pancake before the war. That all changed once Bert got his hands on them. The general idea was that they'd start to turn square by teatime on the second day, which left Jim and Tony to run riot.' Looking at the county's bowling returns even in 1949, it's noticeable how Laker, in particular, seemed to be crowned with greater statistical success in the second innings of a match than the first: one and four wickets respectively against Worcestershire, four and seven against Kent, one and eight against Warwickshire, and so on.

Lock was less consistent than Laker at this stage of his career, and arguably always remained so. As a rule the batsman had to play every ball from the one bowler, and only about half of those from the other. But Lock's bowling was also full of shocks for the batsman, some of them nasty shocks. He could come in, seemingly unhurried, pitch a ball of genuine medium pace on the leg stump and have it snap back to threaten the top of off. He was always in the game. He would shout for lbw both to his own bowling and to anyone else's, and as we've seen his catching of the ball was like having a 12th man in the field. He was never anonymous. Neville Cardus wrote of him, 'He exults and suffers. He rejoices openly at a conquest. He relieves himself by all sorts of lettered words not actually spoken; at any rate, not overheard by the distant spectators. Dull cricket is not to be seen when Lock is on the job.'

* * *

Early in the 1949 season Surrey went up to play Northamptonshire, a solid batting side with the soon-to-be England captain Freddie Brown at the helm. The visitors had not only Laker and Lock but also the Australian orthodox left-armer John McMahon, 31, in their ranks. The popular and convivial McMahon had taken 91 first-class wickets in the previous season, winning his county cap in the process. Never a martyr to false modesty, he had justifiable hopes of a Test call-up by Australia. In the first innings of the match at Northampton, Laker took 1-31 and Lock 4-27, which included removing Brown's middle stump. McMahon didn't even get on to bowl. Always quite vocal, he wasn't happy about this state of affairs. Back at The Oval, McMahon went to see the monocle-wearing county secretary Brian Castor, an equally forthright character who had volunteered for army duty at the age of 50, and subsequently spent the latter part of the war in a Japanese POW camp. Castor was widely considered a capable if sometimes gruff administrator, known for his habit of making public address announcements to any stray pigeons who had invaded The Oval outfield.

McMahon told Castor, 'Lock's taken over. I'm no bloody use to this club, and I want my release.' At that Castor turned purple, reached for the bookshelf, and threw a copy of *Wisden* at his visitor. McMahon duly went on to join Somerset, but this arrangement, too, ended abruptly when, relaxing with his team-mates at the end of a long night spent in the saloon of the Flying Horse Inn in Nottingham, McMahon beheaded the bar's ornamental gladioli display with a regimental sword liberated from a glass case on the wall, crying out, 'When Mac drinks, everybody drinks!' According to *Wisden*, there was also 'an embarrassing episode at Swansea's Grand Hotel' in the same season, following which McMahon thought it best to restrict his active cricket to occasional West

Country league and club appearances, where he sometimes played under Nigel Bennett's captaincy, as well as contributing one or two trenchant, if unsolicited articles to the local press.

Laker ended the 1949 season with 122 first-class wickets at an average below 20, as well as scoring his elusive maiden century – admittedly against Cambridge University – along the way. He also played in the Oval Test against Walter Hadlee's touring New Zealanders, characteristically on that ground taking no wickets in the first innings but 4-78 in the second. It was one of the dreariest summers of cricket in the history of England v New Zealand, or indeed of any series where England were concerned. All four of the Tests were drawn.

Both Laker and Lock were now established cricketers. Entirely different as personalities, what they had in common was the fact that both began from the bottom, with few of the social advantages that helped a man get on in the Britain of that era. Lock had a start over Laker in making his professional debut at the age of barely 17. His father Fred lived long enough to see his younger son make a living as a cricketer. Even so, for the next four years Lock was widely regarded as a player who was more capable of bowling the really lethal ball than of putting in a long spell of mechanical repetition such as might bore the batsman out. He had flight all the time, and spin most of the time, but true precision only about half the time. Laker was the nearer of the two to the finished article, but he'd cruelly dashed the hopes of his admirers during the Australians' 1948 invasion of England, at a time when, to again quote Cardus, 'The proper and consistent means of assessing a Test cricketer, temperamentally and technically, is in the Ashes.' To anyone who came across either bowler before the early 1950s, the suggestion that he would play a major role in post-war international cricket would have seemed improbable.

* * *

Perhaps the following spring's Test trial, played on Laker's old home turf at the Park Avenue ground in Bradford, might have offered a clue that he was at least fast learning the ropes. The match was widely seen more as an early review of the candidates for the 1950/51 tour of Australia than for the immediate home series with the West Indies. Being England in late May, it also rained almost non-stop. The pitch at Bradford was uncovered, and the resulting quagmire bore only the most token resemblance to the arid, camel-coloured strips and oven-like heat of Melbourne or Sydney. Nonetheless, it was a gripping contest in its way. E.W. Swanton wrote of Laker's contribution in the *Daily Telegraph*, 'He utilised a quite hateful pitch excellently, spin[ning] the ball prodigiously and dropping it on the spot every time. If he has a rival as the best of the kind in the country, I do not know his name,' Swanton added, sounding a bit like the tagline of a 1950s commercial. This was a handsome tribute coming from one generally so sparing of praise to any cricketer born later than the Edwardian era, and even at the time came about as close to a papal blessing as you could get in that line of work.

Laker's figures for the England side playing the Rest at Bradford would have impressed an even more severe critic than Swanton, who later came to believe that the bowler had possessed 'considerable merits, [if] not that of excessive perseverance'. In 14 overs of immaculate off-spin, 12 of them maidens, either side of lunch on the the first day, he conceded two singles. And took eight wickets. It's perhaps only fair to note that the Rest XI included one Oxford and three Cambridge undergraduates in their line-up, and had a somewhat speculative feel as a whole. The pitch wasn't so much sticky as it was positively adhesive, and between them the spinners accounted for fully 24 of the 29 wickets to fall in the match. The England fielders served their bowlers well, and Laker also had the distinct advantage of coming on only after

Alec Bedser and Trevor Bailey had thoroughly roughed up the aspiring young talent in the Rest's batting order. Nonetheless, this was a performance of high pedigree for a player who might have considered himself lucky to be included in the presumptive England team in the first place. One of the two runs Laker conceded in the innings was a courtesy, one-off-the-mark to his Surrey colleague Eric Bedser, and the other was scored when the 19-year-old Fred Trueman edged a good-length ball to forward short leg and two fielders collided when trying to catch it. In the next over, Godfrey Evans, standing up, stumped Trueman off Alec Bedser, and Laker then rolled up the remainder of the Rest's innings like a shutter.

England in turn scored 229, leaving their opponents a target of 202 to avoid an innings defeat. The Rest missed this by 89 runs and the match was all over by lunch on the second day. Along with the general head-shaking astonishment among the press and public (despite the later legend, the ground was nearly empty at the start, as a fresh northern wind snapped sideways across the field), the consensus was that Laker had more than risen to the occasion. Writing in the *Evening Standard*, Bruce Harris, whose daily cricket reporting went back to the Great War, said of him, 'He pitched an attacking length with a precision George Macaulay and Hedley Verity would have applauded ... The ball, twisting and hopping all over the place, needed a fly swatter rather than a bat to control it.' It was significant that Harris thought to compare Laker to two former greats of Yorkshire cricket – both victims of the last war – because a number of local supporters were now left to similarly wonder how their native son had ever been allowed to emigrate to Surrey. Alf Burgoyne at the Saltaire club would remark drily, 'When Jim was with us, I picked him out as a batsman. I knew he would make his name in cricket one day, but not as an eight for two bowler.'

Ironically, perhaps the only person besides the shellshocked Rest batsmen not overjoyed by Laker's coup was the bowler himself. As always, he was implacably bored by the trappings of personal fame, as opposed to those of due professional respect. When three or four members of the press gathered in the Bradford pavilion for quotes at the end of the first day's play, Pat Marshall of the *Daily Express* asked the deathless question, 'Would that be your best performance, Jim?'

Laker gave it a moment, before looking up at the journalist through a cloud of cigarette smoke. 'Well, I haven't done it right often,' he replied.

After that there was some more in the same wittily deadpan vein, with talk of it being all in a day's work and how it 'were a funny game'. Then Laker and his sister Margaret walked out of the ground, a large suitcase in his hand, and boarded a local tram for the five-mile journey back to her home in Baildon where he was lodging for the night. No one bothered him to demand a selfie or an autograph, and there were no further requests for interviews or invitations to write ghosted newspaper articles. 'There's nothing really special about it,' Laker again noted before catching the train south the next afternoon, reiterating his central thesis about the vagaries of life as a professional cricketer. 'One day you're on top of the world, next day you get nought for plenty.'

The fundamental truth of this judgement was again harshly demonstrated just six days later, when Laker reported for duty for the full England Test side against the West Indies at Old Trafford. Proving he was consistent if nothing else, he took 0-43 in the visitors' first innings, and 1-43 in the second. England easily won the match, thanks in large part to a sixth-wicket stand of 161 by Bailey and Evans. It seems mildly curious today, when it sometimes seems harder to be dropped by England than to be picked by them in the first place, but the selectors then ignored Laker for the rest of the series. It seems even stranger in light of the fact that he took 166 first-class wickets that season at an average of just 15, helping Surrey to share the championship title with Lancashire.

Laker would long pay a price for his apparently toxic combination of pessimism and bolshiness. Despite his feats at Bradford, he 'seemingly has a very gloomy future', Swanton was left to say of him in September 1950, just four months after he'd rewritten the bowling record book. Swanton continued, 'I am not sure the England Test panel are quite convinced by him.' Laker sometimes said the same thing himself, and wondered just how the selectors came by their decisions. 'It wasn't based on the facts, I'll tell you that much,' he concluded.

* * *

While Laker was experiencing the highs and lows of representative cricket, 20-year-old Tony Lock was establishing himself with Surrey. He helped run through Derbyshire at The Oval, took 6-40 in an innings in the top-of-the-table clash with Lancashire, and another five in an innings against Notts, part of his season's haul of 74 wickets at 23 apiece. He also took 33 catches. Of this total Alec Bedser later reflected, 'Only two of them that I recall were regulation dismissals. Once the ball ballooned up in the air – you could have done *The Times* crossword in the time it hung there – and fell back into Lockie's hands, and the other time it dropped nicely for him at leg slip. On the other 31 occasions he was doing cartwheels and backward flips and generally leaping about like the daring young man on his flying trapeze.' At the end of the season Surrey awarded him his cap, belatedly in his opinion.

'I had begun to despair of ever receiving it,' Lock wrote, 'and was seriously thinking of making a move. In fact, I had been approached by another county' – Middlesex, apparently, which would at least have avoided the need to move house – 'although, looking back, I realise I would have been acting hastily had I accepted the offer.' As a capped player he was earning a basic £550 a year (roughly £7,000 today), which was about on a par with what a junior provincial schoolteacher was then taking home, if slightly better than the average semi-skilled labourer's annual wage of £425. As Lock, among others, would come to reply when periodically asked what appealed to them about professional cricket, 'Well, it's not the money – that's for sure.' Lock himself would often add a choice intensifier before the last word for good measure.

* * *

On Thursday, 27 July 1950 the MCC announced the names of the captain, Freddie Brown, and of 11 other players chosen for their winter tour of Australia and New Zealand. Laker's was not among them. It was particularly bitter timing, because on that same day, playing for Surrey against Worcestershire, Laker took figures of 7-61 in a marathon spell of 45 overs. This gave the cricket press the chance to publish the overnight news from Lord's alongside its report of what *The Times* called, in a veritable hydrant of praise, 'The latest spin-bowling exhibition by the master of his craft, reduc[ing] the most fleet-footed of batsmen to fumbling impotence.'

At intervals between 15 August and 6 September, the selectors would go on to release the names of a further five members of their winter tour party. Still no Laker. They did, however, find space for the 19-year-old off-spinning all-rounder Brian Close, of Yorkshire, who finished the 1950 season with a total of 20 wickets at an average of 33. Close's selection naturally attracted considerable media attention, not least because he then happened to be performing his National Service with the Royal Corps of Signals at a training camp in Catterick, and – less well publicised at the time – was 'confined to barracks' for disciplinary reasons on the day his international call-up was announced. In the event, he managed just 231 runs and 13 wickets in his nine matches on the tour, which could be thought only a mixed success as a whole from the English point of view. Australia retained the Ashes by a margin of four Tests to one, and the MCC successes really boiled down to three players: Len Hutton, Alec Bedser and Godfrey Evans, although Brown himself put up a characteristically stout fight of it in the fifth Test at Melbourne when, while still recovering from a shoulder injury sustained in a late-night car crash, he took 5-49 and 1-32 in 27 eight-ball overs to help England win the day.

Laker was seriously displeased by these developments. Writing ten years later in his book, *Over to Me*, he called Close's inclusion in the Australian tour party 'astonishing', and added, 'I admit I thought – and still think – I should have played,' before going on to share a rumour he had heard about the original selection meeting at Lord's:

> Various names were mentioned until someone, without much conviction, brought up the subject of Brian Close. The idea, mentioned on an impulse, was about to be as quickly dropped, when Freddie Brown, the captain, chimed in. 'Close is just the man for me; I want him,' was said to be the gist of it. Chirpy as ever, Brown had his way, rather to the discomfiture of the others present. Perhaps they had the sort of guilty feeling of a man who looks at some disaster and thinks, 'Did *I* do that?'

Of course this might all have been hearsay, or gossip retailed for Laker's book, but for one impeccable source – Brown himself, who told me, 'Close had bowled tight and steady against my county in a match at Wellingborough, and for determination he was the best all-round English player of that time.' Laker would take the opportunity to further raise the matter of Close's winter employment when, just a few weeks later, he found himself standing at the railing of a ship with Les Ames, the former Kent and England wicketkeeper, who at that time was an MCC selector. To again quote *Over to Me*, Ames told him, 'Your story is quite true – but you shouldn't know about it!'

Even in 1960 Laker's published remarks aroused anger in the Lord's committee room, the deliberations of which were then still as cryptic and sacrosanct as those of a papal conclave. The MCC president – Sir Hubert Ashton, a decorated First World War veteran, and later Conservative MP for Chelmsford – wrote a letter to Laker (by no means the only official censure he received as a result of his book) recommending that in future he conform to the normal customs of 'respect and confidentiality that attend meetings' of the club's selection panel. The 1950/51 tour thus provided the aggrieved bowler a double humiliation. Omitted from the party in the first place, his role taken by a teenager with modest pretensions to Test level bowling, Laker was then publicly snubbed a second time by a magisterial letter of rebuke on the subject. His sourness and truculence on the topic of 'Lord's', as a synonym for cricket officialdom, modified but never totally abandoned in later years, undoubtedly owed something to the events that began that July morning when, in the sepulchral tones of a declaration of war, the BBC announcer read out the first dozen names of 'those players to whom the Marylebone Cricket Club has extended an invitation to represent them in Australia and New Zealand'. At the very least, the question 'When did an England bowler last take eight wickets for two runs in a Test trial, and then ten weeks later not be considered one of the 17 best players in the country?' must be a top contender for a cracking pub quiz.

* * *

In fact, the winter of 1950/51 was to prove a pivotal one in the careers of both Laker and Lock. It might even be said to have defined the way in which most people came to think about them in future years. Feeling aggrieved, Laker now grew even more scornful of what he saw as a snobbish and effete cricketing establishment as embodied by the England selectors. The whole Close matter wasn't just an honest mistake on their part. It was a set of circumstances that appeared to him to offer a combination of deceit, intrigue, ambition and general duplicity of almost Shakespearean proportions. In spite of, or perhaps precisely because of, his obvious intelligence and willingness to offer an opinion, Laker seemed to remain an outsider, still living in his modest digs in Forest Hill and with few if any close friends outside his native Yorkshire. Though obviously talented, the popular theory went, he was an odd bird, and in the final analysis, it seemed, probably a lonely one.

For Lock, that austerity winter of spam fritters, tinned milk and ham salad for high tea on Sunday, soaked in an oil dressing that doubled up as ear-wax remover, proved to be the starting point for a controversy that would dog him throughout the 1950s. It was a debate that centred around the technical merits of his bowling, rather than his own personality. Though relatively muted by today's standards, the ensuing press coverage was enough for Lock to once tell his county captain Stuart Surridge that 'he couldn't look at a paper any more since the terrible smear campaign would kill him. He wanted to get out of cricket altogether and re-enlist in the army.' After matters reached a boiling point in March 1959, an emotional Lock, sounding a bit like a revivalist preacher, told a group of friends, 'Well, let the battle begin,' adding to his colleague Ted Dexter, in even more messianic terms, 'I'll win it or die trying.' Lock was then nearly 30, and it's a tribute to his tenacity and stubbornness that over the next 12 years he played some of the best cricket of his life.

The immediate cause of Lock's protracted anguish was a large, modestly furnished room, really a shed, of critically unusual design, operated by the Allders department store as an annex to their retail flagship at North End in Croydon, south London, where he was appointed a full-time cricket coach over the winters of 1950/51 and 1951/52. By all accounts, the place was typical of the spartan nature of such facilities at the time, with four nets strung up side by side on a strip of threadbare green felt matting, a few shabby chairs and tables rescued from the store's discount warehouse and, fatally, a low-slung wooden beam directly above the bowlers' end. Lock was a shade under six feet tall and found that he had to deliver the ball with a flatter action than before, or else risk it hitting the ceiling. The result was that he spent five days a week for six months gradually acquiring a longer than usual run-up and a slightly but perceptibly bent left arm. 'I wasn't conscious of it at the time,' he wrote later, 'but, not being able to flight the ball as much, I bowled a little quicker. I also found that by "digging" it into the pitch, I was able to produce more turn.' This account is in itself to impart a certain spin on the true state of affairs, which is that when Lock returned to the first-class circuit in April 1951, he was effectively propelling the ball with both his fingers and elbow, or, put another way, chucking it.

During this same period Laker was 5,000 miles away on a Commonwealth tour of India and Ceylon, his first visit to that exquisite if sometimes also gruelling part of the cricket-playing world. 'Like a young man who has just been jilted, I jumped at the next thing that came along,' he later wrote of missing the cut for the MCC party to Australia. As a general rule, budget-conscious tours of the subcontinent of that era weren't notable for their lavish public amenities or pervasive sense of customer comfort. At Poona, against the local maharajah's side, Laker was coming in to bowl when a rat he later insisted was the size of a compact family car ran on the pitch. In the next instant, a kite hawk of even greater proportions swooped down, seized the creature in its beak and wheeled off again. To his credit, Laker kept going in his delivery stride, although he did bowl a double bouncer. Elsewhere on the tour, not keen on flying, he received permission to take the transcontinental train from Lucknow to Bombay, a 900-mile, three-day endurance trial that he shared with several hundred other passengers clinging throughout to the outside of the carriages. 'They gave me a knife in case I was attacked, but the person I was going to use it on was myself,' he would recall.

In later years Laker always rated his last bowling performance of the tour – 5-88 in 65 overs against an unofficial India Test side, played in 105-degree heat in front of 40,000 noisily partisan fans at Bombay's Brabourne Stadium – above even his feat in the previous spring's Test trial. 'At least I got some help from the wicket at Bradford, but bugger all at Bombay,' he summarised.

Then came a step which transformed Laker's life: on 27 March 1951 he married the former Lilly Gottlieb, a petite and vivacious brunette who was then working as a secretary in London while recovering from a recent divorce. Born in 1919, Lilly had escaped with her family from their native Austria in the late 1930s, before acquiring British citizenship with her marriage to a businessman named Walter Gingold and going on to serve with the Auxiliary Territorial Service (ATS) in wartime Egypt. She had first met Laker when they were introduced at a services' dance. On their subsequent date, he'd invited Lilly to a one-day match at the Gezira club, where he took eight wickets – it was her first exposure to cricket, and she asked him if that was a good return – but they then drifted apart again until both happened to attend an ATS reunion dinner in London nearly five years later. 'Oh, hello,' Jim had remarked, with his trademark reserve. The couple subsequently had lunch in a Putney hotel where, Lilly remembered, 'He did nothing but talk about the girls in the West Indies.' Despite this, she agreed to stay in touch. While on tour of India 'he wrote to me every day, and I wrote back every day', Lilly said. In the new year Laker returned home by sea and proposed by silently handing over a large holdall filled with towels and linens, and other goods suitable for setting up a home. The ceremony took place at Kensington Registry Office, with a brief honeymoon at a seaside hotel in Bournemouth, where it rained constantly. In time the newlyweds bought a modest house in south London.

The Lakers' marriage, which produced two daughters, Fiona and Angela, lasted until the end of Jim's life 35 years later, and he frequently used to say that one of the reasons for its success was because Lilly wasn't really a traditional cricket wife, and, as she cheerfully admitted, 'knew as much about spin bowling as I did about the dark side of the moon'. The day-to-day nuances of any such relationship aren't available to a mere author. But it was undoubtedly a love match, and they were devoted to each other. 'I wonder whether two people ever experienced as much love, happiness and affinity as Lilly and I have,' Laker mused to Richie Benaud a quarter of a century later, wretched at being temporarily separated from his wife while visiting Australia.

* * *

When Lock ran in to bowl his first practice ball of the 1951 season on a damp April morning in the Oval nets, and flattened the veteran Surrey all-rounder Jack Parker's off stump while the batsman was still in the early stages of his backlift, there was 'a certain amount of surprise expressed', the bowler himself later admitted. If anything, that would seem to have understated the reaction. Laker, who was standing nearby, remembered, 'The ball hit the deck at fast-medium pace, which was new, and shot like a

Mexican jumping-bean from leg to off,' while Parker himself noted simply, 'Lockie, you fucking threw that.'

It seems almost absurd now in an age of ultramotion cameras, TV umpires and all cricket's other technical apparatus, but in the 1950s the question of whether or not a bowler's action was legitimate was largely a matter of individual opinion. Micky Stewart made his Surrey debut in 1954, and told me, 'Basically, Tony went from being an orthodox left-arm spinner, nice fluid run-up, arm brushing his cheek, to a medium-pacer with a "double whirl" action that could be pretty well unplayable when he really let it rip. But the odd thing is that no one ever really said anything. It was just part of the game in those days. You'd sometimes see films of old players like Harold Larwood and say to yourself, "*That* one looked a bit dodgy," and just chuckle about it. I'm quite sure Lockie wasn't throwing it on purpose. And he didn't do it every ball. No one ever published photos of his action or made a big fuss. So he just got on with it for about the next ten years.'

Nonetheless, the word about Lock soon spread on the county circuit. In June, Godfrey Evans was playing in the Kent side against Surrey at Blackheath, and remembered, 'Jim wheeled away, very correct, as always, while Tony came steaming in and about once an over gave it a jerk like a darts player. The one that got Bill's brother Brian Edrich turned square at about Big Alec Bedser pace. Never seen anything like it before in my life. "How do you bloody play *that*?" Brian asked us in the dressing room, and we just shrugged. It was pretty clear by then that Tony was going to chase Jim up the year's bowling averages.' He did: by the end of the 1951 season Laker had taken 149 first-class wickets to Lock's 105, but 12 months later their totals were 125 and 131 respectively.

Initially Laker seems to have taken a measured view of his colleague's sudden evolution from an orthodox left-arm spinner to an aggressive destroyer of worlds. Summing up the mood in the Surrey dressing room as a whole, he wrote, 'Apart from leg-pulling about how well he would throw the javelin, we did not want to discourage Tony in his new approach to the game. We didn't want to undermine his confidence. So many bowlers over the years had got away with throwing or jerking the ball that we decided that we weren't going to act as a jury. It was up to the umpires to decide.' Laker was even more relaxed on the subject when in conversation with Godfrey Evans. 'Lockie's throwing it this year,' he announced serenely.

* * *

Like many professional sportsmen, cricketers perhaps more than most, Laker had mixed views about statistics. He loved taking wickets and wanted more of them each season, but he had deeply buried resentments towards the sort of journalist, or for that matter Test selector, who brought what he called a 'bean-counter's logic' to the business of assessing a bowler's true worth to his side. Reconciling those two competing feelings was one of Laker's lifelong challenges. In ways that were sometimes uncomfortable to face, he was a purist at heart. In other words, he'd stop worrying about the season's averages so long as he was top of them.

In English domestic cricket of the 1950s, when each county played as many as 30 matches a season, there was often a lively competition to be the first batsman to score 1,000 runs in the summer and the first bowler to take 100 wickets. Now more than merely Laker's support act, Lock was sudden chasing him to the post. Early in the 1951 season the left-armer took six in an innings against Glamorgan, seven in the match with Somerset and six more at home to Essex, and it was still only late May. It was the first time the two team-mates, the one aged 29, the proud holder of nine Test caps and what Cardus described as 'a bowler of the first pedigree', the other still just 21 and figuratively yapping at the older man's ankles, had been seen as serious personal rivals.

As it happened, there was also a third entrant in the race to capture 100 wickets that season, 27-year-old Bob Appleyard of Yorkshire, who had the unusual ability to bowl fast-medium seamers and off-spin with virtually the same action. His performances were all the more notable in light of the fact that he was in poor health throughout, and would spend much of the 1952 season in hospital with an advanced case of tuberculosis. Appleyard scored his 99th dismissal of 1951 in a home match against Glamorgan as early as 28 June, but then fell ill. Meanwhile Laker was in action for Surrey against Sussex at Guildford, where he took 4-53 and 1-54, which brought him up to a total of 90 for the year. On 5 July England began the third Test of the series against South Africa at Old Trafford. The selectors recalled Laker for the first time in more than a year, and he took four wickets in the comfortable home win. Another round of county matches began on Wednesday, 11 July. Laker went out to play for Surrey against Worcestershire on a helpful wicket at Dudley. The home team batted first and he promptly took six wickets, the last of which brought up his hundred. A reporter asked him how he managed to look so relaxed after putting in such a gruelling performance. 'My mother taught me the benefits of perseverance, and other habits that have a positive effect on the countenance,' Laker said, now sounding a bit like a Victorian evangelist.

That same week Appleyard was back in action playing for Yorkshire against Sussex at Hull. Yorkshire batted first, and he had to wait until after tea on the first day to get his chance with the ball. His fourth delivery took the edge of the Sussex opener Don Smith's bat and flew low and hard to first slip, who dropped it. The next morning Appleyard duly bowled Smith to reach his 100th wicket, less than 24 hours after Laker had beaten him to the tape. 'It was the nicest run thing,' *The Times* was left to remark of the contest, echoing the Duke of Wellington after Waterloo. 'There was a good deal of wagering about it,' Laker himself recalled, while adding ruefully that he had shown 'bugger all profit' as a result. The following week Surrey played Yorkshire at The Oval. Appleyard took five wickets in the match and Laker none. The latter hadn't stopped competing, though. Lock fondly remembered a game that same summer when Laker was bowling and the batsman 'picked one off his toes, middled it perfectly, and before I had a chance even to duck I took the fast travelling ball full in the face.

'Jim walked over and said: "Bad luck, Tony – another catch dropped."'

Alec Bedser told me that he'd wandered up to Lock's short leg position in between overs to have a look. 'There were bits of teeth stuck in the grass there.' Lock was eventually persuaded to retire and came back with six stitches inserted in the side of his head. He had to wait until early September before taking his own 100th wicket of the season, but from now on the momentum was in his favour. Laker and Lock both reached their century in the same session of play on 31 July the following year, while bowling in tandem for Surrey against Derbyshire at Chesterfield, Laker about 20 minutes earlier than Lock. Alec Bedser told me, 'There was a lot of ribbing about it in the dressing room … Jim waited while Tony expressed his views about it all, seriously insisting there must have been a cock-up in the scorebook somewhere and that he'd actually been the first, and then Jim crushed him with a few well-chosen points of his own.' 'Crushed' is pretty strong, and suggests that in his quiet way Laker generally preferred to have the last word.

At the end of 1951 Laker's bowling average was 18, and Lock's was 21. Between them they took 254 first-class wickets that season. Most batsmen playing them at The Oval treated them as respectfully as if they were nuns on a pilgrimage to the Vatican. Surrey finished a respectable sixth in the championship table, but took a significant step forward with the appointment that winter of 34-year-old Stuart Surridge as county captain. Surridge would soon come to enjoy the sort of all-knowing, Yoda-like status later conferred on Mike Brearley, if with a more pronounced aggressive streak. He took control of a side which was rich in talent but needed to 'feel the smack of firm government [to] do itself justice', *Wisden* wrote. According to Bedser, Surridge wrote in his diary on the day he was appointed captain, 'Surrey will win the championship for the next six years.' The actual figure was seven, the first five under Surridge.

* * *

While Lock went back to the Croydon nets with the disastrously low beam that winter, thus further deforming his bowling action, Laker took his wife with him on a belated honeymoon cruise to New Zealand, where he was appointed player-coach of Auckland in the Plunket Shield. The terms offered weren't such to encourage thoughts of aristocratic idleness on the visitors' parts. The couple lodged in bed-and-breakfast accommodations, and Lilly found work at a local insurance company office. Laker was regarded as a conscientious if somewhat rigid coach of the old school, who as we've seen was scandalised when one or two of his younger colleagues reported for work in a pair of soft shoes or a cap of excessively florid design. 'You might as well go out with half a bat as wear such costumes,' he griped.

Laker took 24 wickets in the short New Zealand season, eight of them in his first match. Auckland finished a close second place in the Shield. 'J.C. Laker gave uniform satisfaction,' the club's yearbook recorded truthfully, if also a little primly. There was no MCC tour scheduled for the winter of 1952/53, and the couple would probably have returned to New Zealand then but for Lilly's pregnancy. Laker insisted that his children be born in England.

* * *

The Surridge regime at The Oval effectively began with a rainy, two-day rout by Surrey of the touring Indians in early May 1952. Laker took ten wickets in the match, Lock took two and the hosts won by 141 runs. Captained by Vijay Hazare, the season's visitors to England that dank summer were a highly proficient and personally convivial party who divided between those who were 'dry' and 'wet'. Godfrey Evans, himself emphatically in the latter camp, if not actually defining it, always fondly remembered his requisitioning a wheelbarrow to push a well-known Indian seamer down a cobbled mews off London's Regent Street late on the Friday night of that summer's Lord's Test, then going out to the middle the next morning to smash the same bowler for an unbeaten 98 before lunch. 'He admitted he wasn't at his best,' Evans recalled of his bibulous friend. 'In his hungover state, he was seeing two pitches, and having a hard time knowing which one to aim at.'

Surridge's policy towards his own highly rated bowling attack was simple: Peter Loader and Alec Bedser were given the new ball at the beginning of the innings and expected to swiftly get on with it. Loader recalled, 'If we didn't have a breakthrough in the first three or four overs we were on the receiving end of a verbal broadside, after which the spinners promptly relieved us.' Here the Surridge technique employed some more narrowly focused psychology. Alf Gover had now retired but continued to keep a trained eye on his former county colleagues. 'The skipper used to butter up Laker,' he recalled. '"C'mon, I'll give you another short leg." He took another tack with Lock, "I've never seen such fucking awful bowling. What are you supposed to be doing?"' Gover added with that mixture of shock and admiration Surridge typically engendered in his fellow cricketers, 'Lockie would shake his head in disbelief at the Gaffer, redouble his efforts and probably take a crucial wicket.'

As we've seen, the 'spin twins' were in fact quite different personalities. It was partly a matter of circumstances, and partly one of age. Laker had already turned 30 that spring of 1952. Married with his first child on the way, he'd at last moved out of his suburban lodgings, learnt to drive, and bought his own house. Solid and slightly heavy-looking, he had a slow John Wayne way of walking and wore his cricket flannels hitched up high on the waist. He was the more contained, Lock the more histrionic. Laker was the calculator, Lock the gambler. Both men were guarded with strangers and could be fussy and a bit selfish. As Surridge said, 'They didn't much like each other, and consequently I was the go-between.'

In April 1952 Laker went up to Cambridge at the invitation of 23-year-old David Sheppard, the university side's newly appointed captain, to offer two weeks of pre-season coaching in the nets. Sheppard thought his guest 'marvellously disciplined, always neat and punctual, loved a routine, not a huge motivator, but one who inspired you just by his obvious gift for the game'. At one stage a straight-faced Laker gravely informed his hosts, 'I had a bad season last year. I bowled two long hops.' Laker was already legendary in the cricket world, and Sheppard thought him 'all the more impressive because he had a quiet self-confidence, almost always kept his head, and wasn't the shout-it-from-the-rooftops type'.

If 1952 was an important year for Laker, it was a momentous one for Lock: he married his childhood sweetheart Audrey Sage, with whom he would go on to have two sons and an adopted daughter; and he made his England debut. It came in the season's third Test against India, at Old Trafford, and followed performances such as his six wickets against Somerset, five more away to Yorkshire, who included two national selectors, Len Hutton and Norman Yardley, in their side, and no fewer than nine against Worcestershire, all matches Surrey not coincidentally won at a trot.

At Manchester, England batted first in steady drizzle and made 347/9 declared. Lock had just celebrated his 23rd birthday, and admitted to nerves when finally going out to the middle. He was there all of five minutes and made one not out. Off the fourth ball of the Indian reply Vinoo Mankad clipped Alec Bedser round the corner in the direction of backward short leg, where Lock caught it. As he later noted, 'The first time I handled the ball in a Test match, I contributed to the taking of a vital wicket.' Following on, India were then dismissed for 82, which was 24 more than they managed in their first innings. The tourists as a whole weren't keen on 'Fiery Fred' Trueman, who on his own Test debut six weeks earlier had come bounding down the slope on his home Headingley turf and so terrorised the batsmen that the second innings scoreboard at one stage read four wickets for no runs, unprecedented and not matched since. Lock had figures of 4-36, and kept his place in the side for the season's fourth and final Test at The Oval. He did nothing, but in truth nor did anyone else except the young David Sheppard, who made his first international century in his sixth Test. The match ended as a draw, in monsoon conditions, and England took the series 3-0.

On 26 July, in between the final two Tests, the Indians had appeared at The Oval to play Surrey for the second time that season. The ground was full, as it often was on Saturdays in that era, and the tourists, housed overnight in an unprepossessing south London hostel where Mankad remembered the water had emerged from the bathroom taps 'like a sort of sticky-red cough syrup', but now invigorated by a fresh northerly breeze, took the field on the first morning shrouded in their heavy, blue-striped sweaters and in Vijay Hazare's case what looked like a generously cut white woollen shawl or motoring scarf. Among the crowd was a small boy with a broad smile like that of a young model in a toothpaste advertisement who was up from his home in suburban Kent to watch the cricket with his father Joe and younger brother Chris. The boy then called himself Mike Jagger, and was celebrating his ninth birthday. The teams' pennants snapped on the pavilion roof, there was a generous quota of patriotic bunting, and even the iconic Vauxhall End gasometer seemed to have been given a fresh coat of lime-green paint for the occasion. Joe Jagger later recalled that the general atmosphere had been somewhere between that of a 'royal garden party and a sporting battleground': all the ingredients of a good drama, then, and a pitch, meticulously laid by Bert Lock and two young assistants which, on the face of it, looked good for thousands of runs.

As it happened, the other Lock had been the subject of a discreet word of complaint by the tourists' captain following stumps in the Manchester Test a week earlier. Hazare had admitted to his opposite number Len Hutton to having doubts as to the technical excellence of the young England debutant's quicker ball. Hutton had gone on to communicate this concern to his fellow selectors in the form of a notable précis: ''Ee says Tony's chucking it.' Someone in turn must have brought the matter to Stuart Surridge's attention at The Oval, because on 23 July he mentioned it in a note to himself in his diary. Surridge could find no official or semi-official complaint about Lock's bowling in the Test, even so, nor were any incriminating photographs taken. 'There seems to be nothing worth saying against him,' he wrote. Signing the entry with his own initials, as though possibly anticipating doing so for the record, Surridge added that he would 'speak to TL about the necessity, like Caesar's wife, to not be under suspicion'.

It was a forlorn hope. His competitive juices not so much flowing as raging, Lock was straining to beat Laker in the undeclared race to be the first to 100 wickets for the season. Besides, his faster and flatter delivery was generally praised by the critics, 'The nearest thing we have to an unassailable bowler' according to *The Times*, while even the more circumspect Neville Cardus in *The Guardian*, a stickler for cricket etiquette, admitted, 'Lock has a surfeit of vitality, which is perhaps the scarcest thing in the current England side.'

It was this surfeit of vitality that was such a prominent ingredient of Lock's performance in that late July tour match at The Oval. Despite winning the toss and batting, Surrey, captained for the occasion by Peter May, managed just 71 in their first innings. The versatile Ramesh Divecha, cutting his normal brisk medium pace to bowl off-spin, took 6-29. Batting at number ten, Lock scored a relatively respectable eight not out. 'Not our finest hour,' May later remarked with characteristic restraint. Lock took no wickets, and Laker took three, in the Indians' reply of 179.

But that wasn't the end of it. Lock was called three times for throwing in the innings by the square leg umpire, the former Test wicketkeeper Fred Price, and neither the bowler himself nor the capacity crowd were happy about it. In fact there was a lot of booing and other satirical comment. Lock took his cap and wandered down to the boundary at the end of the over. He seemed to be sweating heavily. Once there he suddenly took the cap off again and held it aloft, as if releasing pressure from a valve. After a further minute or two of slow hand-clapping, Price then stopped play and sat down on the damp grass until order was restored. It took a typically blunt loudspeaker announcement by the county secretary Brian Castor – 'he called the display a disgrace to cricket, and reminded us we were all meant to set a good example to our foreign guests' according to Joe Jagger – before play resumed. The Indians eventually won the match by six wickets.

Discussing the whole furore in his 1957 autobiography *For Surrey and England*, Lock wrote:

The umpire at leg, W.F. Price, 'called' me once, and then, a little later, twice more in an over. It appeared he doubted the legitimacy of my delivery. Every umpire has his own opinions and interpretations, and Price was acting within his rights, yet, surely, the least he could have done was to give me prior warning.

I felt like exploding but held my tongue. One of the first things you learn in cricket is to accept the umpire's decision as final. It is a waste of time arguing, or even questioning an official's ruling.

Stuart Surridge, however, helped me by coming up to me and saying, 'Now, Tony, you've satisfied all other umpires about your delivery, so don't get upset and lose control just because one man doubts your action.'

If true, this was a commendably stoical reaction on Lock's part, although set against his published account it should be noted that he was writing some five years after the event, and also that Surridge himself wasn't present at The Oval that day to offer advice on the wisdom of accepting the umpire's verdict or indeed any other subject.

What Lock actually did, immediately after Price's first shout from square leg, was to stand, hands on hips, glaring in that direction for several moments before deigning to bowl his next ball, which was pitched sufficiently slow and short that it bounced twice before reaching the batsman. Alec Bedser later added the detail that Lock had 'unburdened himself' once back in the dressing room at the interval. Gone was the calm, contemplative mood he remembered in his autobiography. 'Tony was disgruntled about being shown up in public, as he saw it,' Bedser recalled, 'and the result was some pretty rich language even by army standards, and a fist-sized dent in the dressing room wall. Mr Castor deducted the cost of repairing it from Tony's wages, I heard.'

In due course, Surrey won the County Championship outright for the first time since 1914. Each of the professional players got a £5 bonus and a plastic watch. At the end of the season, Laker and Lock found themselves on opposing sides in a three-day South v The Rest festival match at Hastings. The weather was dismal, and little of interest happened in between the numerous rain delays. There was at least a small footnote to the proceedings, however, when early on the second day Lock took a tumbling catch to account for Laker off the leg-break bowling of Worcestershire's Roly Jenkins. According to the local *Observer* newspaper, 'The fieldsman involved did not bother to conceal his glee at the dismissal.'

4

Too Much Coffee

A MERE study of the scores gives no idea of the excitement generated from day to day in the 1953 Test series, or of the passion expended in the matches themselves. To John Arlott it was 'the most dramatic Ashes summer' of his memory, which stretched from the visit of Warwick Armstrong's foolproof Australian side of 1921 to Ian Botham's all-round pyrotechnics 60 years later. As a backdrop, the series was played in the wake of the June coronation and the ascent of Everest, both of which contributed to one of those moods of extravagant national confidence perhaps more evident to later historians than they are at the time, but which undoubtedly produced some tangible benefits for England's cricketers. Tony Lock fondly remembered walking in to a pub that September in his native Limpsfield where his welcome had sometimes been ambiguous in the past, and 'they stood me a bottle of champagne nearly as big as I was' in tribute to his summer's work. 'I'd be lucky to get half a shandy in there in the old days,' he reflected. However incongruous it may seem to connect the year's wider events with cricket, connected they were, and in August the celebration echoing over England 'crowned the year', in Jack Fingleton's apt phrase.

There was an unusual curtain-raiser to the series in the shape of what remains Britain's only significant cricket feature film, *The*

Final Test, shot early that spring. Written by Terence Rattigan, the picture offers the timeless comic potential of an English spectator explaining the laws of the game to an American, but in general the script avoids any sort of profundity or even mild narrative twist and relies instead on routine melodrama and stock plot developments: it's like watching a traffic light change. Perhaps the real point of interest lies in seeing 57-year-old Jack Warner playing the fictional England captain, with several real-life Test players in the supporting cast, which at least affords a glimpse of Jim Laker face to face with his character's own screen archetype. It's a slightly odd mixture, the actors and the cricketers, and the audience is left in a kind of no man's land as a result.

In the end, with no time left to let its drama unfold organically, *The Final Test* just does it mechanically. In what seems like the equivalent of chasing 40 runs off the last two overs, the plot's rushed out in throwaway dialogue (some of it John Arlott's) between its players; the Warner character invites his wayward son to be there at The Oval to witness his last Test against the Aussies, but the latter wants to go off and meet his favourite poet instead; the poet turns out to be a cricket buff, and so the lad makes it to the match after all; Warner scores a duck – shades of Bradman in 1948 – but walks back to a standing ovation from a crowd of men dressed in immaculate City suits, with a few beer-quaffing gaffers lurking deferentially in the free seats. It's all about as perfunctory as a checklist, but there's still a certain period charm to seeing the likes of Laker, Hutton and Compton in close-up, along with the knowledge that Godfrey Evans had managed to flub his lines sufficiently often to ensure that the cricketers were eventually on call for two full weeks instead of the originally scheduled three days. 'Not bad, considering we were being paid by the hour,' the wicketkeeper still remembered, with unfeigned pride, some 40 years later.

Surrey were now clearly established as the strongest, and certainly best organised, side in the County Championship. Under Stuart Surridge's unsentimental captaincy they competed not only with their opponents but with each other. Writing in his 1960 memoir *Over to Me*, Laker recalled an incident in a 1953 pre-season practice match (another Surridge innovation) when Peter Loader came out to bat to face Lock's bowling. You can still hear the author's note of dry amusement at what followed:

> 'Be a sport and toss one up, Tony,' asked Loader. 'I just want to hit one six before I get out.' Lock obliged and the ball smartly went on its way towards the pavilion. But it didn't end there. Loader got a taste for the high life, and, five overs later, had hit about 50, mainly off Lock. I can't tell you precisely what was said (it isn't that I don't remember it) but it was an occasion to treasure. Everyone saw the joke – except Lock.

In general Surrey were part superbly drilled sports unit, part feral street gang, and in both cases liberally stocked with short-fused, wiry, intense characters who could be relied on to give full vent to their feelings. Lock was the fire-breathing epitome of this collective spirit, Laker the exception to the rule. Arthur McIntyre perhaps captured the mood best when he recalled, 'Tony was all on the outside, a boiling volcano, while Jim usually just kept his head down. He was a very clever man, very set in his ways, and didn't care for the sort of dressing room larks we did. At the end of the day Laker would just quietly change, adjust his tie, comb his hair and walk off by himself. You never saw him in the pub. It was the opposite with Tony – the problem was sometimes getting him out of the ruddy place.'

Surrey began their home season poorly by scoring just 58 and 122 in two completed innings against the Australians and losing the match before tea on the second day. There was a major swing of fortune when they came to host Warwickshire later in the week. This time the visitors were shot out for 45 and 52 and – for the first time in a county fixture at The Oval in 96 years – the match was over in a single day. Bedser took 12 wickets and Laker took a hat-trick. Lock was bowling with the skin on his spinning finger already rubbed raw in only his fourth game of the season ('If the wound had penetrated further, I would have been bowling off the bone,' he reported graphically), despite which he took 2-9 in his seven overs. He also hit his third-highest score of 27. At one point in the innings Warwickshire's 40-year-old seamer Charles Grove dropped one short, and Lock characteristically went for the hook. The next thing the batsman knew was that someone was muttering sympathetically, 'Have some water, mate. They're bringing the stretcher out now.' Lock was stitched up again in the physio's room, sent to hospital overnight and ruled unfit for the first Test at Trent Bridge, where, literally adding insult to injury, the selectors brought back Johnny Wardle in his place.

Laker was similarly disenchanted when the names were read out for the Nottingham Test to learn that the £65 match fee he and Lilly had been counting on would instead be going to his own Wardle figure, the Lancashire off-spinner Roy Tattersall. It was made even more galling by the fact that Surrey had been up to play a championship match at Trent Bridge just a few days earlier. Laker returned figures of 2-78 in a marathon 46-over spell in the first innings, and 6-58 off 21 in the second. By then he'd already taken 18 first-class wickets in his first four matches of the season, in conditions generally favouring the seamers. Lock had 19 to his account before being poleaxed by Grove.

Laker had the social confidence and forcefulness of character to be an effective subordinate to his hard-driving county captain. He respected Surridge, and Surridge in turn knew that the carrot worked better when it came to his richly talented but delicately wired star bowler than the stick. Lock, by contrast, wasn't the wisest, but certainly the most vivid personality in Surrey's marauding line-up – 'someone who occasionally needed a kick up the arse,' said Arthur McIntyre, who probably saw more of both spinners at close quarters than anyone else in the 1950s, 'but who also had real grit, certainly more of it than Jim did. I respected that.'

Presumably it was this latter quality of Lock's which led him to return more or less straight from his hospital bed to play against Lancashire at Old Trafford, where he took 5-89 in an innings and seven catches in the match. After that it was 3-35 and 4-29 at home to Derbyshire and 6-55 in a continuous 30-over spell against Northants, with Surrey already pulling away from their nearest rivals in the points table. Fred Price umpired Lock in several matches that season, but never again called him. Some, like McIntyre, thought that one or more of the Test selectors had had a word with Price on the subject, perhaps pointing out to him the merits of a quiet life, not to mention of having the feisty left-armer available for future deployment on an overseas tour, such as that to the West Indies in 1953/54, freed of any possible taint of cheating. This may or may not have happened, but from now on the only domestic complaints about Lock's action were those aired by an aggrieved batsman, such as the legendary enquiry by Doug Insole, the Essex captain, to the square leg umpire when he was yorked in fading light at The Oval, 'What was that, then – bowled or run out?'

Meanwhile, England drew the first Test with Lindsay Hassett's Australia, and brought in Statham for his county colleague Tattersall in the second one, at Lord's; it too was drawn, Trevor Bailey famously loitering at the crease for over four hours to score 71 and defy the tourists on the last day. By then England hadn't held the Ashes for 19 years, and their mounting frustration on the point was revealed in a private aside from Len Hutton to his keeper Godfrey Evans as they left Lord's together on the evening of 30 June. Hutton spoke grimly of the future, alarming even Evans, one of life's diehard optimists, with the admission, 'We can't beat these buggers with this team.' There was, the England captain concluded, only one solution: to mobilise a player who might get the job done or, alternatively, might hoist the white flag, depending on what mood he then happened to be in. Laker duly joined the side for the third Test at Old Trafford, not for the first time complaining of a sore finger, and took three wickets in the match, a rain-soaked draw. He had had to leave the field more than once on the first and second days for running repairs in the pavilion. In general Hutton thought Laker was intimidated by the Australian batsmen, and Laker thought Hutton saw spinners only as a last resort. Somehow they never quite hit it off, despite or because of being so similar: both stubborn, inward, given to Delphic utterances, and a bit uptight – 'like two clenched fists', in Evans's opinion.

With three down and two to go, England finally played Laker and Lock in tandem for the fourth Test at Headingley, where Richie Benaud remembered that the pitch was so green you could only barely distinguish it from the square. England made 167 and after that Hutton, for all his apparent aversion to spin, saw fit to pair Bedser and Lock for a protracted spell while Laker bided his time in the Leeds outfield, following the old tenets of feet together and hands behind the ball but otherwise with little chance to impose himself. He did well in the second innings, scoring 48 against Lindwall and Miller at their sharpest, both men regularly bringing the ball back late off the pitch to leave the recognised batsmen strokeless, while playing with yet another injection to numb the pain in his right hand. As a result the tourists were eventually left to chase 177 to win in 115 minutes, failing by 30 runs with six wickets to spare. Bailey was again the anti-hero, seeming to get through his overs like one of those dreams where you're running at top speed but it's as though you're wading through glue, and Hutton took the precaution of meticulously rearranging his field not once but several times as the pavilion clock ticked down to six.

The Times wrote drolly before the fifth and final Test at The Oval, 'It may be hoping too much to realise the nation's dreams of transforming the world order in five or six days. Even the Almighty took seven.' In retrospect the match now seems a, or the, decisive moment in post-war international cricket, the point at which England at last overtook their oldest sporting enemy, then the unchallenged if unofficial champions of the world. To the players at The Oval, though, the Test was less about the great issues of national prestige and global dominance and simply hard but hopeful work – and it was the true apogee of Laker and Lock's partnership.

* * *

To a certain generation, the Test that began at The Oval on that warm Saturday morning of 15 August 1953 remains the ultimate in high-stakes cricketing drama: the one with the overnight queue for tickets wrapped right around the ground, the constantly shifting fortunes in the middle and the hoarse, climactic shout by Brian Johnston on *Test Match Special* that rivals Kenneth Wolstenholme's immortal 'They think it's all over …' as the most famous, most quoted words in 20th-century British sport. Down under, the *Sydney Morning Herald* previewed it as the Test to end Tests:

'There is something a trifle absurd in the thought that the picked teams of Australia and England have now flung themselves at each other four times over a period of 20 days, without so far achieving a single result,' the paper wrote, knocking its report of a first Soviet hydrogen bomb off the front page. 'Today, however, all that will be forgotten. On this occasion, one may feel that it matters very little which side wins provided that one of them does.' Neville Cardus saw it as an almost primordial clash between two national cultures. 'Maybe England have an advantage of all-round technical ability,' he allowed. 'But Australia are the tougher minded and the younger and more virile in outlook.'

The raw details of what followed can perhaps be quickly recalled. England elected to play Lock on his native turf, leaving Wardle – seen smiling thinly, or possibly just gritting his teeth, in the subsequent team photo – to carry the drinks. Lindsay Hassett won the toss and chose to bat, his side fighting back from an unpromising 118-5 to 275 all out. It would have been significantly less if England had held their catches. The spinners bowled only 14 overs between them, with a lone wicket apiece, Lock bounding up with his sleeves buttoned at the wrist, either a sartorial quirk on his part or in order to disguise any straightening of the arm and thus avoid being called for throwing, depending on whose account you buy. Ray Lindwall, batting at nine, top-scored with 62. The fielding in general was dismal, but Lock himself missed nothing hit into his zone of control.

England began their reply convincingly enough, with Hutton and Edrich seeing off the new ball, but then fell into a sort of mid-innings coma with Bailey again at the heart of the action, if it could fairly be called that. As Cardus observed, with that weary mix of exasperation and grudging respect the Essex all-rounder generally inspired, at the close of play on the second day, 'He remained intact, if not invincible, on 35, after two hours of calm obstinacy. I wonder he had not driven Miller mad by this time. He is not only an anchor for England; he barnacles the good ship to the floor of the ocean.' The label stuck. England eventually enjoyed a first-innings lead of 31.

If Hutton truly regarded spin as the poor relation to seam, supplied here by the impressive firm of Trueman, Bedser and Bailey, he was also too much of a pragmatist not to know what to do on a classic Oval turner when he saw one on the third day. Perhaps it had all been no more than the Yorkshireman's native preference for fast-medium reliability over potentially match-winning fancy stuff. Anyway, Laker was soon off the leash again. Bowling with that slightly hangdog expression that seemed to run the gamut for him from utter elation to abject misery, he almost immediately trapped Hassett lbw, for ten. The ball was abruptly turning square. 'You could see Tony pawing the turf with impatience,' Evans remembered. 'There was steam coming from his nostrils. "Give me the fucking ball," he told Len, and oddly enough Len did.' When a team bowls for a whole session with a spinner on at either end, you somehow know they're going for a win. Australia were 59-1 when Laker nailed Hole leg before, and then, menace fairly gleaming from his bald pate, Lock bowled Neil Harvey.

Suddenly three wickets down, Australia were only 29 to the good. The crowd roared every ball. 'Miller, once dangerous in moments such as these, groped his way into the leg-trap of Laker,' wrote Cardus, 'and before the ground had regained breath, Morris padded up without constructive ideas to Lock and died the modern hero's death, lbw.' The tourists had lost four of their top batsmen in 15 minutes and 16 balls for two runs. Lock was quite pleased at these developments, particularly his breakthrough against Harvey. 'My leap for joy measured the ecstasy of the moment,' he later wrote, characteristically shy about it all.

The end result was that just after tea on the third day Australia were all out for 162, an overall lead of 131. Laker took 4-75 in 17 overs and Lock 5-45 in 21. The only wicket to elude them was that of Jim de Courcy, who suicidally ran himself out when backing up too far. Spectators cheered the local heroes all the way to the pavilion when the innings ended. It was sometimes said of Laker that he was altogether too laid-back, with that resigned look he had of placidly expecting the worst, to be really popular with the masses. If so, they didn't seem too bothered about it now. He gave them a brief wave in return, while Lock half ran, half danced up the steps like an excited child heading for the goods on Christmas morning.

Batting in suddenly equatorial sunshine, England crossed the line, for the loss of two wickets, shortly before three o'clock on the fourth day. Australia kept up the fight until the last five minutes. With nine needed to win, Hassett brought himself on for the first time in the series – just four runs ensued – and then threw the ball to Arthur Morris, who bowled much like what he was, a specialist opening bat. There followed one of those common points in England's post-war national experience. By a happy coincidence, Compton and Edrich, the batting world's equivalent of Laker and Lock, were together at the end. Edrich took a single, which brought it down to only four needed and caused a few blue-suited policemen to take up position just outside the boundary rope. As if sensing what was expected of him, Compton promptly tried his trademark sweep, only to see Davidson, fielding as though it were the first over of the series and not the last, fling himself sideways and cut off the four. He tried the shot again next ball, and succeeded. 'Is it the Ashes? Yes! England have won the Ashes!' Brian Johnston yelled, for once abandoning his proprietary air of whimsical understatement. In the end the police proved little deterrent to the crowd, several hundred of whom ran over the field and massed in front of the pavilion, where they shouted 'Speech, speech!' to Hutton and the other players waving down from the balcony. The evening's press headline 'ENGLAND BEAT AUSSIES' was a sort of pre-JFK moment, news so viscerally shocking that the individual would never forget where they were when they saw it. Of the protracted team celebration that followed, even the normally abstemious Laker remarked, 'There was an unforgettable night out, or at least so I've been told.'

It was 19 August 1953, and from that day onwards Laker and Lock would be inextricably linked in the public imagination, not so much as individual halves of a spin-bowling axis, but almost as though they were conjoined as some sort of weird but compelling hybrid creation. Impressive enough even in the normal course of events, like all the truly great players they seemed to rise to the big occasion, the potent and irresistible destroyer of even the mighty Australians. As the later adage went, 'Ashes to ashes, dust to dust. If Laker doesn't get you, Lockie must.'

Speaking privately immediately after the Oval Test, Lindsay Hassett put a rather different spin on the refrain. The Australians' puckish captain, shortly to announce his retirement, accepted defeat with the same equanimity that characterised his batting. 'Not bad,' he allowed, 'considering Tony threw us out.' Much later that night, he amplified on these remarks when he told Godfrey Evans, 'If that bugger [Lock] chucks it, at least he's an accurate chucker,' which seems to have more or less summed up the consensus among the party as a whole. As Keith Miller once added, 'Laker was good [at The Oval], and Lock was even better. He was coming in at medium-quick, pitching on leg and banking to off – it's what the air force boys call angular momentum, and put in plain English it's like trying to bat against a fucking boomerang.' This was expressive enough, but perhaps as a final comment on the events of August 1953 there were the more measured words of Neville Cardus: 'Many great spin bowlers have found themselves unselfconsciously giving an extra flick, to lend to the ball a final decisive vitality. Lock's bowling was on the whole too skilful, is too skilful yet, to suffer a general indictment, merely on the evidence of recurrent lapses from strict conformity ... After all, considering cricket, and especially bowling, as art, the fact that matters most is the technical product, the quality of the ball which comes to the batsman to be played.' Or, loosely translated: Lock's bowling showed the benefits of unlimited aggression, and it seemed almost a churlish technicality to insist he should always keep his arm straight.

Ten days after the summer's climactic Oval showdown, Surrey went down to play their last championship match of the season, against Hampshire in the less pressurised surroundings of Dean Park, Bournemouth. The pitch was so green you could have served it as a salad. The visitors won the toss and fielded. Hampshire lasted for 47 overs and made 82 all out: Laker took 2-37, and Lock 8-26. Surrey managed 151 in reply, and the home team were batting again shortly after tea on the first day. This time Lock took only 5-43, and everyone went home a day and a half early. The following week, Surrey retained the championship by a 16-point margin over their nearest challengers. They were effectively untouchable. For a period in the 1950s it's probably true to say that, as a sporting contest, the annual race for the pennant was not quite fair. One cartoon of the era depicted the Surrey side standing around rubbing their hands with sinister grins on their faces while awaiting their latest guests at The Oval, which might as well have had a sign saying 'Bates Motel' hanging over the front gate.

All this might have been enough excitement for an average professional cricketer, but later in September 1953 Lock followed his triumphs for Surrey and England by volunteering to turn out for his native Oxted in front of a thin but keen crowd there to welcome him back against a Casuals side which included the future England batsman Raman Subba Row in its ranks.

The local press reported:

> Lock took a wicket with his first ball. He proceeded from
> there to show all his skills of flight, spin and change of pace.

His faster delivery accounted for two more wickets and then came Subba Row, who, unfortunately, got an unpleasant ball which rose sharply and he was caught in the leg-trap. The visitors gallantly played out time despite all Lock's wiles, including the fast yorker which petrified batsmen, wicketkeeper and close fieldsmen alike. He was unplayable.

Lock finished the match with 5-27 and returned the following weekend to take four more wickets against Addiscombe, before going on to put the West Kent Wanderers opener out of action with a broken toe. 'Tony wasn't the sort of bowler to put his feet up at the end of the season when he could still be playing cricket,' Trevor Bailey remembered.

On another occasion, Lock was seen, late on the same evening a Test match in which he was playing began at Lord's, wheeling away in the nets at Oxted until, at ten o'clock, the batsman called a halt on the grounds that by then all he could see was the glowing tip of the cigarette the bowler kept permanently clamped in his mouth. What most impressed people was the sheer dedication he brought to the job, whether appearing in front of a packed house at Lord's or a few curious bystanders in rural Surrey. Lock's competitiveness was an engine that never stopped ticking.

* * *

England's contentious tour of the West Indies in 1953/54 already commands a wide literature. It's a frequently repeated fact that there was a full-scale riot in the course of the third Test in British Guiana, whether triggered by drink, gambling or popular resentment at the recent removal from office of the colony's left-wing premier, and that on another occasion the chief minister of Jamaica grasped the tourists' captain by the lapels, hoisted him off the ground, and, apparently in the belief that Hutton had snubbed him, accused the visitors of having insulted the host government.

Things had got off to a poor start when the MCC party, with Laker and Lock for once both included, left London on 14 December 1953, the first of the modern age to tour under a paid captain, and for that matter to travel exclusively by air, only to promptly find themselves stranded by engine trouble in Newfoundland, clad only in their matching Burton tropical suits. 'Not a good omen,' Lock later remarked, adding that he seemed to have experienced all four annual seasons by the time he deplaned in an autumnally wet Bermuda. The many subsequent books on the series invariably include the words 'conflict' or 'cauldron' in their titles. Before leaving home, the tourists had been briefed by the Tory minister (and occasional first-class cricketer) Walter Monckton to expect 'difficulty' in certain Caribbean islands. It was pointed out that the political situation there was delicate, and that under no circumstances should any of the players look for trouble. They soon found it, anyway.

Within minutes of alighting from the plane at Bermuda, Lock had committed the first of the numerous gaffes which would distinguish the tour as a whole and earn the English visitors their possibly unfair reputation as what the local *Gazette* newspaper called 'the high priests of colonialism', 'slavedrivers' and 'utter nobs', among other unflattering terms. As was his habit, Lock had drunk several cups of strong black coffee on the final leg of the flight over, and was perhaps even more animated than usual as a result. Or perhaps he was simply tired and disorientated after the protracted ordeal of the outward journey. In either case, he didn't quite rise to the occasion. There was a full-scale committee on hand to welcome the cricketers, led by the governor of Bermuda wearing his antique military costume, cocked hat, feathers, sword and gold spurs, along with several lesser dignitaries, and bringing up the rear the modestly dark-suited Speaker of the local parliament. Lock seems to have assumed that this last individual was actually an airport porter of some kind, because, asked if there were anything in particular he required while on the island, he replied, 'The luggage would be nice, mate.' It was an honest mistake, but one way or another the tourists would be consistently unfortunate in their efforts at successfully interacting with their host communities over the course of the next 15 weeks. In the great rolling phrases of the *Wisden* of that era, so compelling in their authority:

> In the arrangement of tours Marylebone Cricket Club always has set the furtherance of friendship between man and man, country and country, as one of its main hopes and objectives. As the recognised Privy Council of cricket, M.C.C. firmly maintain their idealistic outlook that the spirit in which the game is played carries greater importance than such transient elation or disappointment as the mere winning or losing of a Test series.
>
> This made it all the more regrettable that the visit of the M.C.C. representatives to the West Indies aroused such controversy and uneasiness. Whatever the gains in other directions, the primary intention for the tour was not fulfilled and the circumstances of its failure were such that all those with the welfare of cricket at heart recognised that the problems arising needed to be tackled boldly but without heat.

Turning from the tour's broader context in order to find out what actually happened: Laker took seven wickets in the first knock-up game, for which Lock was rested. On 19 December, MCC began a full three-day match with Bermuda, a fixture that by all accounts contained a high standard of cricket along with a happy balance of endeavour and humour. 'The charm of the Caribbean fully asserted itself,' Swanton wrote, adding, 'It was played wholeheartedly, but

Jim Laker, standing fifth from left, as a 15-year-old in the Salt Grammar School eleven.

The school itself, which Laker later called a 'thoroughly Victorian establishment'; he meant it as a compliment.

An impish-looking ten-year-old Tony Lock, standing third from left, at school in Limpsfield.

Sir Henry 'Shrimp' Leveson Gower of Oxford University, Surrey and England, who first recommended Lock to The Oval.

Laker's own mentor, Peter Smith of Essex and England. A trim, genial figure, he kept smiling even after being the victim of probably the cruellest hoax in cricket history.

It's widely agreed that Surrey's groundsman Bert Lock (no relation, although he might as well have been) worked wonders in transforming The Oval from the unused but fully equipped wartime internment camp it remained until November 1945, with barbed wire strung across the playing area, into an arena fit for top-class cricket, with a marked receptiveness to spin, just six months later.

Lock in his early days at Surrey, where he made his debut in the week of his 17th birthday.

'You looking at me?' Friendly and often boisterous off the field, Lock always took his work seriously.

Stuart Surridge sets his Surrey team-mates an example in the field.

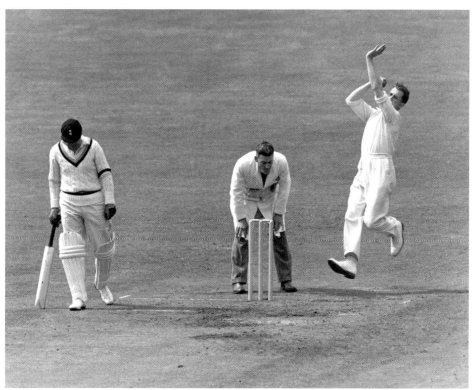

The classic Laker action, left arm cocked like a sniper sighting his target, was always the signal for dead quiet in the crowd. He's seen here for Surrey against Derbyshire in 1949.

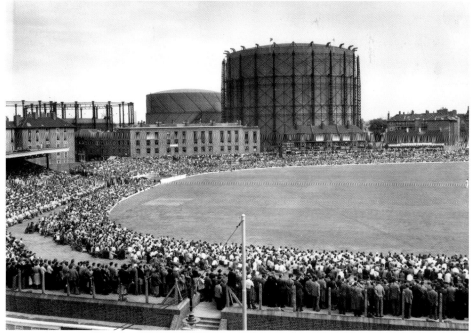

A representative scene at The Oval of the 1950s, where the crowds saw Surrey bring home seven consecutive County Championships.

The Surrey side in 1951, with Laker and Lock separated in the back row by their fellow spinner Eric Bedser. [Courtesy: Surrey CCC]

Len Hutton in relaxed mood, although neither Laker nor Lock ever felt fully comfortable around him.

Much the same thing could be said of Freddie Brown, of Northants and England. Laker later wrote of his management of the MCC side in Australia: 'He started wrongly, and never looked back.'

The young 'Fiery Fred' Trueman, Lock's partner in crime in the West Indies.

Johnny Wardle, who gave Lock a run for his money as England's first choice left-arm spinner in the 1950s. Neither one of them was a shrinking violet. After 13 years' employment, Yorkshire sacked Wardle with the statement: 'He has been warned on several occasions that his behaviour in the field and in the dressing room has left much to be desired. We will not be calling on his services again.'

Len Hutton, Jim Laker and Godfrey Evans offer some last-minute advice to 57-year-old Jack Warner, playing the fictional England captain, in what remains Britain's only significant cricket feature film, The Final Test.

The Surrey team, under Surridge's captaincy, in the middle of their extended purple patch in the 1950s. Laker and Lock took 2,011 first-class wickets between them in seven seasons. [Courtesy: Surrey CCC]

light-heartedly, and with considerable individual distinction ... The English spin bowlers often quietened their opponents.'

Lock took 8-54 in Bermuda's first innings, which must count as one of the more statistically fruitful starts by a bowler appearing on the first day of his first full overseas representative tour. He obviously liked the place, because 48 hours later he went out to play a new match on the same field and took another seven wickets in the brief interval before torrential rain brought an early end to the proceedings. After that the tourists flew on to Jamaica, where Lock promptly took 4-25 against a strong Combined Parishes side captained by George Headley, bringing his total for the week to 20 wickets at 14 apiece. Laker's figures at the same stage were ten at an average of 12. Both players were still doing their utmost to make themselves congenial in small as well as large ways to the tour management. Lock found that he was sharing a hotel room with Fred Trueman, a curious pairing in that neither man had ever travelled abroad, let alone at the quasi-ambassadorial level, before. They were both in their early 20s, and prone to not so much air as bawl out their opinions. 'According to Hutton, I was supposed to look after Fiery Fred,' Lock later wrote. 'I thought this was a very haphazard arrangement. If anyone had to be responsible for some other player, surely it would have been a happier idea for a senior pro to guide the junior one.'

Trueman in turn had a nasty shock coming when he was once woken in the dead of night by the arresting spectacle of a naked Lock, while still fast asleep, standing upright, both arms held high and letting out the piercing appeal, 'Howzat?', followed by the equally shrill verdict, 'Out, damned spot!' and the climactic, 'Come give me your hand ... To bed, to bed, to bed!' before abruptly slumping back again. Trueman did not catch the literary reference, and treated his room-mate with some caution for the rest of the tour.

Like most professional cricketers, Lock was also chronically worried about money. He got a basic £450 for his 15 weeks' work on tour, out of which he paid tax and bought his own kit. 'Without being stood drinks by a shipload of British sailors we would have gone broke,' he later recalled. Nonetheless, it was a pleasure to come off the field at the close of play and stroll down to the beach, watch the sky turn azure and the moon flow up over the water, particularly when it turned out to be yet another of the worst winters in living memory back in Britain.

The West Indies won the first Test, at Kingston, by 140 runs. Lock, like everyone else, didn't foresee England batting quite as badly as they did, particularly in collapsing on the last day when needing just 230 with eight wickets in hand. They were still in with a shout when Peter May was given out caught round the corner. Watching in line with the wickets, Lock believed 'May's bat was at no time within a foot of the ball.' Perhaps it was with this incident in mind that Hutton later wrote, 'Our friends in the Caribbean could be numbered on one hand', and conspicuously 'did not include many of the umpires.'[1] It proved to be a case of after May, the deluge. Evans came in with the score at a pivotal 282/5, still anyone's game. He was upset because the night before Hutton had told his team that he expected them to be tucked up in bed with their lights out at ten o'clock, an hour at which the indefatigable Godders had been known to be opening his second bottle of gin. Now he wanted revenge. 'Play yourself in,' Hutton told the outgoing batsman as he left the dressing room. 'Don't do anything rash.' 'Right,' said Evans, whereupon he went dancing ten yards down the pitch to be bowled by the second ball he faced.

---

1   The situation reached a nadir when the tourists learnt that Harold Walcott would be one of the two men officiating in the second Test at Barbados. Walcott's own nephew Clyde was playing in the game, where he was lucky enough to score a double century.

But perhaps the one really imperishable moment of the Test had come early on the fourth day when Lock was brought on to bowl to the sentimental favourite George Headley, who at the age of 44 had been brought out of retirement in England by public subscription. In keeping with *Wisden*'s lofty ideals, Hutton had told Lock to let the local hero 'have one', and Lock did – a vicious leg cutter of around Alec Bedser pace that a startled Headley just managed to jab away for a single. Behind the stumps, Evans thought it 'about the fastest ball I saw bowled on the tour', adding that he had had to soak his hands in ice water after the close that night. A few minutes later, Headley faced Lock again and had got about halfway through his pickup when he lost his middle and off stumps. 'A faster ball from an alleged slow bowler would be hard to imagine,' Hutton would later write admiringly. But that wasn't the end of it. Lock tried the same thing again in the next over, bowling to Gerry Gomez, and the umpire Perry Burke no-balled him from square leg. It was the first time a bowler had been called for throwing in a Test since the days of starched shirts and waxed moustaches, at Melbourne in January 1898, and the first time ever for an Englishman representing his country.

Hutton promptly walked over to confer with the umpire, and then walked back to where Lock was standing, hands on hips, a violently red-faced figure divorced from the small, defeated voice which gasped out his only comment, 'Not again.' He needed medical treatment at the close for dehydration and heat exhaustion. Hutton advised him to cut out his faster ball until further notice, and as a result Lock, who'd taken five wickets in the match to that point, added only a further nine in the remaining four completed Tests.

It's difficult at this remove to say with any clarity whether the decision to pair Lock and Trueman as room-mates on the tour was wilfully perverse, or perhaps made in the sincere belief that the arrangement might somehow prove mutually beneficial to two young players who thus far in their careers had exhibited all the self-restraining qualities of a Sherman tank. If the latter, it seems to have been only a partial success. The Leicestershire captain Charles Palmer, the man who had once remarked of Lock that he would 'either go to prison or become a great cricketer', served as the tour's player-manager, which put him in the curious position of being under Hutton's jurisdiction in the field but answerable only to Lord's for the day-to-day administration and welfare of the team, including their accommodations.

In later years, Palmer allowed that this particular choice of room-mates might have fallen short of the optimal. 'In fact, it was a joke,' he added, remembering in particular the rest day of the Barbados Test (which England lost by 181 runs), when two 'terrifyingly loud and large English ladies' had complained of having been the subject of certain lewd endearments on the part of Lock and Trueman when riding up together in the hotel lift late the previous night. Although there had been no 'direct carnal indelicacy involved', to quote the official report, one or other of the two cricketers had apparently looked long and hard at the ladies' upholstery before making the comment, 'You don't get many of them to the pound.'

E.W. Swanton, who was on hand to witness the subsequent interview with the beautifully dressed and magnificently irate complainants on the one hand, and the two contrite young tourists on the other, added the descriptive detail that the more robust of the offended parties had proceeded to hold forth 'rather in the manner of Bertie Wooster's Aunt Agatha ... The theme was what was expected of English teams abroad, and I found myself applauding the lady's admirable sentiments, expressed, as I recall, in a fine, manly baritone.' Trueman would devote three pages to the episode in his 2005 memoir *As It Was*, stoutly denying any impropriety, and adding that on the night in question – which happened to have been his 23rd birthday – 'Tony and I had both had a few drinks, after which we had gone straight to our room and taken to our beds at a reasonable hour.' Thirty years after the fact, Lock claimed to have forgotten the whole incident, but could still vividly recall the traumatic experience of being no-balled from square leg a further three times in that week's colony match with Barbados. That, as much as Hutton's edict on the subject, put an end to his less orthodox delivery, and with it much of his usefulness as a bowler on the rock-hard Caribbean wickets. His productive tour of the West Indies was effectively over less than halfway through the itinerary. 'It was not the ideal place to send an immature young player at that time,' Hutton later admitted.

On arrival in Georgetown for the third Test, some of the senior England players requested a meeting with their captain, pointing out to him that they were now two down in the series, with three to go, and thus that there was little or nothing to lose in their henceforth seeking to adopt a more positive attitude to the remaining games. (The exact choice of words may have been more colourful.) Hutton conceded at least some of the logic of this, and, as one practical step in that direction, instructed Tom Graveney to go out and 'bat naturally' in that week's pre-Test colony match. Graveney did so, scoring 231 and sharing a stand with Watson of 402, still an English record for any wicket overseas.

As we've seen, the Test itself was marred by an incident which followed on the run-out decision against the hometown hero Cliff McWatt, a verdict some in the crowd greeted by pelting the ground with an assortment of bottles, fruit and other debris that quickly dotted the outfield like a tropical rash. As a result the remaining batsman and most of the fielding side retreated to form a defensive ring at one end of the pitch, several of them brandishing the uprooted stumps as a potential deterrent, the umpires ran for the pavilion, the president of the British Guiana Association shouted excitedly at everyone through a loudhailer, and Laker stood serenely with his hands in his pockets at long leg, his face deadpan. Someone eventually suggested that Hutton lead his men off, and Hutton declined, adding, 'I want a couple more wickets tonight.' 'You can have mine,' the not-out batsman immediately replied. England eventually won by nine wickets, recording their first Test victory in the Caribbean in 20 years.

The Trinidad Test that followed was indecisive, but not short of incident. England went on to the field in front of a full house, the overflow members of which watched from the nearby trees and hilltops, periodically igniting thunder flashes to mark their pleasure or otherwise at a particular turn of events. The pitch itself was laid over with jute matting, which proved to be a less than ideal surface to bowl on; the West Indies finally declared on the third day at 681/9, with Weekes scoring 206, Worrell 167 and Walcott a mere 124. There are times in life when the miseries of the world threaten to engulf us, when the precariousness of the human condition, far from appearing a worthwhile and even noble struggle, seems an infinite rebuke. Many of us who live on the edge of a North American rainforest feel like this all winter long. Jim Laker's own hour of inner desolation surely came in the course of his stretch of 50 overs, with a return of 2-154, although in fairness Lock's economy rate was only marginally better with 2-178 from 63. Compton and May in turn made centuries, and the captains wearily shook hands on a draw on the sixth and final afternoon. The English batsmen had acquitted themselves well, and, it seemed to them, were also more attentive to the need to entertain the public. Nonetheless, an editorial in the *Trinidad Guardian* declared, 'Our delight as West Indians in the tour is fast turning to dismay.' 'I knew how they felt,' Lock later remarked.

On losing the toss in the final Test at Kingston, Hutton gloomily anticipated a West Indies total somewhere in excess of 500. An hour later they were 13-4, largely thanks to Trevor Bailey, who finished with figures of 7-34 in 16 overs. In the end the hosts managed to score 139, which was 66 fewer than Hutton made in the England reply. Laker finally found his groove in the West Indies second innings, with close fielders leaping around the bat and each delivery looking deceptively like the last one, until the victim was drawn out where the ball no longer was. He took 4-71, and Lock chipped in with a single wicket, that of a 17-year-old debutant named Garry Sobers. Sobers thought they were both very fine bowlers, 'Although Tony definitely used to ping them. He knew that he threw now and again. But he got away with it, so what could you do?' England won the Test by nine wickets, thus recovering from two down to level the series. There were a few more off-the-field mishaps to come, including the possibly apocryphal story insisting that when at a formal dinner Trueman had requested the Indian High Commissioner to 'Pass t'salt, Gunga Din.' Perhaps it didn't really happen, although it fits an image some people had of him. But at the end of the tour Lock received his £50 good-conduct bonus, and Trueman didn't. He never quite forgave Hutton for this, and the two great Yorkshiremen never played together for England again.

In 1966, someone leaked excerpts of Hutton's confidential tour report to the MCC on his players, in which he wrote of Laker:

> He is an extremely able bowler but he has a tendency to be afraid of certain batsmen, instead of adopting the attitude, 'I am a better bowler than you are a batsman.' When a good batsman is at the wicket he is inclined to indicate his unwillingness to bowl. Laker should be carefully considered in committee before future selection for overseas tours.

It might be pertinent to note at this point what Tom Graveney once told me about finding Hutton an 'enigmatical' leader, who, for all his bravura displays with the bat (returning from the West Indies with a Test match average of 96.71), wasn't someone 'whose goodwill and friendly support you ever felt you could rely on'. When I asked him for an example of this, Graveney gave a thin smile and recalled the night when he, Statham, Bailey and Laker had been enjoying a quiet drink in their hotel on the eve of their final departure from Jamaica.

'The skipper came in, gazed around at the four of us with that poker-faced expression of his, sat down, lit a fag, and then started talking quietly about the tour down-under in a year's time.

'"Fancy Australia, Brian?" Hutton enquired.

'"Yes, skipper."

'"Trevor?"

'"Rather, skipper."

'"Tom?"

'"Thanks very much, skipper."'

Then Hutton looked long and hard at Laker.

'Like a drink, Jim?' he asked.

* * *

The year 1954 had one of those summers that make you wonder how the English could ever have come up with a national sport with a minimum requirement of at least halfway dry weather. 'This poor month was less sunny than the preceding winter, with few if any warm days,' the Met Office was forced to admit at the end of June. And moving on to July, 'Days were often cool and cloudy [and] temperatures only briefly approached normal.' The record shows some modest improvement for early August, before, with a certain inevitability, 'The month once again became very wet, and temperatures cool or worse.'

'If 1954 was generally a disappointing year for English cricket watchers, it was similarly a wash-out for me,' Lock wrote in his memoirs. He wasn't picked for a single Test against the touring Pakistanis. This may have had something to do with lingering doubts about his bowling action, although Lock himself admitted, 'My conduct off the field was allegedly under a cloud, and some critics suggested I wasn't a team man.' This was perhaps to understate the official report on his behaviour in the West Indies, which contained a full account of the Barbados hotel lift affair, as well as stories of Lock's personal dining habits: half a dozen cups of black coffee for breakfast ('Tony was like a caged tiger prowling around the room,' Godfrey Evans once told me), much the same for lunch, dinners washed down with beer, and 'a lot of unwise decisions' seemingly made as a result.

Nothing like that could be said against Laker, although he in turn managed to appear in only one of the 15 Tests played between Kingston in March 1954 and The Oval in August 1955. There may have been perfectly sound technical reasons for this, although it's worth noting what Laker's Surrey team-mate Micky Stewart, a successful future England manager, has to say on the matter: 'I thought Jim was a top bloke. By nature he was quite an emotional person. But he deliberately schooled himself to always seem indifferent on the field. It was the stiff upper lip, if you like. The problem was that he just became too bloody good at it. If you didn't know Jim well you might not have thought he was being admirably calm and British. You would have thought he didn't give a toss.'

* * *

Snubbed by England, both Laker and Lock went back to taking an impressive haul of wickets for Surrey. It was the side's third successive year of dominance of the domestic game. As the reigning county champions became more successful, they gradually modulated into a team that could play elegant cricket, but Laker rarely stooped to such frivolity. His stock in trade was simply that he operated as quietly and rhythmically as the workings of a Swiss watch. There may have been some distinctly odd choices made by England committees over the years, particularly those where not all the facts have been broadcast or the needs of an individual Test fully aired. The reader may have his or her own favourite example of the arcane ways of the selection room. But perhaps the strangest case of all was the consistent exclusion of Laker and Lock in the home season of 1954, when they took 260 first-class wickets between them at an average of just 15 and 16 respectively.

In early May a strong MCC side hosted Surrey for the season's traditional curtain-raiser at Lord's. Laker took 15 wickets in the match, which must have impressed even the blazers watching from the pavilion. A week later it was Lock's turn, with a distinctly useful second-innings analysis of 6-22 off 24 overs in a home tie against Leicestershire. Laker then appeared in the inaugural England v Pakistan Test, also at Lord's, in the middle of June. The first three days were washed out, and other than a reception for the teams at Buckingham Palace, not much happened on the last two. The tourists eventually went out to bat on a seam-friendly pitch and scored all of 87, Statham taking 4-18. England replied with 117/9, and that more or less concluded the week's entertainment. Johnny Wardle had taken 16 wickets in his first half-dozen county matches of the season and Lock had taken 27, so naturally the England selectors chose Wardle for the Test. Thirty years later Les Ames summarised some of the atmosphere of the typical England committee meeting of the day, without specifically mentioning Laker or Lock, or any other player. 'As a rule, we didn't dawdle over a lot of statistics, prefer[ring] to stick to a general impression about the man under discussion. "Quite agreeable and pleasant, but not much bloody good in a tight corner" – that was about the gist of it.'

Meanwhile, it was much the familiar story in the Surrey dressing-room. Speaking in 1990, Arthur McIntyre recalled, 'Jim was a perfectly nice, quiet bloke. But he wasn't one to go into raptures of praise or encouragement for you. He kept things battened down. He once told me I had a sensitive soul, and it was as if he was complimenting me on my golf swing.' The Laker–Lock axis was similarly amicable but wary, and McIntyre remembered, 'They largely communicated in grunts.' Laker quietly told a few people that he wasn't unhappy Lock had been called for throwing in the West Indies. Some of those people, like McIntyre, thought that by that 'Jim meant Lockie was too good a bowler to have to resort to chucking, and so his being called was actually a plus – he could devote all his time and energy to being the best left-arm spinner in the world.' Or at least that was one interpretation; but the accounts are as varied and equivocal as the relationship they seek to describe, and the only certainty is that Godfrey Evans later clearly remembered a day on tour in the West Indies when, 'Jim told me that Tony was a bloody good bowler, which I'd already pretty well worked out myself. But he was also "too noisy", and this didn't go over well with some of the other Surrey boys. Jim suggested a solution: to somehow cut Tony's coffee consumption down so that he wasn't always wired up like a ticking time bomb. He admitted there might be practical difficulties to doing this.'

England's decision to dispense with Laker's services in 1954 looks even more bizarre when it's remembered that Hutton, on medical advice, stood down from the second and third of the four-Test series. In his absence the team was led by 25-year-old David Sheppard, the future bishop of Liverpool, a man who appealed to the tradition of appointing amateur captains from the ancient universities. Laker's chief involvement with Sheppard up until then had come in generously offering his services as a coach in the pre-season nets at Cambridge. But even in 1954 international cricket was no place for sentiment. When England met Pakistan for the second time that summer at Trent Bridge, Sheppard and his fellow selectors opted for Appleyard and Wardle over Laker and Lock. They then dropped Appleyard for the third Test and replaced him with Jim McConnon of Glamorgan, a man who made his county debut only at the age of 28 after a football career with Aston Villa. He took three wickets in the match, and just one more in the fourth Test at The Oval which, with Hutton back in charge, England managed to lose. Even then there was no place for either Laker or Lock in the MCC tour party that winter.

Perhaps they had a point to prove, then, or perhaps it was just another extended demonstration of their peerless bowling techniques, and how diligently they worked at them, but from about late July onwards they hit rampant form. Playing Kent at Blackheath, they accounted for all ten wickets, seven-three in Lock's favour, in the only innings possible thanks to rain. The following week at The Oval, Laker took 10-92 and Lock 5-64 in the match against Essex. The Surrey side then took the train up to Kettering, where they narrowly beat Northamptonshire: six more to Lock, 11 to Laker. In ten games they snared 104 victims between them. Their standard field consisted of three slips, a gully, square gully, and a couple of men crouching insultingly close round the corner. They always bowled at the stumps, never to one side or the other just to contain.

It wasn't only the pair's impressive economy rate, or the routine way in which the opposition batsmen seemed to depart the field, as if borne by conveyor belt. They had other positive qualities, too. For one thing, both men could add valuable runs from the late middle order. Batting at number nine, Laker actually hit a full-blooded century that summer against a Gloucestershire side with the sometime England spinners John Mortimore and Sam Cook in the line-up. It's one of the many examples of his essentially dry, taciturn nature that when Laker went home that night he mentioned to his wife only that he had 'got 113 today'. Thinking that he meant a return of no wicket for 113 runs, Lilly tactfully said no more on the subject. It was only when she read about it in the next morning's *Daily Express* that she realised her husband had made what proved to be the highest score of his 20-year career. Since Laker also took 29 catches and Lock no fewer than 42 that season, it's not surprising that both were listed under the heading 'all-rounders' in the Surrey yearbook. In Lock's close fielding the cobra and the shark shared aptitudes in what was one of the most vividly entertaining spectacles on the county circuit, or for that matter in competitive sport anywhere.

At Grace Road, Leicester, the home team went in to bat in the late morning of Wednesday, 11 August; they were all out for 106 shortly after lunch, having been destroyed by Laker (5-27) and Lock (4-28). At least on that occasion they got through a complete session. A fortnight later, at The Oval, the Worcestershire openers went out to the middle at two o'clock, and their last man was back in the pavilion again by half past three. The entire side managed to score 24 runs, and a leg bye, between them; in a neat piece of symmetry, Laker took 2-5 and Lock took 5-2. Surridge then declared the home reply at 92-3, which seemed eccentric to some of his team until he told them that he'd just spoken to the Met Office and been advised that it was about to pour with rain. The county champions just had time to dismiss their visitors a second time, for 40, before the floods came. The whole match had lasted just four hours, and it cemented Surrey's place at the top of the table. One of the visiting batsmen later reflected on having to deal not only with the challenges of the pitch but also the problem of Lock making 'primitive animal noises' from his position a few feet away at short leg, all part of the 'quite extensive' Surrey psy-ops programme. There also always seemed to be a generous amount of appealing, much of it conducted from the direction of short leg. In general, the playing atmosphere had been 'a bit lively', the batsman concluded.

From there the returning county champions went on to a sort of victory lap in their final match of the season, at home to Lancashire, which they won in familiar style. Matters were fairly evenly poised until the last day, when the visitors, chasing 182, were spun out for 86, Laker taking four wickets and Lock five. Lancashire's captain Cyril Washbrook was later to remark, 'Jim was bad enough, but Tony was literally unplayable when he bunged you the fast one,' although against this it should be noted that Lock's friend Fred Price was standing at square leg that afternoon and said nothing.

On 27 July, just as Surrey were running through the Kent batting card at Blackheath, the winter's tour party to Australia was announced. Hutton was captain, and in the measured words of *Wisden*, 'The omission of the three bowlers, F.S. Trueman, G.A.R. Lock and J.C. Laker, who took 15 of the 19 wickets in the victory at The Oval in 1953, occasioned some surprise.' That was putting it mildly. Lock later wrote in his memoirs:

> Several of our boys came up to me and said, 'Bad luck, Tony, you should have been picked.' It was decent of them but I didn't feel like talking about it. As soon as play ended, I changed quickly and hurried away. I had so hoped to go that the news knocked all the stuffing out of me.

Wardle did go to Australia, appearing in four of the five Tests and taking a total of ten wickets. Appleyard also played in the same number of Tests and managed 11 wickets, while Laker's latter-day rival Jim McConnon never made it into the side. The series as a whole followed some of the same trajectory as the West Indies tour before it, England going 1-0 down but then coming back to win 3-1. Thirty years later, Hutton wrote in his autobiography that he'd been 'very unhappy' at Laker's omission from the tour, but that his co-selectors had reminded him of the apparently imperishable trauma of the last day of the Leeds Test in 1948. 'At the time it was standard English thinking that off-spinners were wrong for Australia,' Hutton added. England's captain had nothing to say on the matter of his own misgivings about Laker's commitment, nor on his feelings about the suitability or otherwise of Lock as a de facto ambassador.

* * *

When Laker joined the rest of his Surrey colleagues at the spruce but windswept Fenner's ground in Cambridge for their first full fixture of the 1955 season, he was facing as an adversary the same young students he'd spent the previous month patiently schooling in the game's finer points in the nearby nets. As usual, he made no concession to sentiment. The visitors batted first and scored 328 by tea, with Laker smacking an even-time 44. The university in turn managed 82. The last four wickets fell for the addition of only one run, which meant that in a little over two hours Lock took 6-29 and Laker a comparatively restrained but superbly controlled 2-22 off 25 overs of almost metronomically precise but varied off spin that had the batsmen jumping around the crease like so many cats swatting at a cricket ball-shaped laser light. The students made 176 the second time around, four more to Lock and two to Laker, and Surrey were duly off to the races for a season in which they would win 23 of their 28 championship matches and play what was probably the consistently best cricket in the club's history.

Without dwelling on the accountancy of averages, it's perhaps instructive to note one or two particularly striking examples of the county's venerable spin-bowling firm in action. They provided a stark contrast, Laker solid and naggingly tight, Lock mercurial and capable of the really savage ball as well as the occasional miscue like the one he bounced at Arthur Milton in the MCC v Surrey match at Lord's that the batsman deposited about nine feet above the head of the fielder in front of the leg-side Tavern stand, where it cracked off the drum-tight metal shutter of a pie stall that promptly shot it back again like a trampoline. Lock stood there with his hands on his hips for a moment or two after that. He was fallible, but he was also the man who could turn a match for you. The Somerset team went out to bat against Surrey at The Oval at 11 o'clock on the Saturday morning of 14 May 1955. At lunch they stood at 82-6, and 30 minutes after the resumption they were all out for 99, six wickets to Lock and one to Laker. The home side responded with 224, which was relatively modest by their standards, and at the second attempt the visitors managed 121, Laker 3-44 and Lock 5-53. The carnage wasn't just restricted to The Oval, either. In the next week's tie against Essex at Ilford, Lock took another nine and Laker five. There are often long periods in cricket when not very much is happening, but this was only rarely the case when the Surrey team of that era was in the field.

The 22-year-old Micky Stewart was then breaking in to the side, and would remember how both bowlers were supremely dedicated to the task at hand, Laker with 'less of an obvious display of enthusiasm, but still bloody determined to get his way'. A poignant example of this resolve came in Surrey's match away to Leicestershire in late May. The hosts batted first and scored 114, Lock six wickets and Laker two. The pitch must have been the proverbial bunsen, because Leicester's captain Charles Palmer, of West Indies tour fame, quickly put himself on, throttled back from his normal military medium to bowl gentle off spin, and somehow took an astonishing eight wickets for no runs, which apart from anything else threatened to eclipse Laker's record in the 1950 Test trial for the cheapest such haul in first-class cricket history. No one in the Surrey batting order except the new England captain Peter May had managed to reach double figures. But Laker himself was still in the middle unbeaten, and at one stage played out six consecutive maidens from Palmer before clipping him away for three down to fine leg. Judging from the way he waved his bat aloft as he ran he was well aware of the peculiar significance of the shot. Palmer finished with figures of eight wickets for seven runs off 14 overs, meaning that Laker's 8-2, also off 14, remained intact in the record book. It struck Stewart that there was a curious mixture of shyness and self-assurance about his county colleague. 'Jim was a friendly guy, but let's just say he had very firm views on cricket and on life. He didn't like to be wrong, and he didn't like to be beaten.'

On 4 June Surrey began a match at The Oval with their closest championship rivals Yorkshire. The home team went in first and made just 85, of which Lock top-scored with an unbeaten 21. Yorkshire replied with 131, six of their wickets falling to spin, and Surrey declared their second innings at 261/7, setting a target of 216. The visitors' last man out was, somehow fittingly, Appleyard, who departed caught by Laker off Lock for nine. By all accounts, the Yorkshireman's brief innings had presented the distressing spectacle of a well-groomed poodle attempting to dislodge a rabid ferret from its windpipe. Surrey won by 41 runs. A fortnight later, the same sides met again at Leeds. This time Yorkshire won, but in unusual circumstances. Surrey were shot out for 75 in their second innings in what seems to have been not so much bad light as a reversion to wartime blackout conditions, with Fred Trueman steaming in with only a somewhat sooty, half-size sight screen behind him. Laker and Lock each made 20, which was more than twice the score of any other batsman. It all provided a mild twist on the cherished notion of the solidarity between members of cricket's fast-bowlers' union, because the home side's Ted Lester would remember:

> Fred was bowling a bit quick. Lockie came in as nightwatchman against us. He was staying while in Yorkshire at Fred's house. It didn't affect the rivalry. Fred really let him have it but Lockie stuck it out. There was absolutely no doubt about his courage that day.

This was not to be the only example of the healthy spirit of competition between the recent West Indies tour room-mates and also quite possibly the two most full-blooded English bowlers of the 1950s. Gloucestershire's David Allen remembered a later Yorkshire v The Rest match: 'I was fielding at mid-on when Trueman came in to bat. Lockie said, "I'm going to bounce him."' Allen was aghast at this. 'Careful, Tony,' he cautioned. Lock was unfazed and replied, 'I'm faster than he is. He wouldn't dare try anything.'

In between Surrey's two championship matches with Yorkshire, the England side took on the touring South Africans in the summer's first Test at Trent Bridge. Wardle and Appleyard played, Laker and Lock didn't. In the second Test at Lord's, the selectors dropped Appleyard and gave a first cap to Middlesex's 22-year-old off-spinner Fred Titmus. England won both matches. It seemed to some observers that whenever Laker and Lock were out of the national side it felt slightly incomplete, like watching a David Attenborough wildlife programme in black and white. It was good enough, but something important was missing. Laker himself apparently felt that way, because without getting too personal about it he later admitted to certain doubts about Titmus's inclusion in the side ahead of him. 'If the selectors want to seek out the young players who will make up the team of years ahead, let them revive the idea of the Test Trial,' he wrote, with perhaps unspoken but justifiable pride in the events at Bradford in May 1950.

Lock's unfiltered aggression was too much for some people, with traditional concepts of gentlemanly self-restraint, to take in their stride. But not even his critics doubted his unwavering commitment to the job. He never seemed to let something like a bad knee or a raw spinning finger slow him down, and the sports writer Gordon Ross recalled once seeing him 'strapping himself up like a mummy in the dressing-room which, if Surridge had been there, would have kept him out of the side'. Lock didn't bother much with the finer theory of bowling, and took about as much interest in the MCC coaching manual as he did in the more obscure tracts of Greek literature. But nothing would stop him. 'I was playing cricket,' he once observed, 'because I couldn't help it.' When not bowling his heart out for Surrey, England or any other side that would have him he freely offered his services as a coach, often – something of a pioneer in this area – to aspiring young female players.

A teenager named Julia White, then a schoolgirl member at The Oval, long remembered both Lock's enthusiasm and probity as a mentor, sometimes escorting her around London and helping to arrange her transport to Surrey's away matches. 'My parents had implicit trust in him as a guardian, and so did I,' she later wrote. While there's of course not the least breath of scandal about Lock's relations with White or any of the other impressionable young women he took under his wing in the 1950s, we can perhaps catch a glimpse of the ruinous events that tormented the final months of his life some 40 years later.

Laker was stoked by ambition, too. He clearly cared deeply both about his team's fortunes and his own reputation. 'If you don't want to learn from the best spinner in England that's your problem,' he once informed an unappreciative younger county colleague. On the surface he was the dour Yorkshireman and the antithesis of his slow-bowling twin. At the close of play Lock, gregarious by nature, would often stroll in to his opponents' dressing room and invite one or more of the players to join him in the nearest pub, where he was more than happy to pass hours drinking, talking and playing darts – he was a natural – afterwards reporting back any useful gossip. By contrast, 'Jim wasn't someone you'd normally expect to see propping up the bar,' said Godfrey Evans, who would have known. 'And brilliant as he was, you always had the feeling that life was all a bit of a struggle for him. If I had a criticism of Jim it was that he never really seemed to thaw out, or make playing cricket seem like less of an obvious chore.' It's also true that over the years Laker was sometimes thought to have taken a step backwards, not a step forwards, when the fight was at its hardest and men's steel was most tested. But set against this impression of him, Stuart Surridge, as a rule sparing in his praise of a colleague, remembered years later how 'Jim's power of spin meant that by halfway through a season his fingers were worn raw. I saw him with blood literally pouring down his arm while he bowled. A modern player would be off in a flash if that happened – although it wouldn't, of course, because they don't really spin it anymore.'

Lock was mostly exterior, Laker more elusive. The former ran an endless campaign to command respect and approval, if not outright fear; the latter was an emotionally distant figure, even if hot fires raged just below the surface. Neither man was the epitome of conventional warmth or charm. Their personal flaws were also sometimes cricketing virtues. What could make Laker a stolid and remote personality also helped make him a great bowler; sometimes you have to just shrug when you're being hit around the park and get on with it. What could make Lock an exasperating colleague and a trying friend made him a great bowler, too; sometimes a player's unremitting aggression and utter lack of self-doubt communicates itself to his opponents even before they take the field. They may not have been perfect, and they certainly weren't ideally suited to each other, but English cricket was nonetheless supremely fortunate that Laker and Lock came together when they did.

* * *

When Kent went out to play Surrey at the Rectory Field, Blackheath, on the uncharacteristically sunny morning of 2 July 1955, two distinguished-looking visitors were seen strolling at intervals among the shirt-sleeved crowd on the boundary's edge, pausing from time to time to study the proceedings in the middle and then each to record his thoughts in a black notebook. By all accounts they struck a somewhat incongruous note amidst the more relaxed atmosphere of a warm Saturday morning's provincial county cricket match. The two individuals in question were 52-year-old Gubby Allen, the newly appointed chairman of selectors, and his colleague Les Ames, 49, the former Kent and England stumper, and they were there primarily to cast a trained eye on Tony Lock's bowling action. According to E.W. Swanton, 'They thought that at times his faster ball looked "a bit funny", but neither could see that his elbow was bent prior to delivery.' The bowler took 5-43 in the Kent first innings of 107 all out, and just four days later duly found himself back in the England side to face South Africa in the third Test at Old Trafford.

It has to be said that Lock's comeback was an only mixed success. Although passing his previous best Test score with an unbeaten 19, his bowling figures were a meagre 2-121 and 1-23, and the tourists reached their winning target of 145 with three minutes to go. Nonetheless, England kept faith with Lock in the fourth Test at Leeds – another South African win – and at long last reunited him with Laker for the final match of the series at The Oval. South Africa eventually needed 244 to win, and the outcome was decided in the course of three overs from Laker and Lock in which the tourists' opening partnership was broken and their next three batsmen failed to score. In something of a repeat performance of what had happened on the same ground in 1953, Laker finished with 5-56 and Lock with 4-62. This proved a harder, grimmer affair than even the climax of a closely fought Ashes series. That most genial of cricketers Tom Graveney was left to rue that 'personal relations between the players weren't all they could have been', while Laker was on ground well beyond this when he later wrote of his South African off-spinning counterpart Hugh Tayfield, 'As a [bowler] he was as smooth as they come. As a man, I have less to say for him. He is not the sort of person I wish to have any contact with.'

Meanwhile, Surrey clinched the County Championship for the fourth year running, and at the end of the season took on a Rest of England team that included Lock's perennial Test rival, Johnny Wardle. In general, the players didn't strain on these occasions, instead treating themselves and the crowd to a light-hearted, end-of-summer knockabout. This time, however, fuelled possibly by Wardle's selection ahead of him for the season's first two Tests, and further stimulated by the sponsor's offer of ten barrels of beer to the players with the best batting and bowling figures in the match, Lock decided to let fly. He later wrote:

> At one stage I thought Wardle was caught in the slips by Peter May off Peter Loader. He did not walk, and the umpire said 'not out'. I was livid – and I was bowling the next over. Wardle came to the end facing me. 'I'm after you, Johnny,' I spluttered. 'I'll hit you out of the ground,' he replied. I let him have a faster one and, in trying to put more spin on it, lost control. The ball flew straight at his Adam's apple. He just got his bat up in time to fend it away.

Alec Bedser had taken a rudimentary field surgery course while serving in the wartime RAF, and we have his word for it that in the heated give-and-take that ensued between the two rival bowlers, 'Wardle threatened to brain Lock, and Tony in turn offered Wardle some medical advice that wasn't very practical, I can tell you. I had to separate them in the end.'

When the figures came to be tallied, Laker had 133 first-class wickets for the season at a cost of 17.90 apiece and Lock had 216, of which no fewer than 73 came in August, at an average of 14.39. Of course these are merely numbers, and thus largely inconsequential. But it's a curious fact that when the Surrey team reported back to The Oval in April 1956 it was found that someone had seen fit to glue the list of the previous year's bowling figures, with two particular names on it highlighted in red, to the wall of the professionals' dressing room. It took some little effort to remove this, and a significant amount of paint also came away in the process. It's impossible to say who may have been responsible for this unsanctioned addition to the room's otherwise rather spartan décor, although the county secretary Brian Castor later came to suspect that the 'eternally rivalrous friendship' between his club's two eminent spin bowlers might have had something to do with it.

* * *

'All things considered, the situation is dreadful, we are looked upon as an indisciplined, unruly lot and our opponents assume that we are to be treated by them as little infants by an almighty parent,' wrote an exasperated Nawab of Mamdot, the chairman of the newly formed Pakistan board of control, in a minute tabled to his fellow committee members at the Lahore Gymkhana on 27 November 1955. His note reflected the writer's particular concern about the prospects of his national team in their relations with their English visitors scheduled to arrive the following month.

Perhaps it all stemmed from a distinctively Pakistani intensity of approach, characterised not only by internecine strife but also a lack of fraternity with opposition players and fans alike, peculiar to high-stakes cricket in that part of the world. Or perhaps the situation of which the nawab spoke had deeper cultural roots. The relations between Britain and her former colonial subjects already have a long academic history, some of it quite reputable, that lie outside the scope of a book about two spin bowlers. But it's worth noting here, if only to show how one specific incident on the 1955/56 MCC 'A' tour of Pakistan, which included Tony Lock in its ranks, might have proved the ignition-point of an international sporting furore as epic in its way as the Bodyline controversy of 23 years earlier.

Travelling under Donald Carr's captaincy, the MCC began with a fixture at Karachi's Gymkhana ground which Lock evocatively described as 'an oasis of green in a field of rolled dirt', with a battered grey sight screen tethered in the mud at either end, under which pigs rooted noisily through piles of discarded offal. There were to be several more challenges of a technical or medical nature, Lock reminiscing later on the incidence of 'Karachi tummy' among his team-mates, in the course of the 12-week tour. Nonetheless, he did well; *Wisden* enthused about his 'newfound confidence' on 'pitches generally to his liking', while Carr's primary emotion was one of relief that the home sides 'included so many chuckers [that] Lockie looked like a model bowler by comparison, leaving me one less thing to worry about'. Pakistan won the unofficial Test series 2-1, a result which was broadly congenial to both sides. Lock was the tourists' star bowler, with 81 wickets at an average of only ten, including a return of 11-88 in the victory over the Governor-General's XI, a contest in which he sent down a sequence of 104 balls without conceding a run. For good measure, he also twice did the hat-trick during the tour, averaged nearly 20 with the bat and threw in nine characteristically agile catches. 'For most of the time I was in the best of spirits,' he later reported.

No prolonged overseas trip with Tony Lock could be entirely tranquil, even so, and events took a sharp downward turn during the third representative match with Pakistan played at Peshawar on the Northwest Frontier from 24–28 February 1956. This was the tragicomic episode of the 'kidnapped' umpire, Idrees Beg. Its repercussions would be felt for at least 20 years afterwards, and arguably to some extent still colour Anglo-Pakistani sporting relations to this day.

The whole affair began when, in the course of the keenly anticipated Test, several of the tourists' batsmen came to voice their concern at how receptive Beg seemed to be to the slow left-armer Abdul Kardar's repeated and highly animated appeals for lbw: there were five such decisions in the MCC first innings alone. Kardar's first victim, the young Ken Barrington, once told me that his dismissal had been the worst single injustice of a 15-year career not untouched by shadow. 'You've heard people say, "It would've missed a second set of stumps"? This one would have missed a third set,' Barrington recalled, still a shade rueful more than 20 years later. Another source assured me that Kardar, Pakistan's imperious Test skipper, 'could [have] done no wrong in that match'. He had 'snapped out' his various appeals and Beg, a former military man, had 'obeyed the orders unthinkingly, in the time honoured way'. The strong MCC side were all out for 188, with Kardar taking 6-40 off 28 overs.

On the Sunday evening of the match, a group of MCC players, Lock prominent among them, had finished dinner at a local restaurant and then taken a taxi across town to the officials' hotel, where they went upstairs to Beg's room and invited him to accompany them. The details of what followed are unclear, due to conflicting testimony, but it seems fairly certain that the Englishmen then hustled Beg into a tonga, or horse-drawn carriage, and drove him back to their own hotel, where a bucket of water was poured over him. The Peshawar daily *Mashriq* was later to claim that several of the visitors had been wearing handkerchiefs over their faces, giving them the air of 'brigands' and 'fiends', and that Beg himself had been clad throughout the ordeal only in his pyjamas. (A report that he had been debagged entirely, leaving him to run 'stark bollock naked through the hotel corridors', has proved difficult to verify.) The 'dank and dishevelled' umpire was then released into the night amid 'sundry jeers and catcalls', and made his way home without further ado. There are different versions of some of the fine detail of the story, but the end result was that the next evening's *Mashriq* ran a headline insisting that Beg had been the victim of a 'vile assault'; that the tourists eventually lost the match at Peshawar by seven wickets, leaving the ground under a hail of abuse and with a police escort; and that the president of MCC subsequently offered a formal apology in response to an aggrieved telegram from the Pakistan board.

Whatever the rights or wrongs of the Beg affair, it set the scene for a mutually wary playing relationship between the two countries that, at least on the Pakistani side, lasted well into the next century. There's no evidence that Lock was any more tied up in the outrage than anyone else, although it has to be said that he already enjoyed a reputation for his nocturnal adventures on the tour, which generally revolved around locating the best place for a convivial glass or two of beer ('Eight bob a pint in Karachi', he later noted), and, perhaps as a result, taking the opportunity to then rise to his feet and regale anyone in the vicinity with tall tales, many of which he repeated, endlessly, over the course of the evening. Most of his local audiences didn't mind these monologues. They just wanted the chance to mingle with famous English cricketers. Besides, they were frequently drunk as well. Lock was also widely recognised as something of a practical joker. He was known, for instance, to slip tomatoes into the top blazer pocket of those standing next to him, and to then lead the assembled company in howls of mirth when he clutched the victim tightly to his chest. Donald Carr later remarked, 'Tony was a good tourist in that he was always cheerful, perhaps not so good in that he was sometimes like having a ten-year-old child on your hands … Any room he was in was always full of cigarette smoke, chat and mischief, with a round or two of beer afterwards. But of course the real point was that he was a great bowler.'

Although the MCC offered to conclude their visit in the wake of the Beg affair, and to pay reparations to the home authority for any loss of revenue, in the end the Pakistani board agreed to play the three remaining fixtures, in which Lock took a total of 21 more wickets. The Englishmen's homeward flight, like the tour itself, was not entirely uneventful. Stranded at first Karachi and then Baghdad thanks to fog and engine trouble respectively, the visitors were then caught up in a major earthquake in Beirut. Reaching Heathrow on 21 March after a three-day, six-stop ordeal, the jet-lagged players were met by a bus that took them directly to Lord's for a magisterial dressing-down by the club president, Earl Alexander of Tunis, who had himself flown in that same morning from Canada for the occasion. Only then were Lock and the other exhausted cricketers reunited with the wives and children they had left behind the previous Christmas. 'I'd never seen a man whose face was purple before,' Lock later recalled of his interview with Alexander, the hero of the Dunkirk evacuation 16 years earlier. 'He was so angry I thought he might explode right in front of us.'

In all, it was an inauspicious start to one of the most glorious years in English sporting history.

5

Total War

IT'S USUALLY a mistake to try and assemble random historical facts into a neatly unified pattern that few people would have recognised at the time. Whether in their claim that Britain overnight became a socialist utopia with the advent of the welfare state in 1945, or that the country abruptly succumbed to a sort of priapic frenzy characterised by the sight of bare-thighed young women swaggering around Carnaby Street in their Mary Quant miniskirts to a backdrop of herbally-tinged joss sticks and the wafted strains of the Grateful Dead in the so-called Summer of Love 22 years later, social historians are always keen to identify what seem to them to be the transformative shifts in our communal life. Such judgements are generally only feasible with the aid of hindsight. Few of those confronted with the individual pieces of the jigsaw picture the finished puzzle.

For all that, it's perhaps fair to say that there was an unusually decisive point in the nation's affairs that lay exactly midway between the two pendulum years above, and which truly did impress itself for a variety of both geopolitical and other reasons on our collective consciousness: the year 1956, when no writer of youthful fiction would have dared strain romantic credulity by inventing the turn of events that transformed Jim Laker from a well-known cricketer into one of those great and individual personalities who transcend their craft and attain national treasure status. Laker not only brought off one of the most remarkable personal feats in the history of the sport, but in doing so supplied a much-needed tonic to a public then enduring a relentless diet of news stories detailing the country's greatest foreign-policy debacle of the 20th century and the ensuing end of Britain's major power status.

The crisis in question was Suez. By the time the dust had settled on the whole affair, the prime minister, Anthony Eden, suffering from either a severe abdominal infection or a total nervous collapse, or possibly both, had resigned from office, to be replaced by Harold Macmillan; the pound never quite recovered its old lustre against the dollar on the foreign-exchange market; and the new PM, on a fence-mending trip to Washington, told his hosts that he, personally, was 'very unhappy with the way in which the matter had been handled, [but] had had no real choice but to back Eden'. The British action, Macmillan added, came as the 'last gasp of a declining power, and that perhaps in 200 years the United States will know how we felt'. Since control of the Suez Canal then reverted to Colonel Nasser, who promptly refused passage to most western ships, which led in turn to renewed fuel rationing and power blackouts in Britain, the whole affair could not be called a shining strategic success.[2]

This, then, was the wider context for the events of that same summer's Test series with Australia. Perhaps it's unwise to draw parallels between the state of the nation's prestige and the outcome of a few cricket matches. But perhaps it's not. The fiasco at Suez was humiliating. The whole affair had been an ill-conceived, over-

---

2   Walter Monckton, the Conservative MP who had briefed the departing tourists to the West Indies in December 1953, resigned his position as minister of defence in protest at Suez. He later became president of both MCC and Surrey, and as such would play a starring role in a second national controversy, the disciplining of Jim Laker in 1960.

confident and grisly blunder. Even Winston Churchill hated it. The bitterness and sense of grievance it generated echoed down the late 1950s, and beyond; and in that it was the beginning of Britain's present-day role as essentially an eastern branch office of its Washington headquarters it echoes still. It helped usher in the simultaneously disenchanted and expectant generation of the 1960s, with all that ensued. So perhaps it's not to abandon logic altogether to suggest that England as a whole was particularly receptive to some remedial good news in 1956, and more than usually hungry for a national hero – and that, in the somewhat unlikely guise of a stocky, 34-year-old professional cricketer, whose genius had hitherto been glimpsed only in fits and starts, they found him.

* * *

That there was nothing inevitable or even remotely likely about all this can be seen from the events of the first Test of the series against Ian Johnson's Australia, at Trent Bridge in early June. Laker at least made the cut – he'd represented his country in only 24 of a possible 65 starts since his international debut – his first-innings haul of 10-88 for Surrey against the same opponents just a fortnight earlier having apparently struck even the England selectors as an irresistible credential. He performed there competently rather than brilliantly, with figures of 4-58 and 2-29. In truth it wasn't much of a contest. Rain began to fall on the first morning, and it was one of those occasions somehow peculiar to British cricket when the players walked on and off at regular intervals and much of the batting in between seemed to be done as if in front of a mirror, correct but tediously careful. 'The Australian,' *Wisden* later concluded, 'is mainly a Saturday afternoon cricketer, brought up on hard, true pitches, blazing sunshine and in clear light.' These were not conditions typically associated with springtime Nottingham, and there was never really a coherent narrative to the match. Such cricket as there was tended to substantiate the view that both sides would struggle to bowl the other one out twice on a good wicket.

The hosts batted first and made 217/8, thanks to the successive delays Peter May declared the innings closed only on the third afternoon. Australia replied with 148. May then declared a second time, setting the tourists a sporting target of 258 to win in four hours. They scored a total of 28 runs in the first 90 minutes, and finished at 120-3. Lock was also playing, and threw in four wickets. He was characteristically bashful about his overall performance. 'But for the early rain,' he wrote, 'I'm sure Laker and I would have scythed through the Aussies.' The only real resistance had come from Neil Harvey, who scored 64. 'I had him lbw in the end,' Lock reported. 'Neil didn't look too pleased with the decision, apparently thinking he was out of line with the off stump when the ball struck him. I thought it hit him plumb, and what's more important, so did the umpire.' Harvey later recalled that this was only the second time he'd ever played at Trent Bridge, and that, lest he be unfamiliar with the route, Lock had helpfully given him some explicitly clear directions from the middle back to the dressing room.

On the fourth evening of the match both sets of players had returned to their shared Nottingham city centre hotel. The place as a whole might have struggled to meet the most basic recreational or even sanitary requirements of the modern Test cricketer. There were just two bathrooms on the first, relatively opulent floor, one of which was reserved for the chairman of selectors. Lock was allocated an attic dormitory with Tom Graveney. They shared a bathroom with seven of their immediate neighbours, including several of the Australian players. Lock repeated his Lady Macbeth act later that night, before suddenly coming awake to the sound of more rain lashing down on the hotel roof. This had roughly the same effect as on a child hearing sleigh bells early on Christmas morning. 'I shot out of bed, ran to the window and made sure I wasn't dreaming,' he wrote. 'No, I hadn't been. It was rain, lovely rain. My only fear was that we would get too much of it.'

After bolting down his usual half a dozen cups of dynamite-strength black coffee for breakfast, Lock waved off the team bus and jogged over the nearby bridge to the ground. Rain followed by sunshine would have meant the proverbial sticky dog, a situation ripe for a bowler of his talents, but in the end it didn't happen. Instead it just drizzled steadily, with more stop-start cricket, no real momentum, and the Australians declined the final run chase amid some satirical comment from the sparse crowd. Everyone went home early and the tourists, heading off in their bus just after six that evening, then had a mini pop-up tropical storm to deal with en route to their next fixture at Northampton. Laker had scored nine not out in his only time at bat, and observed drily in the train going back to London, 'I would have made a century but for the head wind.' Everyone laughed, but his place in the side was again under threat. Appleyard had also played at Trent Bridge, and done well, but then went down with a chronic shoulder injury. He never represented England again. 'It's a funny thing,' Lock mused, with just a touch of pique, 'but if Bob had been at his best in the early part of 1956, he probably would have ousted Jim Laker from the off spin berth, and might have won the undying fame that came Laker's way.'

Instead, Lock himself would be dropped for the second Test at Lord's, again replaced by Johnny Wardle. Australia, against the odds, won the match, putting them one up with three to go. Ray Lindwall and Alan Davidson were both injured so 36-year-old Keith Miller had to open the attack with a Test novice, Pat Crawford, right-arm fast of New South Wales. Crawford broke down in his fifth over and didn't bowl again in the match. In his absence, Miller stepped up to take 5-72 in the first innings and 5-80 in the second. Richie Benaud did well, too, holding a spectacular one-handed catch to dismiss Cowdrey off a full-blooded drive and then scoring a swift 97 in the Australian second innings. England were left to chase 372, and had got exactly halfway home when their last man fell shortly after lunch on the fifth day. Laker took a modest three wickets in the match, and Wardle one. Even that eternal optimist Godfrey Evans thought he could detect a hint of panic in the home dressing room, and the selectors duly made four changes for the next Test, at Headingley, recalling both Lock and 41-year-old Cyril Washbrook, who himself happened to be a selector. 'One will do one's best, but it won't be easy,' Washbrook remarked before strutting out to bat for his country, cap set at a characteristically jaunty angle, for the first time in over five years. He made 98, and with Peter May put on a stand of 187 for the fourth wicket, the best England partnership against Australia since the war.

'I am quietly pleased,' Lock apparently told the *Daily Express* of his own return to the Test side, which was either commendably restrained on his part or a notable paraphrase on the paper's. In fact he'd been so distraught to be left out at Lord's that he started vomiting while bowling in the Oval nets before play began in a county match that week, and ended up in St Mary's Hospital. 'Whether the disappointment of being sacked accentuated my sudden stomach trouble, I don't know,' he later wrote. 'All I do know is that I felt violently ill and appendicitis was feared. I had dark visions of missing the rest of the series.'

Lock had heard that he'd been dropped only when the BBC announcer read out the names of the England 12 over the radio on the afternoon of Sunday, 17 June, which happened to be the rest day of Surrey's top-of-the-table home match against Yorkshire. Peter May didn't know about his player being taken ill at practice when he arrived at The Oval at about ten the next morning. The first he heard of the matter was when 'Tony, looking deathly pale, suddenly came bolting back off the field and stopped me, a bit aggressively, as we passed on the pavilion staircase.' Without a word of greeting, Lock steered May into an empty room, where he berated his county and Test captain for the next quarter of an hour. Realising towards the end that the scene was audible to other players, Lock then led May into a less public room for a further ten minutes of recriminations. When the storm was over May said only, 'I can't discuss this now, Tony,' and went upstairs into the amateurs' area to change into his whites. Lock then took 4-29 in Yorkshire's first innings and 5-42 in the second before driving himself to hospital, where he spent much of the next week sitting up in bed smoking and drinking coffee while watching the cricket on television.

In July 1956, Headingley was the scene of vast and often raucously loud congestion, with spouts of white smoke rising from the houses at the Kirkstall Lane End, grey but at least initially dry skies, and a pitch that in E.W. Swanton's measured opinion, had 'perhaps not quite the lasting properties that all concerned had reason to expect'. It was also something of a dress rehearsal for the events at Old Trafford a fortnight later. In the end victory went not so much to the better side as to the side that played better.

England won the toss, batted and scored 325, with a century from May. He was out five minutes before the close of play, and Doug Insole was officially the next man in at number six. But Lock was having none of it. 'When the fourth wicket fell Tony pushed me to one side and said, "I'm bloody well going out." He always fancied his chances as a batsman,' Insole recalled. Ray Lindwall then happened to be bowling at his fastest in fading light, and the chief instinct among other potential nightwatchmen might reasonably have been one of discreet concealment, rather than aggressive volunteerism. Not Lock. From the way he played the first ball, plumb in the middle, there was an authority about his innings quite distinct from the normal tailender's ambition of mere survival. 'He plastered us,' Lindwall noted. Lock successfully saw out play for the day and then began to enjoy himself in the morning. A couple of early bouncers saw the batsman figuratively spitting his teeth into his hand. Now it was personal. One free-swinging blow off the tight and accurate Benaud sent the ball skimming over the pavilion rope, bringing an excited 'My word!' from Swanton in the commentary box. Lock loved to treat the spinners so, and when an over or two later a frustrated Benaud dropped one short the batsman deposited it into the leg-side terrace with the same unhurried venom. He made 21 in the end, which may not sound much, but contained a savagery of stroke that clearly showed the Australians he meant business, and more to the point helped change the whole thrust of the match. 'The Aussies walked back in between innings with their heads down,' Godfrey Evans remembered.

In fact the tourists made just 143, rolled over by Laker and Lock with nine wickets between them. In an hour's play after tea they collapsed from 40-1 to 69-6. It then rained for the next 36 straight hours, completely washing out Saturday's play, and Australia followed on in the markedly changed atmosphere of a damp, half-full ground just before lunchtime on the Monday. 'We were told that rain was falling all round Leeds,' wrote Don Bradman in the *Daily Mail*. 'Watching play in the hazy gloom, a patriotic Australian could not be blamed for believing that it would also fall here at any minute.' The players could periodically hear a rumble of thunder from somewhere over the red brick houses packed together as tight as dominoes. Not knowing the timeframe of the match, Laker and Lock quickly got to work. The tourists were 93-2 at the close, then crumpled again the next morning, all out for 140, Laker and Lock with another nine between them. Lock bowled much more steadily than some people expected him to. Of his 240 deliveries, perhaps six were short-pitched. He sent down 23 maidens.

Sometimes Laker and Lock seemed to take wickets for each other. Broadly speaking, it was a case of 'wait and see' at one end and 'go out and kill' at the other, a double menace for the batsmen. At one stage Lock bowled four consecutive maidens to Keith Miller. It was not in that great all-rounder's nature to defend for protracted periods. The first ball he faced from Laker after his ordeal at the other end, Miller had a go, mistimed the shot and gloved it to Trueman at short leg. Shortly after that Lock came in to bowl to Neil Harvey, who had then scored 69 and looked like he might keep going. His first ball bit and corkscrewed back towards the left-hander's leg stump. Harvey got an edge and the ball popped up around knee high in the general direction of silly mid-off. There being no such man on duty, Lock, in his follow through, somehow reversed thrust, took two or three scuttling steps to his right, impossibly fast, and then, diving, scooped up the ball a split second before it bounced, rolled around a bit and flung it up again in vocal delight while Harvey, after a moment of frozen shock, recovered himself and trudged off to the pavilion in the gloom. That made the Australian score 138/7, and it was all over a few minutes later. England won by an innings and 42, and the series was suddenly square with two to play. Godfrey Evans wrote in his diary that night, 'L[aker] quite pleased with it – mild hopes for the series – but warned of hard road ahead. We should all keep our heads, he said. Tony L and I knocked back some champagne.'

* * *

Tom Graveney the batsman was to some extent the counterpart to Jim Laker the bowler. Both men were prodigiously gifted, obviously, and both were apparently found wanting at critical moments, lacking concentration at the crunch. Neither one could ever be confident of his place in the England side of the day. They were both northerners who played most of their cricket in the south, and both had a pronounced stubborn streak under the acquired surface charm. Each in his own way would fall foul of the establishment, and each felt himself to be an outsider who was tolerated by the powers that be only so long as he was useful to them. Neither one could ever take his career as a professional cricketer for granted.

Graveney, then, spoke with some authority when in 1991 he summed up Laker's character and reputation.

'Terrific man,' he said. 'I played with and against him for about ten years, and then did another dozen with him as a commentator. Jim talked about the game very much like he played it. He never did more than was necessary. He was a sensitive man, and that probably had something to do with certain events in his early life.

'Like me, Laker was a home lover, not one for the girls, although I'm not saying he didn't enjoy a quiet drink or two. He could be a bit puritanical, and I remember him not exactly being chuffed when they once took us all out to a show in Sydney by the name of *Ladies' Night at the Turkish Baths*. Quite miffed by it, Jim was. He was very intelligent, cautious with it, didn't exactly throw money around, nobody's fool, with a good understanding of people and their strengths and weaknesses. We both got buggered about a fair bit by the selectors and one or two others, and like me he didn't much care for it. For an essentially easy-going bloke he eventually copped a lot of grief from the gin-and-tonic boys at Lord's.

'If there was any criticism to be made of Jim as a cricketer it was just that he could sometimes make it all seem a bit of a grind. He wasn't one of nature's optimists. If you wanted someone who was always jumping up and down with excitement like a kid, always wanting to get out there and have a go at the opposition, you'd turn to Lock, not Laker. If it was the end of a long day in the field and the other lot's score was something like 200/1 on a plumb track Jim tended to be the one to avoid catching the skipper's eye while Tony would march up and announce, "Give me that ball. I'll have these buggers out tonight.'"

They were also very different propositions, as we've seen, off the field. When he wasn't playing cricket, Laker was the model family man. He was attentive, protective and irrepressibly proud of his wife and two daughters. As his elder child Angela said, 'He was a hero to me, a loving father and a brilliant man.' Profoundly conservative in his tastes – invited on *Desert Island Discs* in 1956, he chose songs by Vera Lynn and Gracie Fields, with a piano and a cricket ball as his luxury items – Laker padded around in impressively old but well-pressed tweed suits, worn whatever the weather, sometimes allowed himself a glass or two of gin, and liked to unwind on an off-season Saturday afternoon by watching his beloved Chelsea from a reserved seat at Stamford Bridge, his excitement at even a home goal always seemingly well contained. Speaking to the *Sunday Graphic* at the height of her husband's fame in the summer of 1956, Lilly Laker had this to say:

> I'm sorry if it disappoints you, but he's just an ordinary man. He has no fads about food and no particular hobbies. He doesn't like coming shopping with me. He can't – or won't – cook, but he's a generous man with money. Sounds just like any other husband, doesn't he?

In short, Laker was the bank-manager-who-went-to-war type, a calm and thoroughly decent Englishman of sound traditional values, the sort of man to whom you'd entrust your first-born child's welfare if it ever came to it. Lilly added that he was 'very patriotic, proud of his country, and always voted Tory'. There were no airs and graces about him. In later years he didn't much care for cricket's new fixation with the mental aspect of the game. In 1981 a writer on the London *Evening Standard* asked him what his priorities had been as a professional player. The fastidious Laker was as a rule not one for vulgarity, but he permitted himself an exception in this case. 'Hit them as hard as you fucking can,' he summarised. 'Then shake hands afterwards, and go home to your family.'

Though estimable in his own way, Lock wasn't always of the same stoical outlook. Lively and voluble as he was in public, he could be taciturn and moody – and sometimes irascible – off the field. When the England selectors saw fit to dispense with his services in the side to visit Australia over the winter of 1954/55 'Tony basically boiled over', according to Godfrey Evans, who played against him in a match at Blackheath that week. 'Well, no, he didn't basically boil over,' Evans corrected himself. 'He *did* boil over. If the buggers at Lord's had set out to drive him out of his mind, they did it.' Lock's omission was a 'personal betrayal by Len [Hutton], a man Tony admired, a man he'd bowled his heart out for in the West Indies … He'd never forgive him for that.'

And while there wasn't the least breath of impropriety in Lock's private life, the same Evans was one of those who noticed, 'There always seemed to be a different teenaged girl, sometimes with her family, sometimes alone, waiting for Tony at the pavilion door after the close of play.' Clearly these were the young women to whom he'd offered to give coaching classes, often without charge to themselves. It was both generous on Lock's part, and proof that he was ahead of his time in refusing to accept that women should concentrate solely on having babies and not take an active part in traditionally masculine pursuits. All this was greatly to his credit. But in the prevailing atmosphere of the typical 1950s cricket changing room, people talked. Evans was present for a Test at The Oval when one of the other England players saw fit to leave an 'unsubtle' sketch, with a heavily suggestive caption, alluding to his taste in young protégées, on Lock's chair. The attempted levity did not go down well. After a moment's silence, 'Tony grabbed the man by the neck and forced him down' while hissing at him in a 'weird voice' that there was nothing funny about accusing anyone of child abuse. The patent truth of this last remark was to be cruelly reaffirmed in Lock's life, under the most poignant circumstances, many years later.

Both Lock and Laker were supremely successful men who remained to some degree insecure about their chosen path in life. Perhaps this was only logical given the vicissitudes of their Test careers, but it also owed something to their basic temperament. Laker could always recite his season's bowling average down to the last decimal point, and was known to quietly but firmly bring these figures to people's attention years after the fact. Lock was also quite keen on asserting himself with both his colleagues and others. He didn't always accept defeat, or being outdone by a rival, especially well. Johnny Wardle thought Lock was a 'good bowler [but] with a gruff and haughty side that could repel his team-mates as much as his opponents'. Lock thought Wardle a complete twat. He was a competent enough cricketer, he acknowledged, but he didn't have the right stuff for the big occasion.

In the Headingley Test of July 1955, England were trying to play out time on the last day to avoid defeat by South Africa. Lock went out to bat and for once restrained himself, staying for three-quarters of an hour to make seven. He was out with the score at 246/8, chasing a notional 480. Wardle then jogged out with the adoring roar of his hometown crowd in his ears, threw the bat, knocked up 21 in a couple of overs, and got himself out trying to hit Tayfield into the car park. England lost the Test with just over an hour to go. Lock was far from happy at what he saw as this dereliction of collective responsibility on Wardle's part. 'I was annoyed with myself when I got out, but more annoyed by the haphazard strokes of some of those who followed me ... "Our Johnny" just couldn't resist the temptation,' he wrote at the time. 'It's always been my rule to play for the team,' Lock added 30 years later. 'To make every run count. There's no point flashing the bat for 20 minutes if it all goes wrong in the end.'

Notwithstanding the truth of this, perhaps the real heart of the matter is that, like Laker, Lock was basically a soloist. The year 1956 revealed both their finest and most problematic qualities as players: their obvious talent, their general persistence, their combination of high-voltage aggression and honest endeavour, but also their need for personal domination, their aversion to criticism and their contempt for those short-sighted mortals who made the mistake of standing in their way. Each man was in his way a monument to himself, a sensitive, gruff genius, and neither one was particularly inclined to share his hour of glory with anyone else.

* * *

The events at Old Trafford from 26–31 July 1956, fustily dated in some ways, but also existing in a sort of timeless limbo as a yardstick by which other sporting feats are measured, already command a wide literature. Whole books, at least some of them quite readable, have been devoted to the subject. That summer's fourth Test with Australia remains the Battle of Trafalgar of English cricket, the decisive moment in a previously fluctuating and unresolved clash of wills with an unusually determined enemy, even if without quite the same long-term consequences of Nelson's victory; while the Royal Navy proceeded to dominate the sea until the Second World War, England's Test side imploded again as early as December 1958, and seemed to be thrashed pretty comprehensively, both by the Australians and others, at regular intervals thereafter.

But that wet week in Manchester during the Suez summer truly provided a unifying national experience beyond the scope of a mere Test match, and more to the point featured an individual tour de force fit to stand alongside the likes of Geoff Hurst's 'They think it's all over' goal in the 1966 World Cup Final or, if you prefer, Red Rum's serial triumphs at the Grand National, the building excitement and flying finish of Gareth Edwards's try for the 1973 Barbarians against the All Blacks at Cardiff, or Michael Phelps pretty well any time he went near an Olympic swimming pool. They're moments that truly transcend their sports, and, in Jim Laker's case, although there had been previous hints that he had the Australians' number that year, all the sweeter because it seemed to come pretty much out of the blue in the context of his Test career as a whole. There was nothing remotely predictable about it. Up until then Laker had always been that problematical cricketing species, the 'enigma'. The seeds of greatness were there, so he'd kept being picked by England, and then the selectors had kept dropping him again. Even now it was something of a shock to see him in the Test side for a fourth consecutive time. Laker's 12 successive starts from August 1955 to May 1957 represent easily his longest sustained run in the team, and account for more than a quarter of his total number of caps for his country.

In later years there was something of a cottage industry of books, articles and interviews dwelling in almost Percy Thrower-like detail on the physical fitness or otherwise of the Old Trafford wicket that week. Had the whole outcome turned on this factor, affording the home team, and more especially their mercurially talented off-spinner, an unfair advantage? Should there be an asterisk next to Laker's figures in the record book as a result? The bowler himself once remarked that he'd felt 'written off' and 'patronised' throughout his Test days, and that the furore surrounding the Manchester pitch was just another example of how 'certain people, including some of the England selectors, hated to see me succeed, and loved it when I failed'. A bit much, but we can perhaps take his point. As the late American poet Delmore Schwartz observed, 'Even paranoids have enemies.'

Here are the facts of the matter:

When the England players arrived at Old Trafford for a rather cursory practice session on the afternoon of Wednesday, 25 July, the day before the Test, they found an unexceptionally pale-green pitch with one or two visible hairline cracks in it awaiting them. After a few minutes spent watching his men in the nets, Gubby Allen, the chairman of selectors, clad somewhat incongruously for the occasion in a pinstriped City suit with a carnation in the buttonhole, accompanied by Tommy Burrows, the Lancashire chairman, strode out to the middle to confer with Bert Flack, the Old Trafford groundsman. Over the years, certain England selectors have chosen to cultivate a wise detachment from the horticultural minutiae of their nation's Test grounds, but Allen aspired to be fully engaged in the fine no less than the broad detail of his team's performance. Nothing got by him.

Bert Flack was then aged 41, in his eighth year in the job at Old Trafford, a jovial, pipe-smoking sort with Pickwickian side-whiskers who sometimes strolled up to the nearby Salford abattoir for a bucket or two of animal intestines to roll into his wickets. He was always quite clear about what had happened next. 'I'm not satisfied,' Allen had announced, following his tour of the playing area. After a few moments' further deliberation, he'd then walked back to watch his men knocking up in the nets. At that, Burrows had put his arm around Flack's shoulder and gently led him a few yards down the pitch. 'The chairman isn't happy,' he said, lest the point had been missed. 'He wants less grass. Take a little off the top, Bert,' Burrows added, sounding a bit like a customer in a barber's shop rather than the chief executive of a first-class cricket club. Flack did as he was told, albeit under some protest. 'That's daft,' he informed his chairman. 'The game won't last three days. There's no bloody roots growing under the top,' Flack added, in another tonsorial reference. Nonetheless, this was the 1950s, and democracy wasn't the dominant characteristic of the relationship between the typical English county cricket boss and his paid employees. After duly running his mower up and down the track a few more times, Flack told his ground staff to put the covers back on the square. 'And don't talk to the ruddy press, if they ask about it,' he added. 'We're expecting rain,' Flack himself told the *Daily Mail* correspondent Alex Bannister, who happened to pass him walking back to the pavilion, which Bannister thought was odd since the Manchester sun was then beating down in a cloudlessly blue sky.

If Flack indeed shaved the Old Trafford pitch in the late afternoon prior to the start of a Test in the morning he did nothing that would seem to contravene cricket's Law 9, as it stood in 1956, which said only:

> The Ground shall not be rolled, watered, covered, mown, or beaten during a match, except before the commencement of each innings and of each day's play ... Any means may be adopted to cover the whole of the wicket at any time after but not before 11 a.m. on the day immediately preceding a match.

In fact the trio of Allen, Burrows and Flack might even be said to have done no more than diligently conform to the MCC's standing instructions to each of England's 17 first-class clubs, which stated:

All counties must instruct their groundsman that the ideal wicket is one which makes the conditions equal as between batsmen and bowlers without being dangerous ... Under no circumstances should pitches be prepared so as to favour the bat unduly.

Looking down from the top of the tiered Old Trafford pavilion, rather as though in the dress circle of a vast theatre, the field as a whole was a vivid emerald green with one or two biscuit-coloured patches on either side of the covers, with banks of shiny white benches and a pleasantly leafy backdrop. There may be no atmosphere quite like that of an English cricket ground on the opening morning of an Ashes Test. It's true there were mixed views about the pitch itself right up until the moment the first ball was bowled. At around eight the previous evening, no rain having yet materialised, Flack had ordered the covers to be rolled up and carried back to the groundsman's hut at the Stretford End. Laker himself had had a light dinner with some of his team-mates in the pavilion, and following this he wandered out to take a further look at the pitch in the twilight. He found Don Bradman standing there in his capacity as Alex Bannister's assistant on the *Daily Mail*, similarly assessing the wicket. 'Flat and slow,' said Bradman. 'With plenty of runs in it.'

About 15 hours after Bradman's pronouncement, Ray Lindwall came hurtling in to bowl the first ball of the match, which barely rose knee high and bounced twice on its way to the Australians' wicketkeeper Len Maddocks, kicking up a thick cloud of red dust in the process. Keith Miller was standing at slip, and according to Maddocks, 'He immediately burst out laughing and said, "This fucking game will be over in two days."' Some of the other Australian contingent around the ground had to clutch harder than Miller did at what remained of their good humour. Writing in the

Daily Express, Bradman's former Test colleague Arthur Morris had this to say:

> I am not going to claim the pitch was a nightmare, but I have got two main points of criticism. (1) That it should not have shown such advance signs of wear on the first day of a five-day match. (2) Someone slipped up somewhere, and things have not been improved by official statements from the Lancashire club that there was little wrong with the wicket. There was a great deal wrong with it.

In 1993, Colin McDonald, the man who top-scored for Australia with 89 in their increasingly Dunkirk-like rearguard at Old Trafford, added:

> Looking back on it, I still believe the English administration cheated. But not the England team. They played the game perfectly well, according to the traditions of cricket, and they weren't responsible for the conditions.

Australia's Bill 'Tiger' O'Reilly, a spinner who in his day had combined some of Laker's technical fluency with Lock's almost homicidal aversion to batsmen, called the pitch 'a total disgrace', while the tourists' current captain Ian Johnson wrote, in a tone of evocative 1950s vernacular, that his side had been 'trapped on a stinker, the fellows were unhappy, and our batting turned to jelly'. Perhaps Richie Benaud, then a young bowling all-rounder, later the omniscient, Gandalf-like sage of international cricket, put it best when he said simply:

> It was a terrible pitch, but a terrible pitch on which England thoroughly outplayed us. Our batting was, to put the very

best light on it, abysmal. England, or rather one Englishman, destroyed us.

Now to turn from the more agronomical side of the proceedings to the actual cricket.

Peter May won the toss, unanimously accepted as crucial to the outcome, and batted. England's captain thought the wicket, which by then appeared to be a sandy shade of brown, might be good for 'a day or at most two days before it crumbled'; an accurate prognosis, even if it failed to make allowance for the onset of nearly 72 hours of rain. The ground itself was *en fête*, newly painted, flag-strewn and decked out with hanging baskets splashed in red, yellow, purple. The first day was a bit overcast, with rain still being spoken of as a future possibility – this was Manchester in July – but nothing to immediately concern the spectators who had each paid an average eight shillings for admission and sat, decorously capped and coated, while dozens of temporary staff, contrastingly wearing either a gaudy mustard- or plum-coloured smock for the occasion, darted among them like a shoal of tropical fish. The England side, when announced just before the toss, hadn't been without surprises. Tom Graveney had decided he was unfit, so the selectors had hurriedly sent for 26-year-old Alan Oakman of Sussex. These were the golden days before mobile phones, so Gubby Allen had rung Hastings police station and asked them if they knew where Oakman lived. They did. A PC was duly dispatched on a bicycle to knock on Oakman's door and tell him he was expected post haste in Manchester. He arrived in time to take five close catches in the match, which he later modestly described as 'pretty easy – Laker was so accurate you didn't have to worry about being hit, not that I was ever in Lock's class in that regard. I put him in the top three fielders of all time. He caught everything.'

Meanwhile, England made an eminently respectable 459 in their first innings, with centuries from Peter Richardson and the newly ordained David Sheppard. It was a relatively content home dressing room, therefore, although at lunchtime on the second day Laker, who was then getting ready to bowl for the first time in the match, happened to pass the cricket historian Irving Rosenwater on the pavilion stairs. 'Do you realise that all 11 players in the Australian side have scored a first-class hundred, and nine of them have made a Test century?' Rosenwater had asked by way of a greeting. 'That cheers me up,' said Laker.

Australia's reply began well enough, with Colin McDonald and Jimmy Burke putting on 48 for the opening wicket. Even that inveterate bookmaker Godfrey Evans wasn't to suspect that this particular stand would represent more than half the tourists' first-innings total. May then threw the ball to his spinners after less than half an hour of innocuous seam from Statham and Bailey. After an over or two, Laker switched to the Stretford End. McDonald came forward to one that turned and lifted, got an edge, and Lock took a routine catch round the corner. For once he simply threw the ball back without comment. At that Neil Harvey, boasting a Test average hovering around 45, came to the middle. Short, wiry and always impressively businesslike, he took guard, looked significantly around the distant leg-side boundary, and waited for his first ball. Fifty years later, he described it this way: 'That Shane Warne delivery that bowled Mike Gatting, well that wasn't in the same class. It pitched on or about leg and I thought I had it covered, but it turned sharply and clipped the off bail. I never faced a better ball than that.'

There are grounds to believe that a certain amount of disquiet, if not outright panic, ensued in the Australian dressing room following Harvey's dismissal. Richie Benaud remembered that 'one or two of the waiting batsmen exchanged glances', while Keith

Miller was more characteristically blunt in his assessment. 'Well, we're fucked,' he announced calmly, before turning back to the racing pages of his evening paper. Laker himself wrote years later, 'I am not being boastful when I say that that ball to Harvey won the series.'

After tea the wickets came in a deluge, with Lock taking that of Burke and Laker the other seven. 'It was a revolving door,' Benaud was later forced to admit of the visitors' dressing room, as six men returned for the addition of just 16 runs. There was a poignant moment when Burke was on 22 and Lock came in to bowl to him from the Warwick Road End. The ball turned late, brushed the edge and flew at comfortable height to Laker at third slip. He dropped it. The aggrieved bowler expressed his dissatisfaction at this turn of events in terms sufficiently ripe to earn him a rebuke from the Rev. Sheppard, who was standing at mid-on. Luckily, only a minute or two later Lock found the edge again and this time Colin Cowdrey accepted the chance at short midwicket. The Australians were all out for 84 and, following on, went in a second time before the close. Laker's first-innings figures were 9-37 off 16.4 overs and Lock's were 1-37 off 14; remarkably even except for the matter of wickets. The tourists then finished the day at 53-1 after Harvey, possibly still in a state of shock after his earlier dismissal, tamely spooned Laker's full toss – 'easily the worst ball I bowled in the whole match' – back to Cowdrey at midwicket. He was the only fielder within 20 yards, and the departing batsman tossed his bat high in the air in disgust.

It then rained steadily on the Friday night and almost the whole of Saturday. Lilly Laker had come up from London by train on the second evening, with no idea that her husband had just taken nine wickets in an innings against Australia and was already something of a national hero as a result. Making her way through the scrum of press photographers on hand to record the couple's reunion on the Warrington station platform, Lilly asked in all innocence, 'Have you done something special, Jim?' There was only three-quarters of an hour's play on Saturday, during which Burke was caught round the corner by Lock off Laker for 33. Just six runs were added. The monsoon kept the cricketers and their wives confined to their Lymm hotel on Sunday, and they got in only 60 minutes' wintry play on Monday, during which Australia advanced to 84-2. Tuesday morning was at least dry but still sunless, and on a dead pitch the tourists made it through to lunch without further loss: 263 behind, with eight wickets in hand and about four hours to go. As Lock recalled some 30 years later, 'And then, just as we were sitting down to eat, the clouds suddenly parted overhead, and this great ray of sun broke through. You could almost see it sparkling on the pitch. It was like a scene from the Bible.'

When the players went out again it was quickly apparent that conditions had changed decisively in the bowlers' favour. Ian Craig was soon out for 38, lbw to Laker off one that kept low. Mackay and Archer were each caught close in off the same bowler by Oakman, and Miller, having seemingly lost interest in the whole affair, aimed an almighty swing at the off-spinner and was bowled for nought. Australia were suddenly 130/6. Laker had thus far taken 15 in the match, and even the regal figure of E.W. Swanton, usually so guarded in his praise of the bowler, was impressed. Perhaps with an unspoken nod to the events at Leeds in 1948, he wrote in the *Daily Telegraph*, 'There was no room for argument about Laker's application in the second innings at Old Trafford. He sent down 36 overs, practically non-stop, all the time attacking the stumps and compelling the batsmen to play. He never wilted or fell short in terms of length or direction.'

And what of Lock? He tried, certainly. But perhaps he tried too hard. Years later, Bert Flack recalled, 'The more wickets Jim took at one end, the more Tony sped up at the other end. By the last afternoon he was running in at medium-quick and turning the ball so much that it was veering into the hands of first or second slip instead of the wicketkeeper.' The keeper in question, Godfrey Evans, told me that he'd more than once taken Lock aside in between overs and advised him, 'For God's sake, slow down – let the wicket do the work.' He might as well have been asking him to resolve the paradoxes of quantum mechanics into a unified field theory. 'Fuck off,' Lock hissed back through gritted teeth. Richie Benaud, who stayed long enough to score a creditable 18 in the second innings, remembered something similar. 'Tony bowled magnificently from a technical point of view on the last day. We couldn't lay a bat on him, and that was precisely his problem. Our right-handers were able to allow the ball to spin safely past, while with Laker they constantly had to be playing it.' The longer all this went on, the greater Lock's visible displeasure at it. Evans recalled, 'Tony at least made a show of applauding Laker's first two or three dismissals in the final session. But after that he just stood there with his arms folded across his chest each time Jim had another success. "Bastard," I heard him mutter.'

In his 1957 autobiography, Lock insisted that the Old Trafford Test had been just another game for him, and that he had in no way begrudged Laker his career-defining triumph there. In fact he devoted eight closely set pages of the book to an account of his extreme disinterest in the affair. Lock's final public verdict on the match was, 'I bowled as well [there] as I have done on occasions in the past when I've had six or seven victims. It so happened on the final day at Manchester that I beat both the bat and the stumps several times, but the actual wickets eluded me.'

To England's Peter Richardson, who watched events unfold at close quarters, it came down to a question not so much of technique as intelligence. 'I think the more wickets Jim got the more upset Lockie became. The guy had a rush of blood. If he'd pitched the ball up and bowled at a sensible pace, he would have taken at least half the available second innings wickets.'

Instead, Laker of course monopolised all ten. Even so, it was a curiously muted, English sort of success, with none of the ecstatic high-fives or de facto native fertility dances we might expect today. As Laker himself later remarked, 'I've been asked thousands of times what went through my mind in the closing stages, but I have to say I was completely relaxed. Odd as it may seem now, I didn't even consider the possibility of taking all ten wickets.' He added, perhaps just a bit mischievously, 'How could I, when Lock was fizzing the ball with such venomous lift and spin?'

Setting aside the matters of the weather and the pitch, it was of course a wonderful performance by Laker, never hurried, a perfect balance of containment and aggression. He bowled beautifully. His short, utilitarian run, heavy boots clopping, flannels well hitched up, left arm cocked like a sniper sighting his mark, was always the signal for dead quiet in the crowd. The leg trap snapped shut time and again that Tuesday afternoon, with Lock and Oakman pocketing five catches between them. The end came at 5.27pm, with about half an hour to go, when Maddocks was hit on the roll of the pad right in front. England had won by an innings and 170 runs. Laker's figures were 51.2-23-53-10, giving him 19-90 in the match. As Neil Harvey, happily still with us today at the age of 93, says, 'What Jim did at Old Trafford wasn't just a great piece of bowling. It was a bit of sporting history. We haven't seen it since, and I don't think we'll ever see it again.'

The last rites, played out before a small but appreciative crowd of about 4,000, were superbly British. At the death there was a muted appeal and, after a slight pause, the black-hatted umpire Emrys Davies came out of his crouch, long white coat flapping at his ankles, and stabbed his left index finger towards the batsman. At that Laker simply turned, took his sweater from Davies, slung it over his shoulder, and strolled off, his face set, looking for all the world as if he was returning from a gentle session in the nets. Far from being a fire-breathing agent of the Australians' doom, he seemed quiet and faintly embarrassed by the fuss being made over him. A few team-mates offered a handshake, and Godfrey Evans went so far as a genial pat on the back. There was no visible sense of communal or individual elation beyond that. Laker treated himself to a glass of his sponsor's Lucozade and a cigarette in the dressing room, and one or two of the opposition players wandered in to offer their compliments. 'Well done, Jimmy, you've done a great job,' Neil Harvey informed him. 'Well, you've got to get them when you can, haven't you?' Laker shrugged.

One or two others did, however, seem to grasp the extraordinary circumstances of the match. Keith Miller happened to pass Bert Flack, the groundsman, on his way out of the pavilion door, and asked him if the press had been giving him a hard time about the pitch. Flack replied, 'Keith, I've been so bloody busy since the game finished that I haven't had time to cut my own bloody throat.' The *Daily Mail* team of Don Bradman and Alex Bannister left together, and as they were walking to their car they saw 83-year-old Sydney Barnes, sometime of Lancashire and England, waiting patiently at his bus stop. 'What do you think of that?' Bradman asked him. A thin smile came over the face of the man who had taken 189 Test wickets in only 27 matches, 49 of them in a single series against South Africa. 'No bugger ever got all ten when I was playing,' Barnes replied, truthfully enough. Seven years after this exchange, *Wisden*'s 100th edition named both Bradman and Barnes among its 'Six Giants of the Century' list, although the almanack largely abstracted itself from the modern era when conferring its bauble. There was no mention of Laker.

The man of the hour left the ground soon afterwards, walking unmolested across the road to his elderly grey Morris Oxford and then heading south through pre-motorway England. Lilly Laker had travelled ahead by train on the previous Sunday night, and thus missed her husband's date with destiny on the final day. 'It was something we both always regretted,' he admitted. About two hours later, Laker stopped off at a roadside pub near Lichfield for a beer and a sandwich. As he stood at the bar, the nine o'clock television news came on to talk first about Suez and then about the events at Manchester. Laker joined the locals in crowding round the set to watch the match highlights, the first time he'd ever seen himself on the screen. No one recognised him. After that he got back in his car and drove for another four hours to the unassuming house in Portinscale Road, Putney, which he shared with his wife and their two daughters. There was a small group of press photographers waiting there for him of about the size that might nowadays greet a minor internet celebrity best known for what they were wearing or who they were dating. Lilly came out to politely ask everyone to keep the noise down as their girls were fast asleep upstairs. About six hours later, Laker drove himself the short distance back to The Oval where, due to some whim of the fixture gods, Surrey were due to host the Australians. It was raining. Neither Laker nor the visitors could have been too upset at the unexpected opportunity to take the day off. When they finally got going the next morning he restricted himself to taking 4-41 in the tourists' only completed innings, passing his hundred wickets for the season in the process.

Laker's figures at Old Trafford form part of a Holy Trinity of individual Test cricket records. The highest batting average remains Bradman's scarcely credible 99.94, and the best personal score is Brian Lara's unbeaten 400 against England at Antigua in April 2004. One hesitates to venture a bet, but it may be that Bradman's and Laker's are the two which will never be beaten. Even the *Daily Telegraph* loosened the ties of its journalistic corset to remark in September 1956, 'His achievement [at Old Trafford] is a spiritual experience which will linger long after the sun has faded from the summer sky, long, even, after youth has fled.' More prosaically, Laker was paid a basic £70 for his five days' work at Manchester. Of this fee Surrey deducted £17 for each of the two county matches he missed through representing his country. Laker's old employer Barclays Bank and Littlewoods Pools both sent him cheques for £250, and the De La Rue company, the printers of Britain's banknotes, one for £190, representing a tenner for each wicket. Laker later remarked that in addition to this he'd 'made a few bob' by ghostwritten newspaper articles and signed copies of the Test scorecard 'which sold like hotcakes for my Benefit'. Field Marshal Montgomery also sent him an autographed £1 note. Laker later estimated that he'd earned an extra £1,000 thanks to events at Old Trafford, which translates to about £9,500 in today's money.

While Laker drove off alone following the Test, down the dark miles of provincial British B-roads, Lock made his own way south to the small flat above a corner shop and sub-post office at Hamsey Green, near Limpsfield, where he now lived with his wife Audrey, who worked part-time behind the counter, and their two sons Graeme and Richard. Since Putney lay less than 20 miles away, and on a direct line from Manchester, it might have seemed only logical for one of the two Surrey team-mates to have offered the other one a lift. But this happened only rarely in the course of their 13 years as county colleagues. As we've seen, when the England players wandered off the field at the close of play, Peter May had draped a well-meaning arm around his crestfallen bowler's shoulder, and offered him some consoling words of advice, 'Forget the scorebook, Tony. You played your part, too.'

But of course Lock didn't forget it. Some years later, Laker told a journalist on the *Daily Mirror*, 'Tony was so upset at taking only one wicket at Old Trafford that he changed and drove home after the game, not even congratulating me. And for the next month he didn't say a word to me.' Perhaps there was fault on both sides, even so, because some 25 years later Laker told his BBC colleague Bill Frindall, 'Lock was a bit upset after the Test. I think possibly I would have been, too, in his position. And I think one thing I never will forgive myself for was that, amid all the glorification that was taking place afterwards, I didn't spare enough time for him. It was only in later years that I realised that he must have felt desperately unhappy.'

Lock and Laker eventually reconciled in time to join Surrey's celebration of their fifth successive County Championship title at a modest team dinner in London, and then to at least co-exist on England's winter tour of South Africa. In future years both men went to some pains to pay due credit to one another. 'If my performance [at Old Trafford] was unbelievable, then so was his,' Laker wrote late in his life. 'If the game had been replayed a million times it would surely never have happened that way again. Tony bowled quite beautifully without any luck at all.'

Lock for his part offered more measured praise. 'The typical Australian loses heart if he doesn't take a wicket every over or so,' he wrote. 'But Laker plods on regardless. He just puts the ball on the spot and lets it do the work.' It might be fair to say that after 1956 the two men's relationship increasingly came to resemble that between an elderly married couple determined to make a go of it even after a catastrophic betrayal of trust lying somewhere in the past. Sometimes Lock would be conciliatory, even generous, to his old partner, publicly admitting he'd been 'by far the more steady' of the two. Behind the scenes, however, he was still seething. When in later years a well-meaning journalist once told Lock that he'd 'literally decimated' the Australians in the first innings at Old Trafford, in the sense of removing one in ten of them, the still feisty left-armer was unimpressed. 'Bugger off,' he replied.

* * *

The fifth and final Test of the 1956 series, played at The Oval, followed a familiar pattern. England won the toss, batted, made a respectable 247 amid the rain, and then Laker and Lock took a hatful of wickets. They again made a potent combination. As usual Laker had the edge in terms of technical precision, while Lock favoured the carpet-bombing approach of flinging the ball down at full tilt, knowing that sooner or later one of his deliveries would rear up devastatingly off the seam. The two of them may still not have been talking to one another, but they were far too professional not to cooperate in the middle. David Sheppard later recalled that Lock's fielding to Laker's bowling in the Oval Test was an 'extraordinary display of agility and raw nerve', and that in addition to this, 'In Frank's first over, Tony took one of his most fantastic catches – McDonald glanced a very fast ball right off the meat of the bat, an inch or two off the ground, and Lock picked it up right-handed with the ease of a housewife shelling peas for lunch.'

It may not have been an absolutely vintage England team, but few sides can have ever succeeded in pooling resources to the common benefit as much as this one did. In the end the Australians were left chasing 228 to win in two hours on a soft pitch and a dead outfield. May kept his seamers on for a token two overs, and then summoned Laker and Lock. They did their best, but ran out of time. The tourists staggered to 27-5 (Laker bowling nine maidens on the trot, with figures of 3-8) to escape with a draw. England had won the series 2-1, recording a significant chapter of sporting history in the process.

* * *

Cricket is a game often defined by its statistics, so perhaps it's not surprising that Tony Lock might come to be especially sensitive about his own bowling figures in 1956. In all first-class play that season he took 155 wickets at 12.46 each, which, while impressive, was still significantly below his haul of 216 wickets the year before. It's true his average number of overs bowled for each wicket taken was remarkably uniform, 6.6 in 1955 versus 6.8 in 1956. But set against this was his record in the Tests with Australia, where he managed just 15 wickets at 22.46 apiece. Lock bowled a total of nearly 16 overs for each victim in the 1956 series, compared to one victim every 13 overs against South Africa in 1955. For once his competition with Laker had proved counter-productive; as we've seen, instead of throttling back on the helpful Old Trafford wicket he'd pumped it up even more, which may have assuaged his inner demons but did little for his final bowling analysis.

These were all perfectly respectable numbers on Lock's part. Any modern spin bowler to match them would be dousing himself in champagne, if not wallowing in the gratitude of his team's corporate sponsors. But when later coming to review the 1956 season as a whole, Lock fastened obsessively on to a different detail. This was the fact that Laker had taken more than three times his total of Australian Test wickets, at a cost of a mere 9.60 apiece. The press didn't then talk about economy or strike rates, as they did later, but if they had they would have noticed that Laker took an Australian wicket every 37 balls, and that very nearly half the overs he bowled were runless. Lock could take statistical comfort only when his 1956 Test batting average (15.33) and total number of catches (ten) were compared to his rival's figures of 7.40 and zero, respectively. Of course, cricket is really about much more than the tyranny of the scorebook. Trying to assess a player's value to his side in that way is like trying to rate Rembrandt's self-portrait based on its size, or to point out that, whatever Keats had to say on the subject in his *Ode to a Nightingale*, it isn't really possible to fly upon the viewless wings of Poesy, as this would be to break all the known laws of aerodynamics.

Nonetheless, Lock could – and often did – quote this same data well into his later life, reproducing it by way of an explanation of 'Lucky Jim's' pre-eminence over him as a national sporting icon. In his memoir, published soon after the events in question, he paid tribute to Laker's feats in 1956, but still saw the Australians as the architects of their own doom. 'Magnificently as Jim bowled, and keenly though I and others tried to support him, the Aussies should have saved themselves at Leeds and Manchester,' he wrote. 'Too many of them were bowled out from the pavilion – they went out to bat fearing the worst, which is no way for international cricketers to react.'

England's opponents, in other words, had performed ineptly, and Laker had really done no more than to pull the levers that encouraged them to self-destruct. That many if not all of the Australians saw themselves primarily as victims not of the England bowling but of an impossible wicket at Old Trafford can also be glimpsed from two final off-stage scenes of the Test. The first was the moment when Fred Trueman, as England's 12th man, took a bat into the visitors' dressing room for the players to autograph and it came back unsigned, save for the words scrawled across the face, 'Sorry – no comment, head groundsman.' Following that, there was the terse but memorable exchange when Bert Flack himself had approached Ian Johnson, the tourists' captain, to enquire which roller he would like applied for the second innings. 'Please your fucking self,' Johnson had replied.

Lock was also painfully aware that as from 31 July 1956 he would always be regarded as the junior partner in England's venerable spin-bowling firm. To him it was a cruel misconception of the truth. While Lock's stock would continue to rise and fall with each successive series, he grumbled, Laker was now immortal, his performance at Old Trafford seen by some as nothing less than miraculous – quite literally so since the bishop of London, to give just one example, chose in a sermon that August to find the workings of the hand of God in Laker's achievements. From now on the public would always have a fixed image of the two bowlers. Laker was the player of genius, and Lock the one of talent – the 'forgotten man' who had really been no more than the necessary foil to his more illustrious team-mate. If they really were 'twins', as the popular phrase had it, it was only in the sense of an Alec and Eric Bedser, or, climbing a rung or two up or down the cultural evolutionary ladder, the various sibling members of the Bee Gees: civil enough for the most part in their personal relations, but somehow never quite equal in the eyes of the public. In 1956, most cricket watchers were agreed that Lock had bowled well, sometimes spectacularly so, in the summer's Test series. But the same observers went well beyond that in describing the peculiar fate of that year's tourists. There was a certain wry comedy as well as genuine affection in the word people used, which soon passed into everyday language as a sort of shorthand to convey the act of being utterly humiliated by an opponent.

Lakered.

6

Over to Me

NOVEMBER 1956 was an unusually febrile time both in the United Kingdom and around the world. On the second of the month the United States combined with the Russians for the first and to date only occasion in UN history to vote against her wartime allies Britain and France in the Suez affair. Four days later, America went to the polls and re-elected Dwight D. Eisenhower as president. The following week the Soviet Union threatened the UK with atomic weapons unless she cease and desist in Egypt, and, seeming to stray from her humanitarian ideals, then sent in her own troops to crush the Hungarian uprising at the cost of some 22,000 casualties. At a reception in Moscow on 18 November, Nikita Khrushchev greeted his guests from western European embassies not with the traditional vodka and caviar, but the phrase 'We will bury you.' Seven days later, Fidel Castro, Che Guevara and 82 colleagues set off on a yacht from Mexico to start the Cuban revolution. Meanwhile, Britain was effectively adrift on the stormy waters of international affairs until the Tories hurriedly promoted Harold Macmillan through the ranks in January 1957, even that reassuringly Edwardian figure feeling, he wrote in private, 'The physical sensation of the collapse of a universe, that in which one was born, and outside of which there was nothing … The death of all certainty.'

Jim Laker had no known interest in politics beyond his innate conservatism, but if he had it's a fair bet that following the events at Old Trafford a grateful nation would have risen up to appoint him dictator for life. Instead of that, he found himself sharing a second-class inside cabin on the SS *Edinburgh Castle*, bound for South Africa, where he earned a basic £540 for his five months' work as part of the winter's MCC tour party. The side was again led by Peter May, with Doug Insole of Essex as second in command. Tony Lock was also included, but to his eternal chagrin played in only one of the five Tests, losing out to his rival Johnny Wardle. In the event Wardle took no fewer than 105 wickets in all first-class matches, 26 of them in his four Tests, for once making it hard to quibble with the selectors' judgement.

It was also one of the more ill-tempered tours in terms of relations between the two teams. Laker later described the South African captain Clive Ryneveld as 'no more than a fairly pleasant person', before recalling an incident when the home team's Peter Heine had informed the batsman on strike, 'I want to hit you, Bailey,' among other unappreciative remarks, and adding that the off-spinner Hugh Tayfield 'took more liberties with the laws than sportsmanship allows'. These were mild compared to Laker's views as expressed in private. In later conversation, Heine was always 'that Dutchman', quite often with a choice intensifier added, while Tayfield was a 'château-bottled shit', he confided over lunch one day in August 1979.

These were also turbulent times in South Africa's post-war political history, with the state's legally codified system of racism – apartheid – coming under increasing scrutiny at home and abroad. Lord Alexander, the MCC president, had personally briefed the tourists before they embarked on their voyage that autumn. He told them not to mention apartheid. 'The safest thing to talk about is the last British Lions rugby tour, or the beauty of the local scenery,' he added. Still, 'the colour problems of South Africa, even if you don't speak about them, are not things which you can overlook completely', Laker later acknowledged in his autobiography, before recalling an incident on the tour involving Alan Oakman:

> Oakman had borrowed a car to go out for the evening when we were in Cape Town. Driving back, quite late, he saw a coloured man on a bicycle come shooting out of a side turning. Alan couldn't avoid him. The man, his leg broken, lay on the ground, obviously in great pain. A shaken Oakman got out of the car and stood there as a crowd gathered. They started asking, 'Hello, Mr. Oakman, you played a bad stroke today, Mr. Oakman … Will you sign my book, Mr. Oakman?' Then a police officer came along. His first question was, 'He was drunk, Mr. Oakman, wasn't he?' Then the policeman turned to a man in the crowd. 'You live near this nigger … he's always drunk, isn't he?' This, thought Alan, too bemused to do anything, is what white men call justice.

Laker's affection for South Africa was further strained by his experience of the five Tests, which he characterised as played on 'appalling wickets', with a growing English disenchantment at the standard of the home umpiring. He took 50 wickets at an average of 17.50 on the tour, and 11 at nearly 30 in the Tests, in other words eight fewer than he'd managed in a single match the previous summer. His best performance probably came in the second Test, at Cape Town, where he took a frugal 2-7 on the final day to help England win by 312 runs. Rock bottom was the moment when Heine hit him a stinging blow on the shoulder and then enquired, without obvious warmth in his voice, 'Oh, have I hurt you, sonny?' Forced to improvise, the best the Englishman could come up with was, 'I'll hit you over the head with the bloody bat if you ever do that again.' Laker regretted this choice of riposte for years to come, feeling that it had both lacked polish and put him on the same coarse level as his opponent. There was also an extraordinary final Test at Port Elizabeth, played on a wicket which made Old Trafford appear reasonable by comparison. Even Frank Tyson could do little more than hurl the ball down and then watch it shoot straight along the ground. Set 189 to win, England failed by 58 runs. Laker and Lock took just four wickets between them in the match.

Whatever his undoubted personal charm and leadership attributes, it has to be said Peter May had an only modest time of it with the bat, at least in the Tests, managing a total of just 153 runs in the series. Laker was mystified by the non-selection of Tom Graveney for the tour (a view Graveney shared) and only partly impressed by the 25-year-old Jim Parks, of Sussex, whom he remembered on board the *Edinburgh Castle*: 'Several times he would be the first person I met in the morning. Feeling pretty good myself, I'd say, "Good morning, Jim. How are you?"

'"Oh, I don't know," would come the answer. "My back's bad …" Or it might be his leg, or his head. Then, after only one game in South Africa, Parks was found to be experiencing double vision. It was a puzzle to all of us. Was he suffering from nerves? Didn't he *want* to go on the tour?'

Oddly enough, this was very much the sort of thing people would come to ask just a year or two later of Laker himself. Doug Insole later remarked, 'Jim was about the best spin bowler in cricket history, [but] frankly you wouldn't put your mortgage on him in a crisis.' Of Lock, Insole chiefly remembered the white mess jacket he liked to wear at cocktail parties. 'Regrettably, this lost something of its original sheen when an irate South African threw a glass of tomato juice over him,' he wrote.

Despite this incident, Laker had nothing but praise for his Surrey team-mate. 'Tony took his omission from the side very well, and didn't appear to mind the chores of twelfth man,' he recalled. 'This was greatly to his credit, for his "feud" with Wardle was one of the most publicised things in cricket – and Wardle, at least for now, was winning the battle.'

Laker was very possibly sincere in this tribute. Or perhaps on this occasion he felt that he could afford to be generous to a colleague who posed no threat to him. We can note again the essential disparity in temperament that runs as a throughline to their relationship. Lock once burst into a hotel room in Durban with the dramatic announcement that he'd just overheard Peter Heine inform some of the South African players that he was going to go after Peter May in the Test starting the next morning and 'put the toffee-nosed bastard in hospital' for the rest of the tour. 'Bloody hell,' Lock exclaimed, 'this is war!' 'Yes,' said Laker off-handedly. 'I suppose it is.' In the event May was out cheaply to Tayfield in both innings of the Test. Laker took representative cricket seriously enough, but, whatever the extremes of his own career, he kept it all in perspective. 'I flew my wife and two daughters to South Africa, and they thought everything was wonderful,' he later recalled. 'Despite the grim cricket, it was worth it, every moment, just to see my family enjoying themselves so much.'

* * *

The first book-form reviews of the South Africa tour appeared just as the MCC players returned home in wintry late-March conditions and reported back to their counties. For the most part there was only muted approval for the four members of the Surrey contingent. In time, *Wisden* wrote, 'May, like many before him, found that captaining a team abroad was a vastly different proposition than at home ... It appeared that he became over-anxious to do well, and the strain of leadership on and off the field became increasingly severe on him.' Peter Loader for his part had 'generally shown good control [with] the new ball', but had not been crowned by much statistical success. Laker had fallen away from his form in 1956 – he could hardly have done otherwise – and Lock had barely graced the Tests, although 'he again proved his brilliance as a short-leg fieldsman' and was 'extremely keen' throughout.

Nonetheless, these were heady days back at Surrey, whose championship matches in 1957 often presented much the same characteristics of the biblical account of the contest between David and Goliath, but without the surprise ending. When the final table came to be published in September, Surrey had 312 points, which was 94 more than their nearest rival. There were several important constituent parts of the team that crushed all in its path, but no one did more for the overall cause than Laker and Lock. Both men maintained their personal form of the previous season, and in Lock's case actually improved on it, with fully 212 first-class wickets at 12 apiece. As everyone agreed, the great thing about him was that he was never an inhuman, mechanical cricketer merely pegging away like a preset bowling machine. A typical Lock over might contain three pitch-perfect balls, a long hop, one far down the leg side and a climactic bouncer, delivered with a last-second circular whip of his arm, rearing up at the startled batsman's chin. All this cyclone of activity would be accompanied by a lively running commentary on the bowler's part, even as he continued in his follow-through down the wicket, ready to reverse thrust if needed and click out a telescopic arm to field any ball within an arc between about point and forward short leg. Whatever else you could say, cricket was rarely boring when he was in the middle.

While Lock enjoyed sparring with any opponent and on occasion with a select team-mate or two as well, he always especially relished the chance to resume the struggle with Johnny Wardle.

The South African tour had served only to fuel this particular feud. Sports writing is often an arena of partisanship and posturing, your identity wrapped up in both what you love and what you can't stand, but whichever of England's two great left-armers you personally happened to prefer you had to respect the sheer chutzpah they brought to the table. As we've seen, in July 1957 Surrey went up to play Yorkshire at Park Avenue, Bradford, in Wardle's testimonial match. When the moment came, Lock gave the beneficiary one off the mark, as tradition required, but then chased the ball like a whippet fresh off the leash to prevent any thought of a second. Wardle moved swiftly back to his crease, and once there bowed ironically to his opponent. There was a lot of satirical laughter from the crowd, but Lock made his point in the end. Yorkshire were all out for 91, the Surrey spinners taking all ten between them.

Ray Illingworth confirms that any match involving the country's two foremost orthodox left-armers was likely to be a lively affair. 'Wardle won most of his personal duels with Lockie, but not by any means all of them,' he told me. 'We would crease ourselves laughing at those times, because we knew what was coming … Johnny would take delight in giving the treatment to Lock, and Tony always returned the compliment.'

When Wardle came out to bat for the Rest of England against Surrey in September 1957 he drove his first ball from Laker to the cover boundary, then clipped a couple more to leg. At that point Lock came on, measured out his full international run, limbered up for a bit in the mid-distance, then ran in, all bounce and aggression, and let the batsman have it. His first ball nearly knocked Wardle's head off. The second ball was another bouncer, Wardle flashed at it, got a top edge, and Eric Bedser took the catch back-pedalling furiously at square leg, with Lock himself haring up to reinforce the field if required. It was an impressive all-round bit of cricket in its way, and as thrilling to watch in its cumulative rhythm as an

Olympic sprinter suddenly veering off the straight to chase down a bag snatcher catching his eye somewhere off in the corner of the crowd.

The West Indies, under John Goddard, were popular and attractive visitors in what proved to be yet another dismally wet English summer in 1957. Laker played in four of the five Tests, and Lock in three. England dominated throughout and came to the final match at The Oval two up in the series. Here's what *Wisden*, in terms strangely similar to those it used to describe events at Old Trafford just 13 months earlier, had to say about it:

> The ground presented a strange sight before the Test began. The outfield was lush green and in perfect order, but the pitch itself, unusually red-brown, resembled in colour a matting-strip. Whenever the ball pitched on the first day a cloud of dust arose as the surface cracked, and throughout the match slow bowlers were able to turn the ball appreciably. The dust was not so noticeable on the second and third days, [but] the ball continued to spin quickly enough to be really awkward.

There was no need for *Wisden* to add any additional description of the ground conditions beyond this point, because the Test was over shortly after lunch on the third day. England won by an innings and 237 runs. Laker took five wickets in the match, and Lock 11. The latter's 5-28 in the tourists' first innings was his best return for England to date, although in the event the record stood for just 24 hours when he went on to take 6-20 in the second innings. The pitch may have played a part, but it was widely agreed that England's spin bowlers got about their just desserts.

By this time Surrey had already clinched the championship title with nearly a month of the season in hand. The team was known among other desirable attributes for its standard of fielding, particularly close to the bat. Lock took 63 catches in all competitions and Micky Stewart took 77, only one short of Walter Hammond's record established in 1928. To give it some further context, the wicketkeeper Arthur McIntyre took a total of 59 dismissals that season – 50 caught and nine stumped. He once told me that Laker was the harder of the two spinners to keep to – 'on his day, he turned the ball sideways' – and that Lock was as capable of sending down the truly perfect ball as he was of bowling one that they had to fetch from over the third man boundary. 'Tony was a man of blinkered vision who lived and breathed cricket,' McIntyre added. 'He took it all far more personally than Jim did.'

Not that Laker wasn't competitive. He didn't enjoy being hit any more than the next man did. In a championship match the following year at Swansea, Glamorgan's young all-rounder Peter Walker completed his maiden century with an edged boundary off Laker's bowling. Ten of the Surrey team applauded politely, as protocol demanded. The one exception to the ovation was the bowler himself, who stood there, hands on hips, glaring balefully down the wicket at the batsman. Walker thought, 'What an awful bastard.' Later that off-season Laker went out to Hollywood to appear in an episode of *This is Your Life* honouring his fan Boris Karloff, and then to vainly try and explain cricket to Americans, while Lock stayed home and coached among others the 16-year-old schoolgirl Enid Bakewell, who went on to become arguably the greatest all-rounder the women's game has produced. Bakewell thought her 28-year-old mentor 'wonderful, quite opinionated, [and] with a healthy ego'. There was a funny and rather touching example of this last quality when Lock came to the part in his 1957 autobiography where he nominated his side of the 11 greatest cricketers in the world. He was in it.

In the eight months between their first home Test with New Zealand of the 1958 series and their arrival to play that same country as part of their winter's tour, England's cricketers fell spectacularly from grace. Of course, there have been plenty of other such boom and bust cycles before, but this one was special. There were still no such things as formal Test match championship rankings in the late 1950s, but if there had been they would have shown England in a vertiginous plunge from top place to something like fourth or fifth out of the then seven teams, and what was more to have suffered the – to many – unrelieved torment of once again abjectly surrendering the Ashes. The same eight-month span also marked the end of the Laker–Lock partnership at the top level.

The home 1958 series was at least satisfactory, in so far as the word could ever fairly be applied to a summer that somehow always seemed to be cold, grey and *Carry On Sergeant.* New Zealand were outplayed in the first four of the five Tests, and only rain saved them in the final one at The Oval. Laker took 17 wickets at an average of ten in the four games he appeared in and Lock no fewer than 34 at 7.47 in five. There were extraordinary scenes in the second Test at Lord's, where England made 269 and then in a total of four hours dismissed New Zealand twice for scores of 47 and 74. To appease the crowd, the ground authority hurriedly decided to put on an exhibition match. ('I've just fucking *done* that,' said Lock, with figures of 9-29 in the Test.) Laker did not mince his words when he later came to describe the overall course of events.

'The pathetic little pattern continued in the next Test at Leeds,' he wrote. 'New Zealand, batting first, scored 67, then England replied with 267 for 2 declared. Arthur Milton in his first Test hit 104 not out, which told us less about his batting ability than a hard county match would have done. At their second attempt the New Zealanders again foundered against spin' – Lock taking 7-51, he failed to specify – 'totalling a miserable 129. England won the match by an innings.'

Surrey displayed the same sort of effortless mastery in the County Championship as England did in the international series. Their first match of the summer, at home against Gloucestershire, was fairly representative: the reigning champions batted first and declared at 336/7. Their visitors then folded twice to the spinners, Laker stepping up for 7-66 on the last day. There were 'showers and sunshine for the spin twins', reported *Wisden* of another unequal contest at Old Trafford, where Lancashire collapsed to 27 all out in their second innings, which was 147 fewer runs than Peter May had scored on his own. Someone took a picture of them leaving the ground together following the close of play. Lock is about to get mildly trendy, and wears an open-neck shirt with a suspiciously wide collar, tieless, while Laker sports a cardie under his sheepskin coat. They look like a mildly bohemian student walking alongside his chemistry tutor, and neither one seems especially delighted to have just won a championship match against one of their side's closest challengers.

There was an at least slightly more evenly balanced contest later that July against Kent at Blackheath. Unusually, Lock took 15 wickets in the match but still ended up on the losing side. For once the pitch was a beauty, and Surrey were left to chase 252 on the last afternoon. May accepted the gauntlet and set the tone by hitting the first ball he received for six. When Lock bustled out to bat Surrey still needed 104 in slightly over an hour. His innings of 57 lasted just 34 minutes and contained 11 boundaries. It was hard to see what more he could do by way of an all-round contribution, but in the end it wasn't quite enough. Kent won by 29 runs, and Godfrey Evans, the home wicketkeeper, would remember overhearing May 'bollock[ing] Laker after the game because he was strolling around the bar with his hands in his pockets, whistling as if he just didn't care, and Jim said, "Oh really? Would it do either one of us any good if I marched up and down like a ruddy squaddie? Would that somehow put more fucking runs on the board?"'

Laker wasn't necessarily one to react well to criticism, then, nor, to be fair, did he normally stray outside the strict confines of the spirit or laws of the game. But there was a strange incident when Surrey came to play Middlesex at The Oval in the second week of August that year and the teenaged Arnold Long, who was then on the county's ground staff, remembered:

> I was sitting alongside some of the other young players at the ground when Jim was fielding at cover and someone said, 'Have you seen that? Jim has been marking the Test match pitch!' The game was played on a pitch near the Test pitch, and the Test was due to start in a few days' time and, as he walked back and turned as the bowler started to run in, he scuffed a spot on a length with his spikes. We got the binoculars out and you could see it clearly.

If this uncharacteristic lapse on Laker's part really happened, it wouldn't seem to have done him much good, because in the Test that followed he managed figures of only 1-44 in the first innings and 1-25 in the second, and the captains shook hands early on a draw. Perhaps the most striking moment came when Fred Trueman hit the young New Zealand batsman John Sparling, who was playing in his first series, with a bouncer, and at the interval the batsman's father, who had flown in for the occasion, presented himself at the door of the England dressing room to give Trueman a piece of his mind. Godfrey Evans, again demonstrating his Zelig-like ability to be on hand to witness some of cricket's greatest, or at least most poignant moments, later remembered it as 'one of the very few times I can recall when Fred was lost for words'.

Meanwhile, there had been an extraordinary and, as it turned out, significantly more publicised incident involving Laker and Peter May. In trying to assess exactly what happened, we should first acknowledge that both players had what the police call 'form'. Laker thought May 'aloof and distant – a [captain] who does not appear to like mixing with his team', to quote his autobiography, and May, in the relatively greater privacy of his annual reports to the Surrey committee, regarded Laker as a supremely gifted cricketer who was perhaps just a touch more high-maintenance than ideal. There were clearly delicate issues of man-management involved. As we've seen, the two men had already had words following Surrey's narrow loss to Kent at Blackheath, apparently because something about Laker's body language had struck his captain as deficient, and a sharp exchange had ensued. These things sometimes happen in a sports dressing room. Following that the visiting team had simply changed and driven back to London, seemingly thinking no more about it. After all, they were still comfortably on top of the championship table. But apparently that wasn't quite the end of the matter, because Laker was to write that, a day or two after returning from Blackheath, he'd bumped into May in the Oval pavilion. Surrey were then just starting a match against Glamorgan, and both home players were taking a break from the side, May because he was mentally and physically exhausted and Laker because he was having trouble with his all-important right index finger. Lock had also been offered the week off, but missing a game was always a more traumatic experience for him than for most other players, so in the event he turned out and added a further six wickets to his season's haul.

Here is what Laker later wrote of the brief encounter with his county and Test captain that day in the pavilion:

> Our defeat by Kent was plainly still on May's mind. Our conversation had barely begun before it dawned on me that he thought I was to blame for our loss at Blackheath. This, you may imagine, took some digesting. My mind was still

hovering between dismay and resentment when May put his feelings neatly and coldly into words. 'I don't think you were trying to bowl them out,' he declared.

To a professional cricketer, as a reflection on his approach to the job which provides his bread and butter, it was damned near to what the lawyers call slander … Firmly but politely, I asked May to withdraw his remark. He refused to do so.

The conversation took a downhill turn from there. After the inevitable airing of other resentments, Laker, his face now pale with either fury or shock, returned to the specific events at Blackheath. It was clear that beneath his pose of stoic fortitude he was extremely angry. Laker reminded May that he himself had been bowled by a slow full toss while going for runs in the last session against Kent, and May countered that they were talking about Laker's performance here, not his. There was quite a lot more peak decibel debate in this same general vein. Then with a trembling voice Laker repeated his central demand that May withdraw his original remark. May replied that he had no intention of doing so. A minute or two passed – afterward no one could say how many – in total silence. Finally a patch of colour came back to Laker's cheeks and for the third time he again requested a retraction. At that May swept up some papers that had fallen from his arms in all the excitement and without another word on the subject left the room.

In short order, Laker stepped briskly down the corridor to the office of 59-year-old Commander Bob Babb, the man recently appointed to replace Brian Castor as the Surrey county secretary. In the quick verbal brush strokes of what he clearly considered an outrageous breach of protocol by his captain and a contemptible slur on his own good name, Laker outlined the circumstances of the two men's recent post-mortem discussion of the match at Blackheath. He was by no means confident that he could continue to play under May's captaincy, he announced. More immediately, Laker continued, now on something of a roll, he had no desire to spend six months in Australia as part of the coming winter's MCC party with that 'bloody man' in charge. Having missed out on two previous visits to Australia, it seemed he was now sabotaging his chances of appearing in a third one.

As luck would have it, Commander Babb had just that morning been asked by Lord's to confirm the availability of five of his county's players (May, Laker, Lock, Loader and the young stumper Roy Swetman) for the winter tour. Like his predecessor in office, the commander was not one to hesitate, nor dwell unnecessarily on his options, once roused to act. Then and there he picked up the phone on his desk and dialled his MCC counterpart Ronald Aird, a man of similarly crisp, parade ground mien. Babb briefly put him in the picture about the reduction by one of the Surrey touring contingent. 'Before you ring off, Ronnie, I just wanted to check … Rung off,' said Babb, before replacing the receiver and turning to calmly face Laker. 'Well, Jim, you're not going to Australia.'

Like most such affairs, the Laker–May altercation was a mixture of high-minded principle and petty grievance. On the one hand there was the bowler's underlying distrust of the sort of cricketer, however richly talented, steeped in what seemed to him to be the ludicrous social conventions of the era. May, in short, was a toff, at least in Laker's mind, Cambridge-educated and at present engaged to the show-jumping daughter of England's pre-war captain Harold Gilligan, and thus not entirely at ease with the modern vulgar realities of an English professional sports team. It was a caricature, if one that contained a grain of truth. But aside from his lifelong aversion to the ruling elite, Laker also had a more immediate issue with his county captain. This was the tragicomic incident that had followed the summer's third Test against New Zealand at Leeds, when May's car had broken down on the backroads of Rutland while on the late-night journey home, and his passengers Laker and Lock had gotten out to give it a push.

The precise details of what followed are unclear, but Micky Stewart, who heard about it from Laker himself, remembers, 'The upshot was that Peter ended up taking the train back south and Jim and Tony were left to deal with the car problems and get themselves home under their own steam.' All this was just four days before Surrey began their match against Kent at Blackheath, and would not seem to have conspicuously improved the core May–Laker relationship ahead of that fateful encounter. In yet another variant on the whole story, by then Laker was already expressing misgivings about touring Australia as a professional player, and had asked to be specially registered as an amateur for the occasion because of the tax advantages this entailed. It was another twist on the inflammatory issue of 'shamateurism' in English sport, and it seems to have remained unresolved at the time of Laker's showdown with May in The Oval pavilion, possibly adding impetus to his subsequent progress down the hall to his county secretary's office and all that ensued.

In the event, Laker soon seems to have reconsidered his position vis-à-vis Australia, and as a result only a day or two later the interested parties met for a clear-the-air summit with Gubby Allen, Ronald Aird and Aird's assistant Billy Griffith at Lord's. Even then, May still refused to withdraw his central 'not trying' allegation about the Blackheath affair. Instead, he told the room that he expected his opinion as England's captain to be respected, and that if this were no longer the case he would be forced to resign. On that subdued note, the meeting broke up.

Three days later, as in a stage play, May and Laker again passed by each other as one walked in a door and the other one out of it in The Oval pavilion. The intervening home match with Yorkshire, in which May scored a century, and Lock took 11 wickets, seems to have served as a cooling-off period for all parties. In short order the two men repaired to a small room next to the secretary's office, and tried again. The atmosphere was apparently stiff and, after some awkward small talk, May abruptly suggested that Laker should simply forget that he had ever said anything about his industry or lack of it in the Blackheath match. It wasn't quite the same thing as admitting he had been wrong to cast any such aspersion in the first place, but it was enough to invite the well-known British gift for compromise. 'That worked for me,' Laker later wrote, insisting he had then 'forgiven and forgotten' the slight on his character. 'Lord's were duly told I was ready to go to Australia. There were, if I'm not mistaken, sighs of relief all round ... It was a sad and sordid story. But, like all the best stories, it had a happy ending.'

Nonetheless, it would be a stretch to claim that Laker was wholeheartedly delighted at the events of July 1958, and his pleasure at the prospect of touring under May remained well contained. Nor did he forgive and forget, as he insisted was the case. Nearly two years later, Laker wrote of his former captain, 'May was no man-manager ... It was always in his nature to be shy and quiet, but I believe [his problems] really sprang from a fear of the press. He was afraid to do or say anything which might leave itself open to the least misinterpretation.' Lilly Laker told me that her husband eventually came to recognise that he was as upset with himself as he was with his county and Test captain. 'But those were sad days, and it took some time for them to reconcile.'

As it happened, there was to be another example of May's only mediocre talent for media relations, and one with direct consequences for Laker himself, later in July 1958. It seemed that someone had told the *Daily Mail* about the whole Blackheath affair and the subsequent discussions on the Australian tour, and the paper ran with the story just as the England selectors were due to meet to choose their 12 for the summer's fourth Test against New

Zealand at Old Trafford. As a result, Allen and his committee dropped Laker from the team and instead gave a first cap to 26-year-old Ray Illingworth. Illingworth took three wickets in the match and Lock took eight; England won by an innings. 'It was a perfectly reasonable decision by the selectors and, although Allen knew the truth [about Australia] before play started, we agreed in a private talk to let matters stand as they were,' Laker wrote diplomatically, choosing not to dwell on the fact that he had also lost out on his £70 match fee as a result.

Having once resolved the matter of Laker's availability to tour that winter, the MCC almost immediately faced a second crisis involving their party's selection. This one concerned Lock's old nemesis Johnny Wardle. A brief press release from Headingley on 30 July stated, without elaboration, 'The Yorkshire County Cricket Club have informed J. H. Wardle that they will not be calling on his services after the end of the season.' In fact, thanks to Yorkshire blocking his registration elsewhere, apart from one charity match years later in India, he never played first-class cricket again. Wardle's offence was to have put his name to an article in the *Daily Mail* that was sharply critical of his county club, and more generally of a prevailing class system that 'belongs more to the middle ages than the second half of the 20th century'. In a subsequent release, Yorkshire added, 'In past years Wardle has been warned on several occasions that his general behaviour in the field and in the dressing-room has left much to be desired. No improvement was shown [by him] this year.' After some further scathing articles in the *Mail* he had his Australian tour invitation withdrawn by MCC. At the age of 35, with 1,842 first-class wickets behind him, Wardle's career was over.

Meanwhile, Laker's newfound spirit of goodwill extended to playing nearly a dozen more matches under May's captaincy during the remainder of the 1958 season. Surrey were once again county champions, for the seventh consecutive year, with Hampshire, for whom the West Indian opener Roy Marshall scored 2,200 runs and the indefatigable Derek Shackleton took 165 wickets, coming up behind. It was another stellar year for Lock, whose 170 dismissals came at a cost of 12 apiece. He gave the county yearbook the impression of 'sometimes entertaining the crowd and himself while in the field, and on every occasion applying himself to the full with both bat and ball'.

Laker refrained from such exertions, and there were times when he seemed to take his duties relatively lightly. That appearance could be deceptive, and anyway a man as intense as he was was surely entitled to an occasional breather. Like many of cricket's greatest players, it might be fair to say that he was more apt to turn it on in front of a full house at Lord's or The Oval than he was for the proverbial two men and a dog on a wet weekday morning at Ilford.

* * *

In March 1951, 48-year-old Gubby Allen wrote a letter to his friend, the cricket coach and administrator Harry Altham, to discuss some details about the latter's work-in-progress, the seminal *MCC Coaching Book*. Allen's central theme was that the England team was about to embark on an extended period of unrivalled supremacy of Test cricket, which he thought might last for the rest of the decade. Allen based his prediction largely on the basis of the recently played final Test of the current MCC tour of Australia, which the visitors won by eight wickets, as well as on the availability of 'men of known calibre and form' such as Len Hutton, Trevor Bailey and Godfrey Evans. With the addition of a high-class seamer or two (and the young Fred Trueman was already knocking them over for Yorkshire), he thought this run of international success might well go on 'more or less undisturbed throughout the [1950s]', although the natural order of things, with one team reaching its peak and then falling back to regroup, would eventually usher in a new balance of power. 'In the end,' Allen suggested, 'the Australians will probably build up to such a point at which we're forced to again defer to the monotonous and inevitable and relinquish our crown.'

Something very like this happened in the winter of 1958/59, some nine months earlier than Allen predicted. The 12th MCC party to Australia set sail that September in what by all accounts was a dangerous mood of over-confidence. In the new Australian captain Richie Benaud's words, 'At a time when some of his players were on the way down rather than the way up, Peter May was ill served by the pre-tour publicity, which listed his team as the greatest ever to leave home shores. They had an enormous amount to live up to and sometimes that kind of adulation can be worse than criticism.'

It seems implausible now, but it took the MCC tourists nearly three weeks to reach Australia. That the necessary *esprit de corps* might be lacking in the side was evident even on board the SS *Iberia*, the only modestly comfortable P&O liner carrying the players on their extended journey, via Port Said, Aden and Bombay, to Fremantle. These were still the socially nuanced days of gentleman and player, and the great yeoman stumper Godfrey Evans, solidly in the latter camp, remembered a moment early on in the voyage when someone incautiously referred to the team captain as 'Peter' and 'got an earful from our manager Freddie Brown in return'. A man of many sterling qualities, Brown was not to everyone's taste as the chief executive of a travelling national sports team on the cusp of the 1960s. Trueman, for one, later referred to him as 'a snob, bad-mannered, ignorant and a bigot', while Laker thought him 'rude to both the press and professional players at the best of times, and like Hitler when he was drunk'.

Other reviews of Brown's man-management weren't as good as these ones.

Laker, as we've seen, was not in the ideal frame of mind in which to spend six months in close proximity to his county and Test captain, and it seems fair to say that May in turn struggled to get the best out of his gifted but delicately wired bowler. Apart from the lingering fallout of the Blackheath affair, there were simmering resentments about the tour's financial arrangements. The professionals each made £625 for the winter, and for the most part weren't pleased to discover that their amateur colleagues would be paid not only expenses but also compensation for loss of their civilian earnings, and that both these sums would be tax-free. Over the coming months Laker would again take the opportunity to remark sardonically that he would have been better off by simply pretending to play for free. One well-placed observer thought that he showed 'a detachment on the tour little short of mutinous'. Laker's mood was not improved when May went on to win £500 from an Australian newspaper for scoring a century in between lunch and tea in a state match at Sydney. Immediately after that, the England captain announced that he had turned himself into a limited company.

In addition to the feudal arrangements off the field, Laker also faced several stiff technical challenges while in Australia. Richie Benaud later confirmed, 'When Jim came out here we were determined to get after him. He'd destroyed us [in 1956], but he'd never played in Australia before and I can assure you he wasn't going to get another wicket like Old Trafford to bowl on. And we did get after him. He took only 15 wickets in the series, which was four less than he managed in a couple of days at Manchester. But even with him bowling on good wickets and the Australians trying their best to knock him out of the game, he still topped the England tour averages, and generally made our guys look like we were batting with our bootlaces tied together. That's not the mark of a good bowler, or even of a very good bowler. It's the mark of an artist, and I don't use the word lightly.'

Writing only a few months after the event, Laker was nonetheless bitterly indignant about his treatment by friend and foe alike in Australia. 'The tour was badly run,' he noted. 'I'm well aware that there have been plenty of bad managers in the past, but I find it difficult to match Freddie Brown. He started wrongly, and never looked back.' After getting that off his chest, Laker had this to say of the travelling press contingent: 'There were two sorts of journalist on the tour: professional writers and famous players of the recent past, sometimes even of the present. In the second class we had Johnny Wardle, Bill Edrich and Hugh Tayfield. I respected Wardle, although he was obliged to indulge in some personal criticism. As far as possible I avoided Edrich and Tayfield, which gives you some idea of what we thought of the truth and relevance of their work.' There was again an only mixed review of Laker's team-mate Trevor Bailey, of whom he wrote at Brisbane, 'He hit 68 in seven hours and 38 minutes. Trevor's 50 took him one minute over six hours – a record of its kind. Limbering up for this mighty achievement, he paused for a mere 45 minutes on 47. He played himself into a stupor.' In later years, when seeing Bailey use his column in the *Financial Times* to take a modern player to task for being too slow, Laker was sometimes apt to wonder if a printer's error might have been involved.

It's fair to say that Laker, a plain-spoken character who had no time for the coddled, weak or hypersensitive, was slightly behind the curve of our contemporary manners. He simply called it as he saw it. He pronounced himself at first 'stunned' and then 'amused' when the tour committee hurriedly sent for 23-year-old Ted Dexter as a replacement. 'Just *why* they wanted Dexter sent out, rather than one of half a dozen more deserving players, I shall never know,' he wrote. 'I can only assume that they fancied a touch of the gay abandon.' Coming in to bowl at a particularly tense moment at Sydney, Laker froze in his delivery stride when out of the corner of his eye he saw Dexter, so impeccably groomed that his northern colleagues sometimes expected him to break into a chorus of 'I Feel Pretty' in the dressing room, merrily practising his golf swing while standing on the square leg boundary. Something about this struck the bowler as not only ill-advised in the context of the match but also 'all too typical of the public-school attitude that assumes cricket is all a bit of a lark', and a contributory factor to the climate of disharmony on the tour as a whole.

For all this, the run-up to the first Test had been relatively encouraging: an unbeaten score of 177 for Graveney in the drawn match against Western Australia; a nine-wicket win at Adelaide, where Laker took 5-31 in 17 tight eight-ball overs in the first innings and 5-70 in the second; figures of 6-74 for Lock in the tourists' 87-run victory over Victoria at Melbourne; a century for May in each innings and, in something of a Surrey triumphal march, wickets for Laker, Lock and Loader in the crushing win over a strong Australian XI at Sydney; and another tidy performance by Laker in a low-scoring draw at the Gabba with Queensland. Following all that the tourists reported back to Brisbane on Friday, 5 December, where play was due to begin that morning in the first Test, to find a municipal brass band marching across the outfield and a large and generally friendly crowd waiting for them under sunny skies, some of the female contingent among whom shouted out endearments and displayed a large banner indicating how positively they would react to any romantic overtures certain named English players might care to make to them, while from the pavilion balcony Lock (he always remembered this detail) looked down on a 'most impressive' parade of younger local schoolgirls, 'all waving away, and in dresses of the most lovely cut'.

Now all that remained was the actual cricket, which did not go well.

Winning the toss and batting, England managed just 134 in their first innings, an inauspicious start to any Ashes series, and one from which it could be argued they never fully recovered. Trevor Bailey top scored with 27, which took him two hours – almost one of those turns of speed beloved of Jeremy Clarkson on *Top Gear* when compared to his next knock, while coming in at number three. Superbly organised in defence, with a stubbornness that generally appealed to his team more than the spectators, 'the Barnacle' was not otherwise greatly gifted as a top-order batsman. Godfrey Evans once remarked of the England dressing room in that same match, 'Peter May was a very nice guy, but not exactly one for the Churchillian speech. There were long silences where you thought he might have offered a little useful advice, and when you wanted him to say nothing he nattered on about things like the dress code for dinner that night, or how to greet the lady wife of the Governor-General at an embassy cocktail do.' One way or another, Brisbane wasn't England's finest hour. Laker took a total of three wickets in the match and Lock just one. Evans was one of the few people who would have chosen to stand up to the latter's bowling, which in terms of raw speed if not always variety shared many of the more uninhibited characteristics of his friend Fred Trueman. Today's keeper would have been crouching halfway back to the boundary. Eventually set 147 to win, Australia knocked off the runs in three hours for the loss of two wickets.

If anything, matters deteriorated in the next Test at Melbourne. Sound enough in their first innings, England again displayed their time-honoured talent for self-destruction in the second. It was a torrid affair; the 70,000-strong crowd were vocally behind the home team, and Tom Graveney's entry with the score on 14/2 displayed some of the same qualities as the arrival of a Christian at lunchtime in the Colosseum. He lasted for eight minutes and three balls before being caught at full stretch by Alan 'the Claw' Davidson at short leg off a rising ball from the seamer Ian Meckiff. Although typically gracious at the time, Graveney later told me, 'Meckiff flung the ball at you like a javelin thrower. It was about as blatant a chuck as you could ever hope for, and made Lock look like a model straight-armer by comparison.' Australia again won, this time with five hours in hand. Laker and Lock took a total of one wicket between them. Adding injury to insult, Godfrey Evans cracked his finger while batting and as a result England had to call up the jockey-sized Roy Swetman for his international debut in the third Test at Sydney, where he scored 41 and five and dropped four catches.

By then, it seemed that Laker was back on the familiar career rollercoaster: triumph, despair, humiliation, heroism and back to despair again before he knew what had hit him. Now approaching his 37th birthday, he increasingly saw himself being treated like a child. 'First, we had to sign a contract which said players weren't allowed to give interviews to the press,' he complained. 'And by "interview" they meant a single quote. So if you were spending five months travelling through Australia with a journalist and at some stage when you were sitting around a hotel pool together he casually asked you "How do you feel about the Test, Jim?" and you answered facetiously "I think I might get a few wickets", you'd have a purple faced Sergeant Major Freddie Brown yelling at you about it first thing in the morning.' As he waded into team meetings or press conferences, Brown's dark side acquired a pathological intensity, with one journalist depicting him as 'a gold-medal boozer and loudmouth ... Sometimes I thought that he was insane. He was certainly a curious choice as his country's cricket ambassador. Perhaps his experience in the war had upset his mind.'

Nor was Laker too happy when the tour management saw fit to issue a somewhat over-full list of rules and regulations about what the team members could drink (beer was okay, but spirits were out), for how long they could do so, and at what hour they were expected to be tucked up in bed with their lights out each night. 'Tour or no tour, contract or not, it seems to me to be damned cheek to tell responsible adults what they may or may not drink,' he wrote, particularly in light of the fact that 'Brown himself single-handedly put about ten points on Johnny Walker's share price that winter.' These seem to have been contributory parts of Laker's growing restiveness about the whole business of continuing to play professional sport as he approached middle age. While on board the *Iberia* on the outward journey to Australia, he'd let it be known that he would be retiring from the first-class game at the end of the 1959 home season, citing both problems with his arthritic spinning finger and 'feeling knackered after traipsing around the world for 12 years', thus earning another Freddie Brown rocket for being so bloody stupid as to make the announcement on the eve of an Ashes series.

The third Test began at Sydney on 9 January 1959. It was drawn. England faced a deficit of 138 on the first innings, but May (92 in 318 minutes) and Cowdrey (100 not out in six hours) shored things up at the end. Laker took 5-107 and 2-10 for the tourists. Lock threw in 4-130 in the first innings, bowling throughout with an even more than usual look of tight-lipped determination on his face, meaning the Surrey pair took 11 wickets between them. It was the best either they or England managed all winter.

After that there was a noticeable falling-off in fighting spirit within the tourists' camp, one not helped by Brown's increasingly fragile PR sense when it came to handling both them and the press, nor by the feeling among certain players that Peter May's visiting fiancée Virginia Gilligan was taking up altogether too much of his time. Things, apparently already at their darkest, then turned black for England when Laker declared himself unfit minutes before the start of play in the fourth Test at Adelaide. 'I had trouble in my swollen spinning finger to the point where I could bend it no more than 30 degrees from the straight,' he wrote in his autobiography. 'Had I played I would have been letting England and myself down.' Godfrey Evans offered an alternative theory. He told me that Laker had 'never quite recovered from his sense of grievance' at being left out of the two previous tours of Australia, nor from his 'permanent state of being pissed off at Peter May', and had 'decided to make his point in the most dramatic way possible'. Whatever the truth of the matter, it brought back all the old canards that Laker wasn't the man for a scrap; that there were days when, as a bowler, he seemed to get the sulks. Either way, Australia won the Test by ten wickets, and May had this to say in his gracious public tribute to his hosts:

> Congratulations to Richie Benaud's team, they were simply better than we were. I felt that with Laker not fit we had to gamble, and it didn't come off. We never got the starts we would have liked and injuries on the tour generally affected our bowling, but I have no excuses to offer.

After that all that remained were the final rites of the fifth Test at Melbourne. It went to form. Laker, who was now sporting a 102-degree temperature, had chosen to play again and took 4-93 without ever threatening to dominate the proceedings. England dropped Lock from the side and brought in the off-spinner John Mortimore of Gloucestershire for the first of his nine Test caps; one unkind local critic wrote that the latter's bowling was equivalent to giving the batsmen 'a mental, almost a physical, catnap'. The omission of a great cricketer is that much more poignant when he's replaced by a mediocre one. This time around, Australia won by nine wickets.

There was an unavoidable touch of the aftermath of the Lord Mayor's Show to the brief tour of New Zealand that followed. England won the first Test, and the second one was rained off as a draw. But the trip wasn't without its interest for the Laker and Lock story. For one thing, Laker refused to go. Four players were due to be trimmed from the original Australian touring party, and he seems to have assumed he would be one of them. On the rest day of the Melbourne Test, May had asked Laker to come to his hotel room. 'I don't mind if it's for a free drink,' he replied wryly. But when he arrived he found Freddie Brown waiting for him. Without any preliminaries, Laker recalled, 'Brown said, "I want you to go to New Zealand." I said, "I'm not going. My finger isn't fit, and I've already done most of my packing."' Brown's face, richly tinted at the best of times, flushed with anger at this response. 'Are you breaking your contract?' he bawled. 'I told you I'm not fit to bowl and I'm not going to,' Laker replied evenly. At 8.30 the next morning, Brown frogmarched his reluctant bowler down to the local hospital, where a doctor took one look and announced, 'You can't play cricket for at least two months, or you'll run the risk of doing yourself permanent damage.' Three days later, Laker was on a flight back to London; he never spoke to Brown, and never played for England, again.

The other 12th-hour drama involved Lock, who had been somewhat out of sorts in Australia, where the *Sunday Mail* critic described his bowling as 'little more than a joke' (if so, it was at least a practical joke, because he took a creditable 57 first-class wickets on the tour, as well as 24 more in New Zealand). But as usual he was delighted to accept the supreme honour of playing for his country wherever possible. On the evening of 6 March 1959, some of the tourists were relaxing at the Wellington home of the recently retired Kiwi seamer Harry Cave, where Ted Dexter takes up the story:

It was all very chummy, and after dinner Harry invited us to watch some home movie footage of the England v New Zealand Test at Lord's the previous summer. The very first frames were slow-motion shots of Tony Lock, which graphically revealed the very bent bowling arm and then the dramatic straightening, i.e. a rank 'throw'. It was common knowledge that Lock's quicker ball was suspect, but these were standard deliveries. Everyone erupted into gales of laughter and loud jeers, in a highly jovial manner overall. It was just a bit of fun, we thought; no big deal. The moment passed, but the next morning at net practice it was a very chastened and hangdog Lock who at first refused to bowl. He was mortified by what he'd seen the night before. When he finally gave in to Peter May's cajoling, he bowled very slow lollipop balls, not worthy of a Junior Colts school match. Tony was obviously completely shattered. He was literally in tears about what had happened. It was a horrible moment.

Another player might have simply retired, but not Lock. Back in England, he once again set about completely remodelling his bowling action. He took himself out of contention for Surrey's first four matches of the 1959 season, but could often be seen during this period hard at work in The Oval's practice nets. Arthur McIntyre sometimes joined him there to keep wicket, and he remembered, 'Tony used all sorts of styles until he hit on the right one. I don't think I've seen a greater trier than Lockie. Sometimes the blood would be pouring from his fingers as he slogged away to get it right.'

On 24 April 1959, at Surrey's 13th-century Cranleigh parish church, England's captain Peter May married his 24-year-old fiancée Virginia Gilligan. For once the sun was shining, the bride wore a full-length white parchment satin dress, and her long train was held in place by two young flower girls each sporting a garland of daisies, while a few reporters advanced huddled together from the general direction of the local pub. By all accounts it was a gloriously English occasion. The Rev. David Sheppard helped to officiate, and there were several current or former Test players on hand, including Colin Cowdrey, Denis Compton, Godfrey Evans, Peter Loader, Tony Lock and the identical Bedser twins, a popular turn at that night's reception. Jim Laker apparently did not receive an invitation. Surrey began their first-class programme the following day against Cambridge University at Fenner's. Alec Bedser captained the side, Lock was still in self-imposed purdah, and Laker took a pedestrian 2-63 in the only completed innings possible. The match was drawn. Both Laker's and his county's season would end in disappointment.

With a view to the future, Surrey had elected to rotate their three primary slow bowlers – Laker, Lock and Eric Bedser – that year, playing only one or at most two of them at a time. Sound in principle, the strategy soon led to trouble in a dressing room characterised by private grievances and bruised egos. Lock came back in the middle of May, and was not pleased to stroll over to the team sheet stuck on the dressing room wall just before the start of play one morning and only then discover that his services weren't required that day. Alec Bedser was there, and remembered, 'Tony [had] sauntered up, happy as a lark, assuming he was going out to bowl in a few minutes' time, and at that point I saw him look the list up and down and visibly recoil. It was like he'd been struck an actual blow in the face. He left the ground a minute later and that was the last we saw of him for the day.' Lock himself could still recall the incident 30 years later, though giving it a diplomatic spin: 'I considered this a great injustice to me as I was ready to play and had told the captain I was fit to do so, but I thought it best to submit.'

Something similar happened when Surrey came to play Yorkshire at The Oval in a championship match starting on 13

218

June. Laker wrote of this, 'May walked into the dressing room, and pinned the side up on the board. He would have left, as he had entered, without a word, had I not been standing between him and the door. As he walked past me he said just five words, "I've dropped you for today." Just that – and out he went. Not a word of explanation. Not even a private chat beforehand ... An atmosphere quickly developed in the Surrey dressing room that year.'

Lock at least still had time on his side, but Laker was especially bitter to be treated as surplus baggage during his 14th and final season at the club. 'England had washed their hands of me, and I was going out with a basic £800 salary from [Surrey], and little or nothing else. My day was done.' So no lucrative IPL contract offer, no sponsorship and no rewards. Just a mid-level office job to look forward to somewhere, and the immutable fact that he had once been the most famous sportsman in Britain.

At the age of 30, Lock was slowly groping his way back to form. He suffered the indignity of playing several games for the Surrey reserves, but, emboldened by talk of an England recall, steadily built up steam during the second half of the season. He came off the field at The Oval on a baking late July day after taking five cheap wickets against the touring Indians, covered in sweat but triumphant as he passed through the crowd. The former Surrey and England all-rounder Percy Fender was one of those sitting in front of the pavilion as Lock, 'the last of the great left-armers', delivered his verdict on the occasion, looking exultantly back at the packed ground where the fans stood cheering him to the rafters.

'They love their Tony,' he said, thinking aloud.

They certainly did. Whether Lock was now a middle-aged man of easy-going charm, comfortable in his own skin, or a brittle permanent-adolescent type of almost pathological sensitivity, as some thought, is less clear, but of one thing we can be sure: he was, to the tips of his fingers, a supremely dedicated professional cricketer. The 22-year-old Peter Parfitt was then just settling in to the Middlesex side, and came to know Lock well when touring with him for MCC and England. 'He was a great team man, never gave up, and quite a complex guy in his way. I mean, *very* serious on the field, absolutely gutted if a catch went down or the umpire said no, and then a total lad once he was back in the dressing room or down the pub afterwards. I'm not a psychiatrist, but you could just about make a case for saying he was slightly schizophrenic. A bit of a contradiction, anyway.' Other sources remember Lock during this period as a friendly, humorous and generous after-hours companion, if occasionally something of a bore when he discoursed on the events of the day. Even Laker, who kept his distance socially, thought him 'the first person you wanted next to you in the trenches', and invariably leapt to his team-mate's defence whenever the question of throwing arose. The daytime and the nighttime versions of Lock, and also the myth-making that tended to surround him, came into sharp and mildly comic relief in Surrey's match against Yorkshire at Bradford in the middle of July 1959. Laker, who wasn't playing, had this to say of the occasion:

> Tony, I remember, was to stay with his friend Ray Illingworth during the game. The night before, he was delayed and had to knock up his host, who had gone to bed, at about two in the morning. Later that same morning, Lock bowled Illingworth first ball.

It's a good story, and presumably the reason it stuck in Laker's mind is because it neatly conveys the two Locks, the gregarious party animal and the hardened professional sportsman. I once asked Illingworth about the incident in question, and he confirmed, 'Tony did me first ball.' It's possible that both these stalwart England off-spinners simply confused the sequence of events, however, or that their memories spoke more to the Lock legend than to the actual facts, because *Wisden* reports: July 1959. Park Avenue Ground, Bradford. Yorkshire v Surrey. R. Illingworth c. Clark b. Loader 11 in the first innings, and c. A.V. Bedser b. Loader 9 in the second.

Despite losing twice to Surrey that season, Yorkshire went on to unseat them at the top of the County Championship. The title changed hands in dramatic fashion. Yorkshire went down to play Sussex at Hove over the sunlit August bank holiday knowing that the points from an outright victory would assure them of the pennant. Any other outcome would not necessarily end their hopes, but meant that they had to rely on Surrey losing at home to Middlesex. At the death Yorkshire were left to score 215 in just 105 minutes. After the first over the total was 15. After quarter of an hour it was 40/2 and, apparently thinking it might be an opportune moment to step things up, the visitors then put on 141 for the third wicket at a rate of three runs a minute. By that stage Sussex had lost control of the game, giving one of those performances in the field that was so bad it was perversely enjoyable, each successive long hop or dropped catch bringing 'a fresh round of satirical mirth from the ale tent', according to the *Argus*. Yorkshire had seven minutes and five wickets in hand when Illingworth, their number six, made the winning hit, their first outright championship title since 1946. They had earned it.

Surrey meanwhile drew with their London rivals at The Oval, where Lock redux took nine wickets with his third and latest bowling style. It was the end of an era. Peter May again paid gracious tribute to the better side, something of which he had a depressingly wide experience that year, while Laker thought it was all to do with a lack of proper team spirit at The Oval, as well as the fact that 'Bert Lock was under orders [from] Lord's to make better wickets, and it became rare for Surrey to produce a turner.' The spin twins played for the last time in tandem against

Northamptonshire at The Oval early in September. Laker took one wicket and Lock, further suggesting that he was well and truly rehabilitated, took ten. The game was drawn.

'There were not many cheers when Jim Laker finally left The Oval after playing for Surrey for 14 seasons,' Laker himself wrote the following year, in a memoir that was as notable for its rancour as its occasional use of the third person. 'It's not for me to tell in detail now of my record over those years,' he continued. 'Suffice it to say, frankly, that I am proud of it and will never cease to be. But candidly, I was not so proud of Surrey's farewell to me. It would have been nice to have had a letter of appreciation from the club president, Lord Monckton. It would have taken little effort. It would have cost no more than a stamp. I got no such letter. That wasn't all. A week after I left, the club held a cocktail party for players and their wives. I was not invited, even though I was still technically on the books until the end of the year.

'I can only offer one clue to treatment that seemed to me more than slightly off-hand. I had resigned – I didn't wait to be sacked. That put me in bad odour with Surrey. To them the professional would seem to be very much a paid lackey who bowls when he is told to bowl, then, when the match ends, is forgotten until the next. They have little time for you off the field. Once a player has finished his active cricket they could hardly be less interested in him.'

It's quite easy to get depressed thinking of a once great cricketer having to scratch a living outside of the game, although at least in Laker's case he seems to have driven away from The Oval in his trusty grey Morris on the evening of 4 September 1959 without so much as a backward glance of regret. Somehow it seems only fitting that he should have chosen to hang up his spikes at the end of the old decade rather than staying to witness the era of swinging social etiquette, heightened sexual promise and increasingly silly shirts that characterised the 1960s. Even as a young man he'd been a bit of an old fogey. Nowadays he tended to shuffle around in his usual neat but shopworn suit, a biro or two still on display in his top pocket, very much the image of an Englishman of the old school, outwardly genial and inwardly reserved. He had a new 'all Swiss' gold watch presented as a parting gift from Surrey (it was stamped 'Made in Taiwan' on the reverse), but little else in the way of personal ostentation. One Christmas, he was delighted when his wife gave him a book token and some woolly socks – his idea of wonderfully practical gifts.

Even in retirement, Laker's life still revolved around routine. He was always up early, whatever the season, walked the family dog, read the *Express,* listened to the Home Service, and drank copious amounts of tea. He enjoyed a cocktail or two in the evening, but forsook anything more chemically potent than the occasional Disprin. He was known to sing along to his favourite show tunes in a karaoke-like style. He was also famously happily married, with two well-adjusted, sporty young daughters. Laker seemed to have it all, but in a grave misstep he put his name to an instant memoir, a familiar enough tactic for a retired cricketer, but one that in his case strayed from the usual, uncontroversial formula of wallowing in a jacuzzi of nostalgic reveries and affectionate pen portraits of friends and colleagues, and instead seemed to be dipped in vitriol. As a result, he set himself up as an inviting target for critics, and was effectively sent to Siberia by the authorities at Lord's and The Oval.

While Laker worked on his book and helped run a ladies' dress shop in south London with his wife Lilly, Lock joined Surrey's brief off-season tour of Rhodesia. He took 15 wickets there in two matches. The home captain David Lewis, who'd played university cricket in England, remembered of this visit: 'Tony seemed dimly aware that there were ten other Surrey players on the field besides him, but he was so highly wound up it was as though he operated as a one-man demolition team. When he bowled he carried on right down the pitch to you, hands stretched out wide like a couple of buckets ready to collect the ball, and he always seemed to cover great swathes of the park anywhere from about gully to square leg. You felt you were playing extra opponents when he was around. Back in the pub he was friendly enough, liked a drop, usually let you know what was on his mind. He referred to Jim Laker as "that bowler". It was clearly a love–hate match. "I don't know if we'll ever see that bowler again," he said. "Some of the boys never want to see him. We didn't even see him much last season. That's all right. On his day he was still the greatest bloody bowler of his kind in the world. No one could top him.'"

Summarising these remarks, Lewis said, 'Tony was a constant bolt of energy, while Jim was temperamentally cool, reserved, cautious, amazingly patient, but in the end a bit stubborn and inflexible. No wonder they were work-mates rather than friends.'

* * *

Probably the first thing to say about Jim Laker's incendiary memoir *Over to Me* is that its author, whoever it was, could really write. Books put out by sportsmen about their careers are usually, in the words of the football reporter Brian Glanville, 'disingenuous ghosted pap'. It remains a matter of debate whether Laker engaged the services of a ghost for *Over to Me*, but the book was published in his name and, whatever else, you could never accuse it of excessive pap. Its author was fearless in his denunciation of the second-rate but, at the same time, he celebrated all that was worth celebrating. And he clearly knew what he was talking about, too, which helped.

Why did Laker write it? On one level, for the money. Shaped by a childhood of uncertainty, he rarely passed up a chance to feather his nest. Like almost all professional cricketers of the day, Laker was far from a wealthy man. He'd had a successful benefit season in 1956, but he qualified even this comparative windfall by later writing of his testimonial match at The Oval, 'The gate receipts for the game were £800, and the expenses were £1,200. If I hadn't insured myself against rain, I would have had to pay Surrey £400 out of my own pocket.' As it turned out, Laker's book more than fulfilled his commercial hopes for it. Even in those days, most celebrity memoirs tended to get politely noticed in the trade before going on to a long and peaceful retirement in the bargain bins. *Over to Me* did altogether better business, quickly selling out its first run of 9,000 copies and ultimately netting its author around £3,000, some £28,000 today, which was more than twice what he'd earned in a typical season for Surrey.

Another reason Laker pulled the pin on his literary hand grenade in May 1960 was one of pure revenge. While there were plenty of astute sketches of fellow cricketers and perceptive remarks on the game as a whole to be found in *Over to Me*, the takeaway theme of the book was that of the smell of bridges burning behind it. The entire 75,000-word text was strewn with the anger, the bile and above all the sense of injustice Laker had accumulated over the previous 13 years as what he called a 'lackey' of Surrey and England. Doug Insole once told me that Laker had shown him the advance proofs of the book 'and I said, "You've come up with some pretty strong stuff," and at that point Jim admitted that he hadn't personally written, or even read, every word, but that nonetheless it was an accurate reflection of his honest views on certain matters.' Laker went on to inform Insole that he 'intended to follow Shakespeare's immortal advice on these occasions, and "publish and be damned"', which was all sound enough, even if the adage is traditionally credited to the first Duke of Wellington.

Shrewd as he was as an observer of the wider trends in cricket, Laker proved less gifted when it came to an objective assessment of his own career, not least when rehearsing his many criticisms of the English game's ruling elite. His list of grievances about the 1958/59 Australian tour, in particular, was long – very long. We've already noted Laker's reservations about his manager Freddie Brown and captain Peter May, which were one thing, but some of his comments on his fellow professionals crossed the line from the merely acerbic into that less attractive world of the bitchy. One such barb resulted in a formal complaint, and the subsequent statement by *Over to Me*'s publishers:

> Frederick Muller Ltd. wish to note on behalf of themselves and Mr. Laker that Mr. W.J. 'Bill' Edrich is, in their opinion, a highly responsible and skilled cricket journalist, and the text of the book has now been amended to remove any possibility of misunderstanding about this point.

Some of *Over to Me*'s critics were as displeased with it as Edrich was, and both Brian Statham and Denis Compton were among those who considered legal action. Taken as a whole, the entire 238-page book read as a protracted suicide note in terms of its author's future welcome, if any, in the average county dressing room. In an extraordinary turnaround, Laker now found himself ostracised not only by the game's entrenched elite, but also by many of those who had either watched or played with or against him in the recent past. One way or another, it was a precipitous fall from grace for a man who had been hailed as a national hero only four years earlier.

To say that the MCC were displeased at the book's contents would be an understatement broadly on the order of noting that the United Kingdom had had a small misunderstanding with Germany in the years 1939–45. Laker's honorary membership of the club was promptly revoked, while the prevailing mood music at Surrey was one of almost Wagnerian malevolence. At a meeting of the county's general committee on 18 May 1960, chaired by Laker's old friend Errol Holmes, and attended by, among others, Jack Hobbs, Alf Gover and the club secretary Commander Babb, it was noted:

> With reference to J. C. Laker's recent book, the President has now read all the contents and has approved the wording of a letter to be sent to Laker. The committee considered this draft and agreed that it should be sent by hand to Laker forthwith and a copy released to the Press.

The letter in question went out that same day over Babb's signature, and is worth quoting in full if only for the faint but discernible whiff of contempt, or at the very least its lack of any residual goodwill, towards the county's recently retired employee.

> Dear Laker,
> The Surrey Committee has carefully considered your book and in particular its attacks upon the M.C.C., the Surrey Club and a large number of individuals in the cricket world.
> The Committee particularly deplores your criticism of many of your team mates and others at the Oval who have worked so hard to ensure the success of your benefit of over £10,000. There have been other books recently which lovers of cricket have regarded as harmful and in bad taste, but in the opinion of the Committee yours has done a greater disservice than any of them.
> In the circumstances, I am instructed to inform you that the right of entry to the Oval given by your Pass has been withdrawn.
> The Committee feels that it is necessary to make its attitude quite plain to its Members and the cricket public. It is therefore sending a copy of this letter to the Press.

Laker always felt uneasy about venting anger or making an egotistical show of protest, as opposed to retreating into a morose silence. Even as a child, he'd learned to camouflage his displeasure behind a studied calm. Yet this stinging blow rankled, as he admitted when he said, 'I am completely unrepentant … My only regret is that Surrey should have taken such action without asking for a response from me. Even a man on trial for his life is entitled to a hearing.' Laker went on to write to the MCC offering to donate every penny he earned from sales of *Over to Me* 'to the furtherance of the cause of cricket in any part of the world' – and presumably also that of his own rehabilitation – a proposal they rejected. Perhaps the very fact of Surrey's pettiness in revoking Laker's free pass served to prove his point that 'All I did in my book was to offer criticism of what I thought was wrong, especially the fact that the counties don't treat their professional employees as they ought.' As a direct consequence, the man who had achieved the greatest bowling performance of all time, and taken some 1,400 wickets for Surrey along the way, would now be obliged to line up and pay half a crown at the turnstiles in the event he fancied watching cricket at The Oval or any of the county's other grounds. Nor, unsurprisingly, would there be any mention of Laker's name in the 1960 Queen's Birthday Honours, or at any other time in the remaining 26 years of his life.

Perhaps the most balanced verdict on the whole affair came from the poet and journalist Alan Ross in *The Observer*. He was not uninhibitedly in the Laker camp. Ross wrote, 'He quotes Oscar Wilde's "the truth is rarely pure and never simple" to justify a string of personal disparagements sometimes barely short of libel … It makes one wish that professional cricketers would get themselves better literary advisers, with more of an eye on their client's reputation and less of a one on sensation and short-term financial success.'

But Ross also spotted a truth the luminaries at Lord's and The Oval had chosen to overlook; it wasn't so much Laker and his book on trial, as it was the whole system.

'Somehow, as so often before with professional cricketers, it's all ended in bitterness. Why? The answer lies, I think, in the curiously obsolescent fashion in which professionals are still treated. They are not, as should be the case with a person of Laker's eminence, regarded as part of the upper hierarchy but simply as one of the paid staff for whom, rather as with a Non Commissioned Officer, too much knowledge is deemed to be a bad thing.'

As it happened, Laker wasn't the only Surrey and England spin bowler to be adversely affected by *Over to Me*'s publication. Tony Lock had now cut his speed but restored the loop to his bowling action, and duly took 9-102 in Surrey's opening match of 1960. This was an auspicious start, because it was also his benefit season. Bowling some 1,200 overs, Lock would take a further 139 first-class wickets during a summer unfavourable for spin. We needn't dwell on the individual details of each match, except to say that in one three-week purple patch in June he took ten wickets against Nottinghamshire at Trent Bridge; seven more the following week away to Worcestershire; a haul of 6-90 in an innings against Kent at The Oval; 5-74 away to Essex; and 3-45 and 4-26 at home to Hampshire, before running riot against Oxford University at Guildford, where he added 12 more wickets, including that of the future India captain 'Tiger' Pataudi in both innings, as well as taking a handful of reflex catches while squatting more or less under the batsman's nose and throwing in a brutal cameo of 13 off five balls faced. One way or another, Lock wasn't the sort of player to lapse into anonymous inactivity. His messianic self-belief and need to be in the thick of the fray almost seemed like an addiction. The veteran cricket writer Derek Hodgson remembered Lock being hit in the head while fielding against Gloucestershire that season. 'Tony had to be helped off, spitting blood and teeth on the ground as he went, though refusing to go to hospital. He was sitting in the pavilion, being revived, when he noticed that Eric Bedser, who bowled off spin, had turned his first delivery a long way. Lock, still groggy, leapt up, insisted on returning to the field, demanded the ball and took six wickets in 15 balls.'

Yet when all the figures were added up that autumn, Lock's benefit reaped just £3,700, which was a third of what Laker had managed four years earlier. It was the lowest such return for any Surrey player since the war. In a future book, Laker wrote of this, 'No one player in my time deserved a benefit more than Tony, yet when it came it proved to be something of a disaster. His tremendous efforts for the county should have been rewarded with the sort of sum that had come the way of Alec Bedser and myself.'

There were several contributory factors to this outcome. It was another dismally wet summer, for one, and Surrey had now fallen far enough from their 1950s pedestal to finish only seventh in the final championship table. But some observers thought there was another explanation. With all the hostile publicity directed against Laker, the theory went, it was not the ideal moment for the public to be asked to reward the player's long-time bowling partner. This guilt-by-association scenario may sound dubious at best, or hopelessly speculative at worst, but it had one significant backer: Lock himself, who wrote, 'I fancy I caught the backlash from Jim's book. He had let his hair down in print on his retirement, and as a result the public weren't exactly enamoured with temperamental star cricketers … I was shocked when my benefit was the smallest one for years. I had overcome two crises, an operation on my knee and the throwing shemozzle, and I was banking on security from a good payday.'

On the rest day of a late-August championship match at The Oval, Lock went back to play for his native Oxted & Limpsfield in a game against a Present & Past Surrey XI he invited down to help raise funds. The visitors fielded a strong side that included the Bedser twins, Peter Loader, Micky Stewart, Roy Swetman and the young John Edrich. A crowd of 2,000 endured a mixture of sunshine and showers to watch a keenly fought contest that produced 416 runs in just over four hours' play and ended in a narrow win for the Surrey side. Laker did not participate in the day's proceedings. Whether he wasn't invited or instead chose not to make himself available is a moot point. Lock never commented on the matter one way or another, at least in public, though once the final fruits of his benefit were totted up he wrote to Alec Bedser, 'I can't understand why this streak of bad luck should come my way when that bowler [Laker] made a fortune.' In other correspondence, he sometimes elongated the term 'that bowler' by adding a choice adjective.

It must have seemed cruelly unjust to Lock that while he still struggled to make a living playing cricket at Surrey, his old team-mate was raking in the money from a book roundly criticising the club. While the one man was 'cursed with bad luck', the other one seemed to move through his charmed life 'piling up the cheques from the newspapers and sponsors' even in his controversial second career. Time would moderate Lock's view of his former county colleague, but in the charged atmosphere of September 1960 he felt that he'd been poorly compensated for his years of untiring service, while 'that bowler' was essentially rewarded for his self-promotion.

7

Salvaging the Wreckage

ON THE evening of Friday, 16 June 1961, 31-year-old Tony Lock, wearing his usual ill-fitting grey suit and a pair of well-scuffed brown suede shoes, stepped down from a Southern Region train pulling into London's Victoria station, which was packed with visitors arriving in the capital for a night's entertainment and with commuters departing in the other direction. The train itself was painted royal blue and green, with a thin cream stripe, and consisted of four carriages, a second-class at each end with a third- and first-class in the middle. Lock travelled third-class. He'd spent the previous three days helping Surrey win a county match against Sussex at Hove, where he took three wickets in the first innings and five in the second, as well as scoring a typically robust 61 not out. As a batsman he remained vulnerable to high-class spin and his defensive limitations always made his innings unpredictable, but in the words of Micky Stewart, who captained Surrey that season whenever Peter May was absent, 'Tony was worth his weight in gold because he could turn the course of a game in half an hour.'

Lock did not linger after alighting from the train that warm Friday evening at Victoria. Just 20 minutes later he was climbing out of a taxi to step through the Grace Gates four miles away at Lord's. By that time the light was fading but still playable. Lock patted down what remained of his hair, buttoned the jacket of his rumpled suit – the reflex of many professional cricketers in that hallowed spot – passed through the back door of the pavilion at a trot, and prepared to launch a charm offensive against Gubby Allen.

The invitation to a private Test trial with England's august chairman of selectors was almost certainly the result of Peter May's enthusiastic report describing his county colleague's determined efforts to completely remodel his bowling action. The throwing issue was more than usually germane just then, because Allen had recently joined with Don Bradman to draft new international guidelines on the matter. When Australia toured England in 1961, it was agreed that no bowler whose action was thought suspect would be included in either team. As a result, Lock now needed to pass his chairman's personal inspection, which was primarily a technical bowling one, but also to establish that he was 'the sort of chap who could represent his country without incident', as Allen privately put it, before any possible return to Test colours.

'It was a little unreal,' said John Murray, the Middlesex and now England wicketkeeper, who was called on to hurriedly join the small party who assembled at the Lord's Nursery End nets in the midsummer twilight. 'Lockie took off his jacket and tie, but was still wearing his suit bottoms over a pair of gym shoes. A couple of the lads from the ground staff, one right-handed and the other left-handed, took turns batting. I did my best behind the stumps. Allen took up position at about silly mid-off, with old Jim Swanton, I remember, and one or two other nobs, obviously clocking Tony's action.' It must have gone reasonably well, because Murray recalled that at one point Swanton had shouted out 'Plumb, sir!' with Dickensian gusto.

After a few minutes, Allen challenged Lock to a specific test. Pulling an elegant handkerchief from the top pocket of his City suit and laying this on the wicket, the chairman of selectors invited his grey-trousered bowler to pitch the ball on it as many times in a row as he could. Lock duly sent around 20 balls at the target, hitting it with about three-quarters of them and narrowly missing with the others. 'Anyone who happened to have walked by and seen us would have thought we were bonkers,' Murray recalled. 'By then you could barely see your hand in front of your face, but Lockie kept firing them in time after time, right on the mark, while the old boys off to the side stood there making their very pukka, Varsity Match remarks –"*Bowled*, that man!" – until Tony finally slipped in a short one that bloody nearly knocked the poor batsman's block off. That concluded the evening's entertainment.'

At 11 the next morning, Lock was back in action for Surrey against Yorkshire at The Oval. He took nine wickets in the match, and held four typically deft catches. On the rest day, he learned he had been recalled to the England side to meet Australia in the second Test at Lord's. It was his first appearance for his country since March 1959, an interval of more than two and a quarter years. Perhaps as a result, there was a certain amount of anticipation when he came on to bowl early on the second day of the Test with the tourists on 112/4 in reply to England's 206 all out. The colourful *Daily Telegraph* columnist Ron Roberts wrote of the occasion:

> Defiantly rolling up his sleeve – he used to have it buttoned at the wrist – to show no offending kink at the elbow, he wheeled his left arm over in a nice, unbroken arc. The ball did not whip through, in consequence, with its old venom, but length and direction were good, and not a run was yielded by him before lunch.

In short, Lock was back, having reinvented himself as the bowler's bowler. He may not have routinely beaten the bat by sheer pace or malevolence of bounce anymore, but he had the newly acquired virtues of control and consistency. He bowled 26 wicketless but immaculately tight overs at Lord's, of which half were maidens, and kept his place for two of the three remaining matches of the series, which Australia won 2-1 to retain the Ashes. Gubby Allen wrote at the end of it, 'G.A.R. Lock never cared to bowl at a standard below the very best of which he is capable.' It was to be the start of a seven-year-long Indian summer for England's mercurial left-armer, and included probably the most consistently polished performances of his career.

Jim Laker, by contrast, played no serious cricket in 1961, other than lending his services to charity with a few Sunday afternoon matches for the Lord's Taverners. Instead, he kept his hand in with a regular column in the *Daily Sketch*, which he delivered, invariably punctually, written out in neat longhand, each Tuesday and Thursday afternoon. That wasn't all when it came to Laker's literary efforts that summer. Just 16 months after *Over to Me* came a new book, chiefly on the Australian tour but also offering a range of opinions on other subjects, which began on a note of contrition and ended with the wry comment, 'I feel I can now give this advice to future cricket writers: complete your career before going into print, and most emphatically take your time to publish a book which will truly be the work of the author's name on the cover.'

The 200-odd pages in between these two statements contained some radical ideas filtered through a conservative sensibility. Laker was an early advocate of one-day cricket, for instance, wanted teams to step things up in general with a minimum bowling rate of 100 balls an hour, and even suggested introducing penalties against slow-scoring batsmen. But he still thought cricketers should first and foremost be ambassadors of their sport, hated the idea that they might be turned into human advertising boards by corporate sponsors, and deplored the creeping trend for players to be seen slouching around in 'casual trousers and sandals'. Any such sign of weakness was the quickest way for an opponent to size you up and take advantage, he felt, besides which a cricketer owed it to the paying public to always give it his best effort.

'That was my motto in 13 years as a professional,' he added.

* * *

In 1961/62 an England team under Ted Dexter toured India, Pakistan and Ceylon, playing 24 first-class matches including eight Tests. Lock was one of the side's acknowledged successes, with a total of 59 wickets at 23 apiece. But statistics tell only half the story when cricketers find themselves thrown into close proximity with one another for four or five months at a time in often profoundly trying circumstances. What counts most is spirit. Lock scored here, too, because Dexter would remember, 'Tony was a great man to have with you in that part of the world, where things can become pretty ropy (dodgy transport, accommodation, food, etc). He would willingly bowl all day, and often came off at the close pink in the face and covered in bright red dust from head to toe. One of the most agreeable customs on tour was to decorate the best all-round performer at the end of the day with a garland of flowers. Tony must have been the man honoured at least 80 per cent of the time.'

It's sometimes curious to be reminded that this fearsome individualist was also a tireless team player. Peter Parfitt of Middlesex was also on the tour. 'Tony was absolutely the guy you wanted at your side,' he told me. 'He'd walk, actually jog, out at the start, grab the ball and you'd have to eventually wrench it away from him again to ever give him a rest. It was a little like taking a bone from a dog. Then he was always the life and soul of the party back at the hotel. As soon as he arrived he'd clown around, and people responded in kind. He'd sing comic songs, tell army jokes, do impressions, or even recite limericks of his own composition. Tony was quite a childish man in some ways, and I say that in the nicest sense. In my experience he was either shouting with joy or crying with frustration. He didn't do neutral.'

It always mystified Lock that there could be any doubt as to his rightful place in the England side. 'There was no other left-arm bowler in my league in the world,' he once remarked, truthfully enough, if for once throwing modesty to the wind. Like Laker, he never quite got over the sense of precariousness that seemed to linger like a cold mist over his international career. Lock's name was missing in May 1962 when Ted Dexter's MCC side took on the touring Pakistanis at Lord's, usually a good sign of the selectors' intentions for the coming series, but to some surprise he was back for the summer's first Test at Edgbaston. England won by an innings, and Lock acquitted himself well enough with five wickets. But he had a sorry time of it in the next Test at Lord's, of which Dexter wrote:

> Came a lull in the speed of falling wickets and the crowd began to chant, 'We want Lock, we want Tony Lock!' Now against my better judgement, Lock had been included in the side. He did not get to bowl in the first innings and when this cry went up in the second I thought, fatally, 'We're here to entertain them, I'll give Lock a bowl.' I didn't like his first over very much but I reasoned, 'Well, I've put him on and I can't just take him off again, it would be an insult to a great cricketer.' So I let him go on and the more he bowled the bigger thrashing he got.

Lock's figures were 0-78 off 14 overs, and Dexter told me that he and his fellow selectors hadn't lingered long when it came to dropping him for the next Test at Headingley. He was then recalled again at Trent Bridge, before being axed once more for the summer's final Test at The Oval. He could count himself unlucky not to have played on his native turf, where Illingworth and Allen turned the ball square in the second innings and the England close fielding was often untidy and sometimes downright inept, a state of affairs Lock would never have tolerated. Over the course of the wet summer he took 108 first-class wickets, only six of them in the Tests, at a cost of 26 apiece. Surrey finished fifth in a championship race again won by Yorkshire.

Laker seems to have come to question the merits of a life now largely devoted to selling ladies' dresses and writing books, meanwhile, because in February 1962, in the same week he celebrated his 40th birthday, he wrote to the Surrey committee volunteering his services to play as an amateur in the coming season. Had the county accepted his offer it might have raised the delicate question of whether their star bowler would even be allowed into The Oval without first paying his entrance fee at the gate, but in the end there was no problem: the committee turned him down flat. Two years after the publication of *Over to Me*, its author remained in officially imposed exile, an MCC sub-committee recording on 2 August 1962 that while it looked with favour on the matter of distinguished overseas players joining their club, it was 'not inclined to reinstate J.C. Laker as an honorary cricket member'.

No one at Lord's or The Oval wanted him. But Trevor Bailey, the captain-secretary at Essex, had seen enough of Laker over the years to continue to look on him as 'probably the greatest off-spinner the world has known', rather than merely the author of a poorly received memoir. As one or two of the book's most stinging blows had been aimed at Bailey himself, it was magnanimous of him to act as he now did.

'I was speaking at a sporting dinner with Jim in Manchester and we travelled back together by train the following morning,' Bailey remembered. 'Over a very good breakfast I casually mentioned that

Essex were short of a spin bowler and was he interested in helping us out? To my delight and surprise, he agreed to play a few games for us as an amateur and we duly registered him.'

Bailey must have acted swiftly in the matter, because Laker himself later recalled the same conversation in slightly different terms. 'Trevor made a good sales pitch, so much so that when I picked up the *Daily Express* the next morning I was surprised to discover that I had been signed to play for him as an amateur.' Whatever the truth of the affair, the deal nearly foundered at a stormy meeting of Essex members held in Chelmsford on 23 March 1962. Pat Marshall of the *Express* wrote, 'Several of the attendees walked out. Others said that this decision would lead to resignations. One man took to the stage to say that he hoped the MCC would refuse to allow Laker's registration, [and] there was general applause at the sentiment.'

The matter seems to have been settled in Laker's favour only by the intervention of Arnold Quick, the Essex treasurer, who pointed out the salient fact that the county was effectively bankrupt 'and we sorely need this player's drawing power'. Years later, Bailey recalled, 'It was hard to accept the criticism because I had acquired a very great cricketer and personality for little more than petrol money. It was like signing George Best at the end of his career and persuading him to turn out for nothing.'

Laker made his Essex debut on 12 May 1962, against Derbyshire on a seaming pitch at Ilford. It was a modest start; he took 2-74 in the first innings, and didn't bowl in the second. The visitors won by seven wickets. *Wisden* reported, 'Laker did well, but had no luck.' His new team-mates saw him as someone who was quietly self-confident rather than aggressively histrionic. 'He basically kept the same poker face whether seeing a catch go down or taking a wicket,' Bailey remembered. 'Merely having him in the side was enough of an inspiration.' Laker once used the arrival at the crease at Romford of his old friend Tom Graveney – then scoring a century roughly every other match – to put on a characteristic show of aplomb. 'Don't worry about him,' Laker muttered to the close field as the batsman approached. 'He won't last an over. He doesn't fancy off spin.' Graveney duly shuffled around the crease for his first three balls and Laker bowled him with his fourth one.

There was something typical about this performance. As Bailey remarked, the 40-year-old veteran still clung to the quiet confidence – 'a sort of dry stoicism' – he'd acquired as a young man. Nothing seemed to fluster him very much. Laker was in the middle of playing another match at Worcester in August 1962 when a messenger arrived at the dressing room door with a telegram for him from the MCC. Taking it and handing the boy sixpence, he read the contents without even a twitch. Finally, he put the envelope in his pocket and said to his team-mates, 'You know, I think it's beginning to turn out there.' At first, nobody dared to ask him the question on everyone's mind, but then Brian Taylor, the Essex wicketkeeper, screwed up the courage. 'What did Lord's say, Jim?' 'Still out indefinitely,' Laker answered evenly. Then he gestured towards the pitch and said, 'I fancy having a go this afternoon.' Sure enough he took three cheap wickets in the session, and to the watching *Daily Mail* correspondent, 'It [was] quite clear he would have strolled back into the Test side again if it was chosen solely on merit.'

Laker took 51 wickets in only 12 matches that season, and pronounced himself quietly pleased with the outcome. He was even happier at the news that winter of the final abolition of English cricket's gentleman and player status. 'It's the best thing to have happened to the game in my lifetime … I'd rather doff my cap to a professional like Len Hutton than an undeserving amateur,' Laker wrote, before giving a broader statement of personal principles. 'One respects a man in life for what he does rather than who he is.'

In the end Laker played three seasons at Essex, adding a further 111 wickets to his career total in the process. He rarely seethed with enthusiasm for the job, and as a general rule padded mournfully out to the middle at the start of play each day looking as though his pet dog had just been run over. The teenaged Keith Fletcher was just coming into the county side in 1962. 'Jim was a big bloke with great, beefy hands, a definite plus if you're a spinner,' England's future captain told me. 'He was still a class act as a player. As a man, he tended to keep to himself. There was never a lot of obvious excitement going on from his quarter. He'd watch the young lads in the nets sometimes, and you couldn't tell from his expression whether he was favourably impressed or not. He was one of those blokes who equate silence with strength. Lesser bowlers would break into a war dance when they took a wicket, while Jim just shrugged, hitched up his flannels and stood there waiting for the next man. I think "dry" is the word I'm looking for.'

One mild curiosity of Laker's time at Essex is that for one reason or another he missed all six opportunities to represent his new county against Surrey. He may have had his differences with The Oval authorities, but he later wrote that he 'never want[ed] to be in a position of doing anything to harm the club where it was my honour to play for so long'.

* * *

On 14 July 1962, Tony Lock took the field for Surrey in an away match against Gloucestershire. He took five cheap wickets in the first innings and two more in the second. Despite these figures, and the evidence of a numerically successful season as a whole, his name was missing the following week when the MCC announced their winter tour party under Ted Dexter's captaincy to Australia. Lock was beyond disappointed at the news. He was inconsolable. Peter Parfitt saw him on the night of the team's announcement and remembers, 'We went out to dinner and Tony was literally in tears. He just couldn't understand it. "Why?" he kept asking, like a child who'd just been told that Christmas was cancelled. It was awful.'

A day or two later, Tom Graveney saw Lock in the lobby of the Nottingham hotel where they were both staying while, poignantly enough, representing England in the summer's fourth Test against Pakistan. 'He told me that he just couldn't get his head around the fact that he suddenly wasn't considered one of the best 17 cricketers in the country, and I fell back on the usual lines about persistence being its own reward, and that the man who expected loyalty from the England selectors was in for a long wait. Tony's only reply, which he hissed at me with a slightly odd look in his eyes, was "Don't I fucking know that?"'

Lock was not pleased, then. Perhaps the selectors still had doubts about his ability at that level – his Test wickets since refurbishing his action had been noticeably more expensive than before – if not about his particular effectiveness on Australian pitches. If so, it was a curious turn of events in the light of what followed. In September, Lock appeared in the last Gentlemen v Players match, where he took seven wickets, and then almost immediately set off to play a highly successful winter of first-class cricket. In Australia. Perhaps with a touch of drama, he'd remarked in an interview late that August that he considered himself 'jilted' by England, and would accept any reasonable alternative offer for his services. This duly came from Barry Shepherd, the 25-year-old double cricket and hockey international recently appointed captain of Western Australia. Shepherd had seen enough of Lock to think of him as 'a fighter but also a thinker … He may not have spun the ball much, but he was a master of flight and control. And as a bonus it was like having a human bulldog in the team in terms of aggression. When Tony first came here he pinned up a notice on the dressing room board in which he set out ten tips about undermining your opponent. Tip number one read, "Get in the batsman's face right away, and always remind him he won't be there long." The other nine tips were pretty much in the same vein.'

Shepherd later remarked, 'In some ways Tony was more of a typical Aussie than we were. You could see how he might have rubbed people up the wrong way back at some tea party at Lord's, but he was exactly the kind of no-bullshit bloke we loved.' Asked how he'd responded to the state's initial offer, Lock replied with a metaphor, 'It was like a man in a passing dinghy asking a drowning swimmer if he was interested in a lift back to the shore.'

As a result, Lock, his wife Audrey and their two young sons took up residence in Perth from late September 1962 to early March 1963. Audrey helped to run a small fish and chip shop to supplement the family income. Lock's first match for his new employers began in the same week in October that the Cuban missile crisis saw American B-52s armed with hydrogen bombs circling over the Norwegian Sea, ready to move on their commander-in-chief's order to their pre-assigned targets in the Soviet Union. Western Australia's opponents that day were none other than the visiting MCC team. The tourists' stumper John Murray remembered strolling across the practice pitch before the start, 'And there was Lock coming the other way. When Dexter saw him he flipped Tony the ball and cheerily invited him to come bowl at us in the nets, and Lockie gave him a thousand-yard stare and flung the ball straight back like a ruddy Cruise missile. It nearly knocked Ted's head off.'

Lock took 4-68 off 21 eight-ball overs in the first innings of the MCC match, and didn't bowl in the second. A few days later, the Soviet politburo agreed to 'remove the arms [in Cuba] which some describe as offensive', and Washington in turn ordered its bombers back to base. The world was safe for cricket again. In his eight Sheffield Shield games that season Lock finished with 32 wickets at 29 apiece. Don Bradman was there to see him take 7-53 in an innings against Victoria at Melbourne, and told Dexter and some of the other Englishmen that he thought this the finest piece of bowling he had seen since Old Trafford in 1956.

Both Laker and Lock were back on the county circuit in 1963, although they managed not to meet. Each insisted he was now enjoying his cricket more than at any time in the past. As if he were living his life backwards, Laker, despite his undertaker's gait on the field, seemed to find a youthful enthusiasm for the game in his fifth decade. It was as if after all his record-setting exertions for Surrey and England he'd finally attained the one quality always beyond him: true relaxation. The 20-year-old Robin Hobbs was then coming into the Essex side, and remembered, 'Jim kept to himself socially, but he still had the most classical action, was a joy to watch, and a very generous guy in his way with the ordinary fans and supporters.' A local reporter named Tony Gill once saw Laker climb behind the wheel of his car when leaving the ground after a long day's bowling at Romford, and then pause briefly at the main gate to speak to the steward on duty there. 'As people walking by recognised Jim, they pressed their faces to the car window and started taking pictures and asking for autographs. Far from minding this attention, he seemed to love it. He wasn't exactly tooting a party horn, maybe, but you could see a definite smile.'

Lock, too, was now in danger of becoming something of a genial elder statesman. The teenaged Pat Pocock was bowling in the deserted practice nets at The Oval one hot afternoon in 1963, when, 'Suddenly there was a noise behind me and I looked up to see Lockie, a bit red in the face, saying, "What are you doing?" I expected a bollocking of some sort, but instead he rolled up his sleeves and for the next two hours gave me a master-class in the art of spin bowling. It was the sort of priceless advice you can't get out of a coaching book, and I thought it an extraordinary gesture

SALVAGING THE WRECKAGE

to show to a kid who was struggling to get into the county second XI. I'd heard Tony could be a moody bugger, but I have to say there was something endearing about this guy, now probably on the down slope of his career, taking the time and trouble to help a young bowler when he had absolutely no need to do so.'

Lock finished with a relatively modest 88 first-class wickets that season. He played in three of the summer's five Tests against West Indies. On the whole he bowled unexceptionally but did well with the bat, scoring 56 against an attack of Hall, Griffith, Sobers and Gibbs in the home win at Edgbaston, and 53, including six fours and a six, at Headingley. As a result he had a better batting average for the series than Colin Cowdrey, but a worse bowling average than Ted Dexter. He played his 385th and last game for Surrey, at home to Warwickshire, in September 1963; the match was rained off as a draw. The county finished a modest 11th in the championship table, one place above Essex.

* * *

For someone supposedly easing into retirement, Lock kept himself busy. He was back in Perth in October 1963 for a second term with Western Australia. Admittedly it wasn't one crowned with much success: he took only eight first-class wickets, and his side finished in last place in the Sheffield Shield. But Lock's new life in Australia evidently appealed to him enough to convince him to stay on when the season ended the following March. Or to be more exact he went back to England, settled his affairs, collected his family and returned with them via a five-stopover Qantas flight to take possession of a neat, three-bedroom detached house in the north Perth suburb of Embleton.

When it became apparent that Lock had now emigrated rather than just taken temporary winter employment, some of the British press ran eulogies of him as though he had just died. Both there

245

and elsewhere in the cricket world virtues were discovered that had somehow previously failed to surface. It was obvious now that serious commentators took to this testy, sometimes truculent bowler in a way which few people had ever suspected. Like Laker before him, he'd become a sort of national treasure. *The Times* wrote, 'He had character as well as greatness, two commodities which English cricket will be loath to export,' and Laker told the same outlet, 'Tony was one of the very best of his kind the game has seen,' someone who had 'transformed himself completely from a raw medium-pacer into a genuine left-arm spinner who made intelligent use of his resources [and] will be much missed by his former comrades'. Seldom did Laker strike such a poignant note. For all his occasional doubts about Lock's behaviour over the years, he recognised his old team-mate's supreme achievement in prevailing against odds which would have crushed a man of lesser spirit.

Perhaps Laker himself had now mellowed, because Ted Dexter remembered:

Jim was one of my sterner critics at the start of my career. He had me down as a dilettante, flash harry hitter with no great talent. Flash forward to an International Cavaliers tour of the West Indies in early 1964. We were playing against Jamaica, who were captained by Frank Worrell, and had the great left-armer Alf Valentine in their ranks. Both sides wanted to win, so there were no giveaway runs. I was in top form, down the pitch one moment, right back and spearing the off side field the next. If it wasn't 100 it was certainly in the eighties or nineties [actually it was 120] at about a run a minute. Back in the pavilion I suddenly sensed Jim at my elbow. 'I just thought you would like to know,' he said, 'that was the best innings I have ever seen.' Praise indeed!

In June 1964 Laker went back to Lord's to play for an England team against an all-star XI in a match to raise funds for the National Playing Fields Association. His opponents for the day ranged from the recent Australian captain Richie Benaud down to the frequently trouserless actor Brian Rix. Laker had initially been invited to represent the celebrity side, but Billy Griffith, the MCC secretary, intervened. 'If Jim's to play here, it will be for England,' he announced just before the start, perhaps the first hint of an official olive branch being extended in the bowler's direction. The Surrey committee voted to restore his privileges at The Oval later that season. Like Lock's, Laker's bowling figures for the year were only fair: in eight matches for Essex he took a modest 17 wickets at 34 apiece. The county at least managed to finish tenth, an improvement of two places in the table. Trevor Bailey told me that he had no regrets about 'signing a man who had graduated to the status of a British hero'.

John Arlott thought Laker still showed vestiges of the old greatness. Watching him bowl for the Cavaliers one Sunday afternoon was one of those bittersweet experiences when you see cricketers of a certain age come out of retirement and go through their paces one more time, a bit like visiting a once magnificent palace whose roof has caved in. When called upon, Laker limped stiffly up to the wicket, a martyr to affliction. His first delivery, sent down to a young Cambridge University batsman, pitched on a length and eased off gently to leg. The second delivery did the same thing. 'The third ball,' Arlott wrote, 'looked identical to the two before, and the visibly happy young batsman moved unhurriedly across to play it, only for it to bite, turn, hurry through and hit his stumps while his bat was only half-way down.'

In the normal course of affairs a three-day match between Northamptonshire and Essex starting on a wet Wednesday morning would qualify only as a sort of routine courtesy call by one county side on another. However, in July 1964 this particular fixture took on new significance. It proved to be Laker's final appearance in English domestic cricket. He took 2-56 in 19 overs in the only Northants innings necessary, and left the field to a standing ovation from the small but appreciative crowd. Laker again briefly toured the West Indies with the Cavaliers that winter, and that concluded his first-class career. He'd taken 1,944 wickets at just over 18 apiece in 17 years at the top level. Some 166 of these had come in a golden spell from early May to mid-August 1950. Along the way, he'd also dispatched ten or more victims in a match no fewer than 32 times. Very nearly half his total number of dismissals were either bowled or lbw.

Buried within the overall numbers is the fact that Lock took 124 catches – significantly more than any other fielder, including the Surrey wicketkeeper Arthur McIntyre – off Laker's bowling. Some of these were routine, but many others were half chances at best, taken at full stretch or in swivelling one-handed grabs from close to the bat. Although Laker could sometimes be possessive about his achievements, he was always happy to share due credit with Lock. 'Tony's fielding was often the difference between Surrey and our opponents,' he wrote, in the course of extolling the 'greatest fighter and trier a cricket team has ever had'. No one could ask for a better epitaph than that.

Just as Laker was finally hanging up his boots in July 1964, Lock was in discussions about playing a third season with Western Australia. In fact, the local committee wondered if he might be interested in taking on the state's captaincy from Barry Shepherd. He was. There are perfectly good leaders of cricket teams whose devotion to the cause doesn't necessarily stem from any statistical success in the middle. Lock wasn't one of them. He wanted to win, at all costs, always. Lock's Western Australia colleague John Parker later recalled one teatime pep talk after a long, unproductive

session in the field. '"Let's try something different now, lads,"
Lockie suggested, looking us all up and down. "Three things: bowl
fucking straight. Bowl fucking straight. Bowl fucking straight."
And that did it for the motivational speech.' Lock himself took 25
wickets in the short Australian season, and his side climbed one
place in the Shield.

While Lock and his family were putting down roots in Western
Australia, a group of English county cricket officials met 9,000
miles away at Grace Road, Leicester, to discuss how to improve
the playing performance of a side that had finished in 16th place
in the previous season's championship table. The driving force
behind this initiative was 30-year-old Mike Turner, the county's
dynamic new secretary (today's equivalent of a chief executive),
the man behind the first regional limited-overs competition for
English clubs, whose success had in turn led to the introduction
of the knockout Gillette Cup and all that followed. Lock always
admired this colourful, plain-spoken character with his relentlessly
go-ahead vision of the future. 'He was all business and his mind
was centred on putting bums on seats.'

Turner thought his county's bowling resources were in a
particularly woeful state and urgently in need of repair. To
him, therefore, the news of Lock's Australian renaissance was
providential, raising as it did the prospect of 'Tony returning
to play for another season or two in the English summer, and
stiffen our side's backbone in the process'. Turner was lucky that
Leicestershire's president at the time happened to also be the
chairman of a successful local engineering firm, and willing to
invest large amounts of money to boost the club's playing fortunes.
The county duly made a three-year offer to Lock, worth roughly
£4,000 plus living expenses, and he readily accepted it. According
to Turner, 'In all the excitement, Tony forgot to mention that he'd
also just signed a contract as player-coach of Ramsbottom in the

Lancashire League.' It was an 'unfortunate start', Turner admitted, and in the end Leicestershire agreed to use their new signing only on weekdays, and to send a side to play at Ramsbottom as partial compensation for their loss. By some further oversight, however, the match in question never took place, which was doubly regrettable when it emerged that the cash-strapped Lancashire League club had also previously paid Lock's full travel expenses from Australia.

Whatever the administrative issues involved, Leicestershire's new recruit made an immediate impact at the club. Lock's debut match was against Lancashire in early May: he took six wickets, threw in a catch scooped off the grass at silly point, and scored a rapid 40, driving lustily and relentlessly chewing gum, in the Australian fashion, in his one innings. In the end he dismissed 35 batsmen in eight matches that season. But more important than the raw figures was the effect Lock had on his new county colleagues. Mike Turner remembered, 'Tony was now a genuine spinner of the ball, with a flowing action that was more Bishan Bedi than Derek Underwood.' Despite his more sedate bowling style, he could, and did, exhibit 'visionary daring in [the field], always urging the captain to declare the second he safely could, if not earlier, and to go for the runs in a chase'. Lock wasn't a man for a prolonged debate about the state of the wicket or the potential for rain to affect the proceedings at some future stage of the match. 'He was a very here-and-now kind of guy,' Turner summarised. 'It was basically a case of get rid of the batsmen, whatever it took, then knock off the winning runs as fast as you could, and everyone down to the pub.'

Micky Stewart played against Lock in his Late Period, and thought him a 'rough diamond [with] a loud voice and a big heart'. Once, while on a private tour together of Rhodesia, Stewart 'saw Tony turn up wearing a slightly spivvy bright mauve suit every day. One afternoon, our hosts arranged a trip on a pleasure boat down the Zambesi, and as we were going on board we noticed that Lockie was AWOL. It was about 110° in the shade, and we weren't going to hang around. So off we went. About an hour later we're drifting down the river with bloody great crocodiles on either side of us and I look over and there's Tony waving merrily from a small canoe. He's still wearing his mauve suit and holding a bottle of gin in one hand and a glass in the other.'

Back in the relative civilisation of the East Midlands, Stewart found himself facing his former county team-mate in a match at Grace Road in August 1965. It was Lock's first championship appearance against Surrey. Perhaps the pitch, an unhealthy-looking pasty grey colour, played a part, because Leicestershire made just 77 all out and the visitors replied with 135; Lock 5-32. The game was all over in two days. Stewart was hit on the head while batting, but recovered to join Lock for dinner at Leicester's Grand Hotel. It was a good-humoured occasion. Somehow it was also quintessential Lock, the oddly gauche perpetual-teenager who coexisted with the basically kindly man now in his 20th year as a globetrotting professional cricketer.

Stewart recalls:

There were quite a few of us, players and wives, at the table. First, Tony loudly announced that he was paying for everyone's meal, and then very courteously asked permission of his guests to be allowed to smoke during the first course. We all said yes, but then Tony managed to open his box of matches upside down and liberally spray the contents into his brown soup. Next came the challenge of the wine. Lockie studied the list for a long time. A bloody long time. The waiter came to the table three times to take the order. Three times Tony irritably waved him away again. Finally, the poor man approached for the fourth time, and Lock came to a sudden decision. 'All right,' he shouted, as we all awaited the verdict. 'Red!'

Leicestershire finished the 1965 season in 14th place in the table, which was poor, admittedly, but almost imperial status compared to their recent standards. They had a freshly relaid pitch, a new pavilion, and in Tony Lock a newly appointed team captain. He'd somehow also found the time to play a few Saturday matches for Ramsbottom, finishing with the tidy figures of 92 wickets at nine apiece. He still attacked cricket, whatever the level, with the same intensity he had brought to his days at The Oval.

Jim Laker, for his part, played only a few charity matches that season. In late August he went back to The Oval to represent Old Surrey, under Peter May, against the Lord's Taverners. Laker took five wickets, and as they were leaving the field, his captain said, 'I'm glad we're just playing for fun, Jim. I'd hate to see it if you were really trying.' That May dared to joke about such matters – and that Laker dared to throw back his head with laughter – says much for his newfound relaxation. The one-time prickly first-class cricketer and professional curmudgeon was fast becoming a certified national treasure, and his more cheerful mood reflected that.

As if illustrating the fact, the famously unsentimental, supremely pragmatic Yorkshireman now suddenly developed an interest in astrology. An Aquarian, he was deemed to be 'not in awe of tradition or authority, [nor] of turning on those in higher office, particularly when in search of the truth'. Soon Laker was thumbing through the index of names in *Wisden* to discover the star signs of his former Test match colleagues and opponents. Then he started producing lists of players grouped together by their tropical zodiac. He found that Peter May and Colin Cowdrey, for instance, were Capricorns, 'ambitious, determined, materialistic, and generally upholders of tradition', that Denis Compton was Gemini ('social, talkative and whimsical, with an aversion to repeating oneself') and Lock was Cancer ('highly sensitive and self-protective'). Increasingly, everything now struck Laker as a sign of fate. His mind latched obsessively on to the number of lines in a letter or the number of times a given word was repeated, or even on to the dates it was sent and delivered.

Johnny Wardle remembered his surprise when Laker invited him to lunch one day later in the 1960s, and promptly began the meal by asking him to supply his zodiac sign and an exact time of birth so that he could determine whether the 'numbers were right' for their meeting, or, conversely, if the very act of human communion was itself an arbitrary convention and the concept of liking or disliking someone else merely an illusion. ('I thought he'd been drinking,' Wardle told me.) Without the pressures of day-to-day cricket, it seemed Laker could finally give rein to some of his long-suppressed interests, and talk about himself, his life, his hopes and perhaps even sometimes his slightly dotty New Age enthusiasms.

Meanwhile, Lock was back for a fourth campaign with Western Australia in 1965/66. His first appearance of the season came in late October, against Mike Smith's MCC tourists. It has to be said it wasn't Lock's finest hour. He scored a total of four runs and took no wickets in the match, which the visitors narrowly won in the final session. Nonetheless, he finished the season with 44 victims, which was more than any other bowler in Australian cricket. Not coincidentally, his state moved up two further places to finish as runners-up to New South Wales in the Sheffield Shield. The man with the ravenous craving for success was about to impose his iron rule on the slightly ramshackle team who had been the poor relations of the Australian game for much of their 80-year history.

Lock delivered what amounted to a brief sermon more than a standard pep talk at the end of the season, exhorting his team-mates to work hard and not stray from the straight and narrow in their home lives, as 'We can't afford any personal distractions if we're going to win the title.' It's possible some of his remarks, which one player told me had reminded him of an Old Testament prophet, might have surprised those who knew him only as the former *enfant terrible* of English cricket.

Lock returned as Leicestershire captain in 1966 and made an impact with his full-throttled batting and newly controlled bowling, but more than anything else by his fielding close to the wicket and dynamic leadership style. The year revealed both his finest and most trying qualities as a team player: his infectious enthusiasm, his courageous persistence, his ability to think in strategic terms, but also his occasional petulance, his messianic self-belief, and his contempt for lesser mortals. Leicestershire finished eighth in the table, a rise of six places, and Lock, now approaching his 40th birthday, took no fewer than 109 first-class wickets and 38 catches, figures that rivalled his glory days at The Oval.

That there was a peppery side to Leicester's new captain was no newsflash. But there was a childlike one, too, as seen in the way he liked to read intellectually undemanding comic books or cowboy yarns in the dressing room, gleefully passed out exploding cigars, and had the slightly odd if endearing habit of volunteering to mow other people's lawns, being dissuaded only with some effort from doing so at Grace Road itself. Lock's essential approach to captaincy was one of unquenchable optimism. He always believed that he was playing the greatest game on earth, and that at any given time he and his colleagues were the greatest team on earth. Were they really? Not always. But in Lock's mind, if they believed they were, they were. Essex's Robin Hobbs told me, 'Leicester's pitches were so doctored with sand those days, I remember Trevor Bailey taking a deckchair out to the middle before the toss there one morning with a sign saying "Southend Beach" fixed to it. We somehow scored about 150, which was roughly twice what we thought we would, and then back in the pavilion I heard Lockie telling his batsmen, "Right, lads, we'll knock these runs off in an hour and then go down the pub.'"

The young Leicestershire stumper Roger Tolchard thought there was 'something bordering on the superhuman – perhaps the inhuman – in Lock's constant, over-the-top self-confidence', although when the moment came he found he could be surprisingly benign as well.

As Tolchard remembers:

> In 1966 I was 19, turning 20, and Lockie had me in the office and said I was in for the first six games of the season and then they would evaluate. I was in awe of the man, and never said a word. I was just grateful to be playing. Anyway, I remember it was a bloody awful summer for weather. A few weeks in we were playing Somerset at Taunton, Leicester were fielding, and sure enough we came off for rain. My mum and dad had come to watch, so I slipped round the back and sat in their car for a few minutes. The next thing I knew, I looked through the gap by the pavilion and they were playing! Bloody hell, I thought, there goes my career. I raced round, bawling my eyes out, thinking, my God, I will never play again, old Clive Inman had already put all the wicketkeeping gear on, and I literally sprinted out to the middle, still crying, and of course they all thought it was the funniest thing ever. I was terrified, but Lockie just smiled and shook his head. He kept me in the team all right. In fact, that was the beginning of the best 18 years of my life.

* * *

While Jim Laker insisted that his retirement years were just that – 'I'm simply too ancient to play competitive sport,' he wrote in

The Sketch in May 1966 – his many admirers in the game never quite accepted the fact. The county secretaries at Hampshire and Middlesex both enquired about his availability that season, and while Laker declined their offers he turned out with some success in a dozen or so games for a variety of charities. Richie Benaud wrote of one appearance at Cranbrook school in Kent that July, 'One of my fondest cricket memories is to have fielded at leg slip to Jim that day, when he was aged 44, and gave a bowling masterclass against a strong South African XI.' Perhaps Laker also continued to grow more sentimental with age, because Pat Pocock remembers going to his house a year or two later, 'And there was just a single, well-scuffed cricket ball displayed on the mantlepiece. I assumed it must be from Old Trafford in 1956, or some other great Test occasion, but, no, when I asked Jim he just smiled and said with a note of unfeigned pride, "It's the one I used in my first match for Surrey."'

Recalling this same incident, one biographer informs us that Laker 'now felt the subterranean pull of tender Oval memories'. That may be true, but it seems fairer to say that he was becoming more relaxed, even nostalgic, about his days at Surrey. As we've seen, the club had brought him back in from the cold in 1964, and now, more than seven years after the publication of *Over to Me*, the MCC finally followed suit. A few friends and admirers threw Laker a celebration party that night at the Cricketers Club in central London. Godfrey Evans, a virtual fixture on the premises both then and for much of the remaining 30 years of his life, said, 'Once Jim lost the chip on his shoulder he was a thoroughly nice bloke. I remember he told me that he always tried to treat people well, not that they necessarily deserved it, but because it was the right thing for a Christian gentleman to do. You wouldn't have heard *that* in the old days.'

Lock, too, seemed to lighten up in the mid-1960s, and relish his role as a jet-setting cricket commuter for whom it was permanently

Laker in 1955, the season in which he took 133 wickets but only once got into the England Test side.

Lock's 'double-whirl' action remained the subject of debate throughout the 1950s.

Len Hutton welcomes Ian Johnson, the Australian captain, on his team's arrival in England in April 1956. Johnson only rarely smiled quite as broadly again that season.

Laker and Lock walk on, all business, at the start of play for the third Test at Headingley, July 1956.

Laker leaves the same field, to the applause of his female fans, after taking 11 wickets in the match.

Enjoying a cigarette and a glass of his sponsor's Lucozade on the Headingley balcony.

Lock catches Australia's Jim Burke on the third day of that summer's legendary Old Trafford Test. It was Laker's 11th wicket of the match, and eight more would follow.

Neil Harvey tosses his bat in the air to express his disgust at being caught off a ball Laker described as 'easily the worst one I bowled in the whole match.' Lock's own excitement seems to be well contained.

Jim and Lilly Laker at Old Trafford on the Saturday evening of 28 July 1956. Lilly took the train back to London on Sunday night, and thus missed her husband's date with destiny on the final day. 'It was something we always both regretted', he admitted.

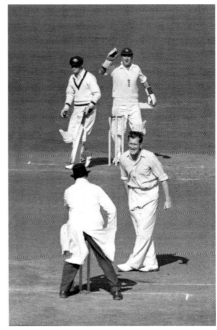

Laker and Godfrey Evans appeal for lbw against Australia's last man in, Len Maddocks, giving the bowler 19-90 in the Test.

Laker walks off, his face deadpan, after setting his world record. Stopping at a roadside pub later that night, he joined the locals in crowding round to watch the match highlights on television. No one recognised him.

Signing autographs at the wheel of his elderly grey Morris Oxford while on the journey from Manchester back to London. 'It was a pretty ordinary day,' Laker later remarked, telling people that he'd made a basic £70 for his work in the Test, and that Surrey had deducted £17 from this for each of the two county matches he missed by representing his country.

Lock, Laker and Frank Tyson arrive at Lord's before their departure to South Africa, October 1956.

Lock says goodbye to his son Graeme and wife Audrey while catching the boat train that night.

The MCC party on board the SS Edinburgh Castle, *bound for Durban*. Lock, seated third from left, looks euphoric, and even Laker, standing fourth from left, seems quietly pleased with life.

Laker and his captain Peter May, as Tweedle Dee and Tweedle Dum respectively, carry off first prize in the ship's fancy dress competition. Their relations weren't always this good.

Lock waves from The Oval balcony at the end of the fifth Test against West Indies in August 1957. He took 6-20 in the second innings, and the tourists were all out for 86.

Laker and Lock get their tickets punched at St Pancras station on their way to Australia, September 1958. The tour was only a mixed success, and ended in a showdown between Laker and the England management; he never played for his country again.

Laker proves that he at least read Over to Me, *even if he didn't write it.*

The elder statesman, whose views on cricket revealed some radical ideas filtered through a conservative sensibility; Laker in 1980.

The following letter has been sent to
J. C. Laker by the Surrey County Cricket
Club.

18th May, 1960.

Dear Laker,

The Surrey Committee has carefully considered your
recent book and in particular its attacks upon the M.C.C., the
Surrey Club and a large number of individuals in the cricket
world.

The Committee particularly deplores your criticisms
of many of your team mates and others at the Oval who have
worked so hard to ensure the success of your benefit of over
£10,000. There have been other books recently which lovers
of cricket have regarded as harmful and in bad taste but in
the opinion of the Committee yours has done a greater dis-service
to cricket than any of them.

In the circumstances, I am instructed to inform you
that the right of entry to the Oval given by your Pass has been
withdrawn.

The Committee feels that it is necessary to make its
attitude quite clear to its Members and the cricket public. It
is therefore sending a copy of this letter to the Press.

Yours truly,

(signed) B.O. BABB,

Secretary.

Colonel Babb's superbly contemptuous 1960 letter to Laker

Lock bowls for Leicestershire in 1967.

With his Western Australia team-mates.
[Courtesy: Western Australia Cricket Association]

Lock in Australian retirement.

summer. Off the field, at least, his geniality grew more pronounced with age. Eleven-year-old Richard Lock, in particular, was awed by his father, whom he regarded as a marble figure on a pedestal. To his younger son, he always seemed to be of heroic proportions – not only as a brilliant cricketer, but exacting in matters of personal integrity, serene in the face of criticism, and profusely generous when it came to giving something back to the game. 'Dad liked nothing better than going down to work with autistic children, teaching them hand-to-eye coordination,' Richard recalled. 'He had untold patience with these kids. His rapport with them was, I think, because he responded to their innocence.'

But if Lock had mellowed in his private life, he still remained the same fiery competitor of old the moment he strode on the field. Northamptonshire's burly young schoolteacher-cricketer Colin Milburn joined the Western Australia side for the 1966/67 season. He long remembered a match against South Australia in Adelaide when an 18-year-old Greg Chappell declined to walk after patently nicking a ball from Lock straight back to the wicketkeeper. 'That was the first time I'd ever heard anyone sledging,' Milburn recalled, 'and it was pretty rich stuff. Here was this middle-aged bloke from Surrey giving one of the Aussies some verbal on his own turf. No quarter was asked, and none given ... Tony was completely brazen.' Indeed, Lock was as fearless in body as he was in mind. In another Sheffield Shield match that season the batsman went for a scything blow to leg, caught the edge, and the ball hit the Western Australia skipper, who was characteristically crouching nearby, full on, breaking his nose. As his team-mates rushed forward to help, Lock rose groggily to his feet. 'It's nothing,' he insisted, smiling grimly as blood cascaded down his face, before inviting his colleagues to 'bugger off back to your marks'.

Lock had a thoroughly conventional, eyes-on-the-ball approach to fielding. But it took the sort of skill you can't learn from a coaching manual for him to routinely pocket not just edges and nicks but also full-blooded slogs, strokes which would have split the boundary board without his intervention. Nor did he ever flinch, let alone budge, from his preferred kamikaze position at short leg. Literally an 'in your face' catcher, Lock conquered not just the actual odds in the field, but conquered himself, also, by sheer grit and guts. In his entire 25-year career no one would ever remember him admitting to being hurt or the least incommoded by a small matter such as a fractured nose, or ever leaving the field unless explicitly required to do so, and Lock would no more have worn a helmet than he would a tutu. He took 51 Sheffield Shield wickets that season, the first bowler to reach the half century since before the war. Western Australia slipped back to fourth in the table, even so, and Lock had some blunt words for his colleagues before they left the dressing room on the last day of the season.

'You were fucking awful out there about half the time,' he told his exhausted, sun-blistered team-mates sitting silently by their lockers. Then he lit the inevitable cigarette, pausing to look each of the players up and down before he continued, 'But the other half you were fucking brilliant. *That's* what I want to see more of next year.'

The 1967 English season opened with bitterly cold winds and grey skies. Lock was back for his third year with Leicestershire. It proved to be one of the best of his career. He took 128 first-class wickets, twice dismissing 13 batsmen in a match, as well as adding 603 runs and 33 catches. But more important than any individual success was the collective improvement in his team's fortunes. The county finished as joint runners-up behind Yorkshire, and might have fared even better but for some cruel luck with the weather. At Hastings in late July, for instance, they ended the second day with a lead of 238 and five second-innings wickets in hand. Lock had planned to declare midway through the next morning's session and then set Sussex to score 300 in five hours on a turning wicket. 'A piece of piss for us,' he remarked to some of his colleagues over dinner.

The players returned to the ground the following morning and could scarcely believe their eyes. The first two days of the match had taken place in an atmosphere that was roughly akin to looking through the pinhole of a scenic souvenir charm at some late Edwardian garden party, with a parade of Henley-style blazers and floral bonnets jostling with that summer's 'trendy' new gear, not infrequently splayed open at the chest as if for imminent heart surgery, a splash of summer pastels distinguishing the ground overall with its flag-strewn marquees and patriotic bunting, the whole scene shimmering under a cloudless blue sky. The players returned to find the place shrouded in an impenetrable mist. The sides never got back on the field, and Leicester were denied a vital 12 points which would have put them ahead of the eventual champions at the top of the table. The county suffered one or two other bad breaks with injuries and absences, but they signed off in style with an emphatic home win against Northamptonshire in early September. Lock took 7-75 in the first innings and 6-43 in the second. It proved to be his final appearance in English county cricket.

'There was a big crowd that day,' Mike Turner recalled, 'and I'll always treasure the memory of Tony looking out across the field from the players' balcony. He raised his arms time and again to acknowledge the applause. He just looked like Jesus standing there.' It was Leicestershire's best championship finish in the county's 72-year history. No wonder Lock beamed down as he did, occasionally jabbing the air in delight, until someone handed him a microphone. 'Next year we'll do it!' he shouted, somehow keeping the ubiquitous cigarette clamped between his lips. The roar that met this remark was truly deafening; he had clearly struck the most responsive possible chord. But in the event Leicester would have to wait until 1975 to finally win their first title, and then they did so without Lock's help. A note in the county archives reads, 'The captain was offered £1,650 basic salary for 1968, increasing to £1,750 in 1969, but after due reflection he chose not to return.'

Twenty years earlier, Jim Laker had watched the teenaged Lock fumble a chance in the field and promptly informed the Surrey captain, 'The kid will never be a short leg as long as he plays the game.' Misjudgements could hardly come any greater than this. By the end of his career Lock had taken 830 catches, the vast majority of them close to the bat. Somehow fittingly, Laker and Lock met on the cricket field for the last time that same summer, as opponents in a Sunday afternoon charity match at Grace Road. Lock took three wickets, Laker took two, and neither of them scored a run. No one made a fuss of the occasion, and few of the small crowd present could have known what they were witnessing. But Ken Barrington told me he'd heard the two old bowlers reminisce at a players' reception at The Oval later that season. 'Tony used to soak up all the aggro he'd taken over the years, and I think it helped him to get it off his chest because underneath his hard shell he was a sensitive guy, but he ended up by saying, "Well, Jim, sod it. We've been successful and these other buggers [the critics] haven't."' It almost seemed to Barrington as if the two of them were in a sort of very exclusive club, and that only they truly understood the pressures and challenges each of them had faced over the years.

After that it seemed Lock's long goodbye to cricket couldn't get any more Hollywood, and yet it did. He went back to Western Australia in 1967/68, and duly captained the state side to their first Sheffield Shield title in 20 years. As usual he led from the front and took the stigma of being an Englishman playing cricket in Australia in his stride. There was a moment in the season's climactic match against Victoria at Melbourne when a perhaps over-lubricated supporter shouted the time-honoured 'Go home, you pommie bastard!' Lock turned and bowed elaborately in the man's direction, and then proceeded to take five quick wickets, including those of the Test players Paul Sheahan and Keith Stackpole. The general feeling in the dressing room was that the spectator's intervention had been spectacularly counter-productive, as the visitors went on to win the match early on the last afternoon.

There were Beatlemania-like scenes when the Western Australia players flew home to Perth, which they did by way of a brief but well-oiled layover in Adelaide. The team's 26-year-old all-rounder Ian Brayshaw remembered stepping a little unsteadily from the plane at their final destination. 'I estimate there were 5,000 people waiting to greet us. A live telecast was organised by Channel Seven. Tony was so pissed that he could barely make himself understood to the viewing audience. We were celebrating a stunning victory which paved the way for Western Australia to become a cricketing force then and in later years.' Having said what he could, Lock stumbled into a taxi, leaving others to further brief the media.

The globetrotting veteran, now just weeks short of his 39th birthday, showed no signs of slowing down. Lock still gave his heart and soul to cricket, and was never going to be one of those hands-off captains who operate largely in the shadows, a spectral figure whose presence is mostly felt, not seen. Western Australia's seamer Sam Gannon remembered, 'Tony was then bald, a bit pudgy, and he walked around in the most diabolical clothes, wrinkled strides, shirt always hanging out, usually in a pair of knackered brothel creepers. He looked like someone's slightly dodgy old uncle, daft, maybe, but harmless. And frankly his appearance was as much at odds with his real character as a furry bunny is with a charging rhino.' In fact, as anyone who had incurred Lock's wrath during a match, or survived one of the frenzied appeals with which he still regaled umpires, would testify, a rhino might conceivably have had the edge in manners.

No self-respecting scriptwriter would have dared contrive what happened next. Just 48 hours after returning in triumph to Perth nursing both the outsized Sheffield Shield trophy and an incipient hangover, Lock was on the first of a series of five flights that took him to join Colin Cowdrey's England team 11,000 miles away on a tour of the Caribbean. He arrived just in time to take three cheap wickets in the drawn colony match with the Windward Islands. The selectors had taken the unusual step of calling up an almost pensionable-aged bowler from his winter home on the other side of the globe only after a freak boating accident had deprived Fred Titmus of four toes on his left foot; the Middlesex off-spinner eventually received £90 compensation (about £600 today) for his loss, or £22 10s a toe, from the MCC's insurance policy. Even so, Lock's fairytale comeback had its critics. A note in the MCC files of 21 March 1968 records the 'Resolution to call up G.A.R. Lock to the team to tour the West Indies, and the expression of regret by the Treasurer [Lock's old friend Gubby Allen] at the choice'.

Two days after the Windward Islands match, Lock was back in the England side to play the West Indies in the winter's fourth Test at Trinidad. It was his first appearance for his country in nearly five years, and admittedly wasn't his finest performance (1-129) with the ball. But he was at least there to witness one of the most dramatic moments of post-war international cricket. Set a target of 215 runs in slightly over two and a half hours, the visitors crossed the line with just three minutes to spare. Geoff Boycott, of all people, not generally as pugnacious with a bat as he later was with a microphone, scored 50 in 90 balls. The unexpected result clinched the series.

Perhaps it was just something about dinners, but after the protracted saga of the wine at the Grand Hotel in Leicester, Lock now faced another challenge when he sat down for a convivial meal with Essex and England's Robin Hobbs at the Pegasus Hotel on the last stop of the tour in Georgetown, Guyana.

'Tony started off calmly enough and ordered a curry,' Hobbs recalls. 'But then he took a mouthful and promptly returned it to the waiter, claiming it wasn't hot enough. A few minutes later it came back from the kitchen. Still no good. Tony eventually sent the food back three times, each time complaining that it was too mild.' On the fourth time this happened, the waiter, with a note of panic in his voice, regaled Lock with a list of the ingredients in what was now a visibly steaming pile of vindaloo, obviously aware of the consequences of a drunk middle-aged cricketer ingesting this thermogenic dish.

But Lock refused to heed the advice and, like the wilful schoolboy he was, held a forkful of the explosive matter in front of his mouth, his eyes darting around the room to be sure everyone was watching. 'Tony took a bite,' Hobbs recalls, 'and then without a further word he picked up the plate and hurled it against the wall. It hung there for a while in a multicoloured mess, a bit like an abstract painting. "When I say hot," Tony observed, in a surprisingly level voice, "I mean hot."' Lock made no other comment beyond that, although, under cover of the nervous, stilted conversation that finally resumed around the room, Hobbs heard him emit a series of weird grunts.

Tom Graveney once told me in broadly this context that he always felt an affinity with Lock, relishing his bonhomie and outlandish behaviour and calling him 'one of the most upbeat men I ever knew. He would crack jokes and have more to say in one conversation than Laker would in a week.' On the other hand, Graveney conceded, 'Jim was very much a wise old bird, while with Tony you always had the sense you were dealing with a bright but touchy teenage delinquent.'

Lock kept his cool, even so, in the wake of the Test at Georgetown when he was quietly walking away from the ground with Pat Pocock and one or two other team-mates following the draw which gave England the series. 'Suddenly,' Pocock says, 'a crowd gathered behind us and handfuls of pebbles started to rain down at our feet. They were followed by chunks of house brick, then by a steel chair, which hit and cut the teenaged lad who was helping carry our bags.' Stunned and temporarily blinded by pouring blood, the boy was seized by two or three of the players and half dragged across a wide open expanse of gravel driveway, difficult to navigate in their spiked boots, back out of the main gate. Then they ran.

'By that point it was getting bloody frightening,' Pocock continues. 'We rushed for our car, and the driver promptly took off at about 60mph, his hand leaning on the horn as he did so. God knows how we managed to avoid hitting someone in the chaos. By then we were all in the back, crouched down on the floor, or at least most of us were, because I looked up and there was Tony still sitting bolt upright, now bleeding from a cut to the back of his neck but his face otherwise completely deadpan. I'm pretty sure he was still smoking a fag. We eventually got back to the hotel, and I remember shaking with shock. Not Tony, though. He just calmly wiped away the blood and went about his business. He'd seen it all before. It was as if it was just one of those things bound to happen from time to time in cricket.'

Lock had earlier scored a whirlwind 89 in the England first innings, his highest ever first-class score in what proved to be his 49th and final appearance for his country. Jim Laker later wrote, 'If I know my Tony, that knock in Georgetown probably gave him more satisfaction than any bowling performance of his career.' The match itself ended in one of those thrilling stalemates seemingly unique to cricket when Glamorgan's left-arm seamer Jeff Jones, with a lifetime first-class batting average of 3.97, managed to scramble through an over from Lance Gibbs, then the most feared spin bowler in the world.

* * *

The following English season ended in some disarray when the olive-skinned Basil D'Oliveira, fresh from a score of 158 while representing England against Australia in the summer's final Test at The Oval, was conspicuously missing from the list of 16 names selected to tour South Africa in the winter. There was an immediate outcry that his exclusion was the result of some behind-the-scenes deal with the Pretoria government to protect their policy of strict racial segregation. In time the plot thickened when Warwickshire's Tom Cartwright, a bowler who could bat a bit, withdrew from the tour through injury, and D'Oliveira, a batsman who could bowl a bit, was called up in his place. This was too much for South Africa's state president John Vorster, who announced, 'We are not prepared to receive a team thrust upon us by people whose interests are not in the game, but to advance their political goals.'

Jim Laker was always outraged by any suggestion of racism, whether in cricket or elsewhere, quietly donating his time and money to several charities for minority causes. It testifies to his sometimes paradoxical nature that he was both deeply resentful at being left out of the 1948/49 MCC tour of South Africa ('a typical establishment fit-up', he later remarked), but delighted to then be invited to visit the Johannesburg townships as a private citizen to coach underprivileged black youths. 'I worked as hard as I ever did in my whole career,' he said of the experience. 'I was in the nets from nine in the morning until seven at night six days a week, paid peanuts, and I had the time of my life.' England took Charles Palmer with them as their sole off-spinner that winter, which, after he took a total of five wickets on the tour, Palmer himself described as 'probably a mistake'.

Laker made his debut as a BBC television commentator that same summer of 1968. He brought much the same note of dry authority to the air as he did to his now regular journalism. It was as if he and his fellow broadcasters were merely sitting over a glass of sherry in the lounge bar of their local pub, casually exchanging a few views on the day's play. He was a natural, all parties agreed. It was the beginning of an association with the BBC that was to last for nearly 20 years. Lock had no similar platform to boast of, but somehow he could at least still claim to serve as an occasional irritant to cricket's powers-that-be. A note in the MCC archives of August 1968 reads:

> Correspondence, telegrams, collection notice relating to the Australian tour of the British Isles, [and] continuing discussions about the arrangements for G.A.R. Lock's luggage to be returned to Perth with the Australian Cricket Team.

Lock's own mind, meanwhile, had fastened obsessively on to a different detail. Thanks to his emergency call-up to play in the West Indies, he ended his career with 66 more Test runs than Laker did. In later years, Lock never let people forget this fact, although as a rule he failed to mention that he had also finished with 19 fewer wickets, the same number Laker had taken in the match at Old Trafford in 1956. No matter how many international awards or trophies Lock won, it seemed the competition that mattered to him most was the one he still played in his head against his old Surrey and England team-mate.

'My World was Completely Shattered'

AS JIM Laker was busy consolidating his latter-day place in the British establishment – a tweed-suited cove with a Conservative Party membership, and a job at the more refined end of the BBC – Tony Lock was showing his old wanderlust, still travelling restively around the world in search of a game of cricket while increasingly calling Western Australia his family home. A frontiersman at heart, he gravitated to a society, if not the stereotypical outback, known for its informality, anonymity and general lack of hidebound tradition. Unrelenting as ever on the field, he was otherwise a generally cheerful figure. Lock threw himself into his coaching, quite often of underprivileged local youths, enjoyed a beer, still read cowboy books voraciously, kept a variety of dogs, all of whom he adored, had to be physically restrained from mowing any nearby lawn, and remained a loving, protective husband and father. As someone once observed of the great jazz saxophonist Stan Getz, he was a nice bunch of guys: loud, voluble and titanically competitive, with a touchingly puerile side that perhaps helped explain some of his later-ruinous fondness for adolescent girls.

Lock was back for a seventh season with Western Australia in 1968/69. He took 46 Sheffield Shield wickets in just eight matches, more than any other bowler in the competition, although in the end his side had to settle for second place in the table. In the second innings of a match with Queensland at Brisbane, he finished with figures of 7-61 off 22 eight-ball overs. He still got prodigious bounce and turn on the cast-iron Australian wickets, and never seemed to tire of the demands of playing six-day-a-week cricket at the age of 39, now with two badly deteriorating knees to cope with. His club's annual report referred to his 'Uncanny control and accurate bowling, sustained for long hours under trying heat conditions. Any match in which he plays is stamped with his personality … Lock's keenness in the field, the voicing of demands which test his own vocal chords and the nerves of opposing batsmen and umpires, and the gamesmanship in his batting all delight crowds in Australia.'

As a bowler, he appealed roughly every other ball. But, conversely, when batting he always walked the moment he knew he was out without even waiting for the official's decision. As a captain, he was old-fashioned enough to insist on being called 'Mr Lock' or 'Skipper'. His team-mates in general seem to have been impressed and frightened by him in about equal parts, which was presumably how he liked it. The 20-year-old Dennis Lillee came into the Western Australia side later that year and said of him:

He didn't suffer fools gladly. If he didn't like you, it was better to keep your distance. Fortunately, he took a shine to me. Perhaps he saw something of himself in my personality. Lock made a major impact on me in terms of my aggression and professionalism.

Since Lillee went on to take the small matter of 355 Test wickets, Lock's career could be said to have ended with a bang and not a whimper for that reason alone. Either way, it wasn't a bad legacy. The idea that Lillee's fundamental approach to cricket was a sort of logical, chronological extension of Lock's might be a stretch, but it has one important advocate – Lillee himself, who once told me, 'I tried to consciously copy Tony in the way he had a take-no-prisoners attitude to the game. So, yes, in a way you could blame him when I started knocking over batsmen against England.'

Lock's eighth consecutive season of chosen exile followed in 1969/70. This time he took a relatively modest 27 Shield wickets (Lillee had 32) and Western Australia again finished as runners-up. He was as pugnacious as ever, caught everything that came his way in the field, and let out a loud, Jimmy Connors-like grunt on releasing the ball. But he could now be hit, and his batting was hampered by an increasing aversion to running singles. Ian Brayshaw would remember of a match at Melbourne, 'We were chasing a target and needed quick runs … I pushed one firmly past short leg into the wide-open spaces. The solitary close fielder had to get up from his haunches to retrieve the ball. We ran five.' At the end of the over, a beetroot-faced Lock summoned his batting partner for a mid-pitch conference. 'Brayshaw,' he panted at length. 'If you ever do that again, I'll fucking kill you.' After bagging a pair in another match, Lock registered his dissatisfaction by marching smartly back to the dressing room, where he pulled out his cigarette lighter, turned it up full blast, and set fire to the offending bat.

Partial to old habits, Laker also continued to play a few semi-competitive matches each summer, including one appearance for the Cavaliers against Yorkshire in his childhood haunt of Fartown. He took 1-27 and scored five not out, which at least included a hooked four off Fred Trueman. Still vigorous, Laker could send a golf ball sailing 200 yards down the fairway, and turned out for a charity football side most winter Sunday afternoons. Then his strength began to wane, and he gradually had to curtail his appearances. With typical precision, he reduced his playing time each match to 60 minutes, then 30, then 20, before retiring altogether around his 50th birthday.

Laker also continued to quietly support several charitable causes and individuals. In May 1969, Colin Milburn was involved in a car accident which cost him the sight of his left eye, thus depriving English cricket of its most exciting young batsman. Laker and a few others formed a benefit committee, which quickly raised £19,473 (roughly £130,000 today), leaving Milburn to remark, 'Jim was the kindest of men, who wanted no fuss made of him at charity matches or dinners. He probably worked 20 hours a week for me that summer without a penny's pay.' This diligent, behind-the-scenes exertion on behalf of a friend was a Laker characteristic. Tom Graveney told me that he was one of several cricketers with young children who had found gifts anonymously delivered to their homes each Christmas, and added, 'The general feeling was that Jim was behind it.'

Laker also graduated to the full BBC international commentary team when England hosted Pakistan at Edgbaston in June 1971. It proved to be the first of 111 such assignments, which was more than twice the number of his Test caps. His colleague Don Mosey said of this second chapter of his career: 'It's difficult to say that his confidence grew over time because Jim was perfectly confident from the start. He had been asked to talk about cricket; he knew cricket, so he was simply talking about something he was well qualified to discuss.' Laker's comments were always carefully rationed. Sometimes he said literally nothing between deliveries, allowing himself only a throaty chuckle. This, perhaps, was where the patience of certain viewers was most extended. But taken as a whole it was increasingly obvious as he entered his sixth decade that the newly mild-mannered Laker was the kind of man who had used to be disgusted but now tried to be amused, in the immortal words of Elvis Costello.

While Laker was perfecting his Hemingwayesque commentary style of unspoken emotion and hidden wisdom, mixed with a touch of Harold Pinter's comic menace, Lock was embarking on his ninth and final season at Western Australia. He took 31 wickets in eight Sheffield Shield matches, and his team finished third out of five in the table. Not the full Disney ending, then, although he still had his moments – such as dismissing both MCC openers (admittedly after they put on 215) in the latest tour match at Perth, or taking seven wickets away to New South Wales while throwing in a typically deft catch round the corner, clutching the ball off the full meat of Doug Walters's bat, slipping it unobtrusively in his pocket, then peering down to long leg as if following its progress to the boundary. The crowd looked puzzled; Walters departed with a smile on his face. At 41, Lock could still have got in most first-class sides solely on the strength of his fielding.

Meanwhile, Australia had rather sheepishly introduced its first domestic limited-overs tournament, a six-match competition underwritten by Vehicle & General, in 1969/70. It was not an immediate success. A total of just 20,780 customers, an average of 3,463 per game, paid at the turnstiles to watch a guest team from New Zealand go on to win the inaugural trophy. The figures were better for the contest's second year, the sponsorship was more generous, and the final – Queensland v Western Australia at Melbourne – attracted a crowd of around 7,000, who sat in an intensity of silence some way removed from today's frenetic, floodlit slogs deliriously cheered on by men and women dressed as bananas.

Lock and his side rose to the occasion. Western Australia scored 170 in 38 overs, then knocked over the opposition (which included the 43-year-old Tom Graveney) for just 79. If not quite the full Sheffield Shield, it was still a significant moment in consolidating the state's position as a force to be reckoned with in Australian domestic cricket. A sort of resigned lethargy had seemed to hang over the team at the time Lock had first joined it in 1962. Western Australia's finances were running low, as was morale. They had finished in last place in the previous season's Shield. By the time he left again, they were consistently serious contenders in the long format of the game, and pioneering champions at what was then still regarded as the cheap and cheerful sideline of the knockout version.

These were broadly comparable accomplishments to those Lock had brought about at Leicester, and between them they represent a solid legacy. The *enfant terrible* of English county cricket in the 1940s had turned out to be the *éminence grise* of the game in Australia as it embarked on its revolutionary decade of the 1970s. One well-placed source at Perth told me, 'Tony was a brilliant captain, always up for a scrap, and at times bloody terrifying to team-mates and opponents alike.' Recruiting him to the side had been a bit like adopting a pet tiger; exciting, certain to command respect, but not necessarily the safest option.

By the time Lock retired he had played a total of 654 first-class matches spread over four decades. He took 2,844 wickets and scored 10,342 runs, the game's highest career total without a single century to show for it. Little more need be said about his close catching, or his reserves of courage and aggression, or the fact that he clearly appeals to a peculiarly British school of sport by struggling through a series of crises that might have led a lesser man to consider the merits of early retirement. He was not born with genius like Laker. But he was the man you would want next to you in the middle when watching a batsman like Harvey or Sobers take guard at about 3pm, when tea seemed far and the boundary near. There was a gradual post-war movement away from the diffident, gentlemanly type, in cricket as in other walks of life, towards one whose will to succeed eclipsed his sometimes fragile social skills. Lock took this trend to an advanced stage. He had few equals when it came to making the most of his resources, and would surely feature in any all-time XI in which self-confidence was a condition of entry. 'People responded to his energy, his rawness, his fury,' one paper wrote.

'The club was very fortunate in having Tony's services in the last years of his career,' the Western Australia annual report noted, more drily, in 1971. Lock went out on 1 March of that year, after a drawn Shield match against Victoria at Perth. His final first-class wicket came when he trapped the visitors' Paul Sheahan leg before for a duck. The local *Sunday Times* correspondent said that there had been a primal fury in the bowler's appeal that had made the eruption of Krakatoa seem gently muted by comparison. At the end of the match the president of the home club presented Lock with a clock and a mounted ball and, to loud applause from the crowd, informed him that he was an Australian hero.

For a man who had played 49 Tests for England, and once gave it as his opinion that 'beating the Aussies, really grinding them down, is the greatest joy to be found on a cricket pitch', this was a singularly generous testimonial on his hosts' part.

Having devoted his own career to eliminating risk and perfecting a number of undemonstrative but supremely effective skills on the field, Laker brought much the same attributes to bear in his new role. His friend Don Mosey captured the essence of the act when recalling a pulsating Gillette Cup semi-final between Somerset and Essex in which Viv Richards thumped a century that passed, with lightning speed, from rout to orgy. The ensuing television commentary may have lacked something in wit, grace and imagery, not to mention the simulated frenzy of certain modern-day broadcasters who, even in their quieter moments, sound like their trousers are on fire. But these defects were more than offset by Laker's directness and authority. He took the finer points seriously.

'Richards started on his way to a brilliant ton by crashing a flurry of fours from the first few balls he received,' Mosey recalled. 'Sitting in the passenger seat, so to speak, all my radio commentator's instincts cried out for a description of this strokeplay. Words, phrases, formed in my mind and pleaded to be uttered into the microphone which Jim Laker held – silently. When the fourth four in rapid succession raced to the boundary, Jim finally spoke: "He doesn't hang about, this chap." The words were uttered with a little smile and they seemed to be addressed as much to the other two people in the box as to the world at large. In that instant I understood the true difference between radio and television commentary. What was almost an aside – "He doesn't hang about" – summed up what most viewers were thinking. It was, in fact, a thought, spoken aloud, rather than a professional observation, and it was couched in terms with which just about everyone could identify. Jim had captured the moment.'

It's possibly only to state the obvious to note again that the steady, precise qualities Laker brought to the commentary box were also those that had served him well as a bowler. 'Jim won a position of respect in cricket by his sympathetic interpretation of the game and laconic asides as a pundit,' his sometime critic E.W. Swanton acknowledged. Swanton was struck by Laker's strong populist streak, how he was intrigued by common people but indifferent to the high-born. 'He still blamed what he called "the establishment" for many of his problems as a player, but as time went on he appeared to be a more relaxed character, prepared to discuss the indignities of *Over to Me* and the rest with a faint smile on his lips.' Laker's newfound serenity didn't preclude an occasional spat with his BBC colleagues. The nature of the job meant that he sometimes had to yield the floor to what he considered the patronising or banal truisms of his fellow commentators, or even descend to a little laboured comic double-act with them. 'This only strengthened my resolve to show them that I could pedal my own bike,' he once noted.

The former Glamorgan and England all-rounder Peter Walker had this to say of his first experience of sitting alongside Laker in the commentary box:

> It came at the start of one of my earliest appearances fronting the BBC2 Sunday cricket programme. The match was at Tewkesbury and, as always, we went on air five minutes before play began at 2pm. I'd prepared what I thought was a marvellously descriptive piece about the area, and I was still in full flow when the umpires appeared and with time running out before the start I then expounded on each player. By the time I was finished, the bowler was about to run in and I said, 'And now for commentary, here's Jim Laker.' I sat back smugly, pleased with my opening until Jim responded, 'Thank you, Peter, you've said it all.' And he didn't speak again for five minutes. It was a hard lesson – never steal Laker's thunder.

Peter Parfitt had a broadly similar experience when working alongside Laker later in the 1970s. 'Jim had a habit of hogging the microphone during the more lively passages of play, then suddenly handing over to you when things were at a lull. Don't forget there was a strict pecking order at the BBC in those days. You just didn't upstage the senior man, even in jest. Your job was to back up whatever he said on air, and you could look forward to a bollocking from the high-ups if you strayed off script.'

Another BBC commentator who knew a certain amount about cricket, if not quite as much as Laker did, found this out the hard way. 'Jim remarked casually of one delivery in a Sunday game, "That was an off-spinner that didn't turn," and without thinking I said,

"Actually, Jim, it looked more like an arm ball to me." Laker didn't speak to me for the rest of the day. I mean, *total* silence. I went home, and the next morning there was a phone call telling me to report to Broadcasting House. I went in, and there was our producer and a couple of other characters in posh suits waiting for me. I was led to a back office and stood there while they took it in turns to tell me I'd committed the ultimate sin of contradicting Laker and what was I thinking, etc. It was like being back at school again. I half expected them to tell me to bend over for six of the best.' In those days, conforming to the nation's public service broadcaster's code of standards was sometimes fatally to blur the distinction between professionalism and absurdity. As the man was leaving the room, one of the suits added with a touch of bombast that his behaviour on air had been 'an affront to the good name of the Corporation'.

* * *

Laker wasn't one of those sportsmen who never quite adjust to retirement or civilian life. He continued to offer his thoughts on the game, and be well paid for them, until very nearly the end of his life. In general these views grew more resistant to change with the passage of time. He thought most modern-day spin bowlers negligible – 'none of them give the ball enough air' – and that, with covered wickets and shortened boundaries, batsmen now had the better of the struggle. 'When I started, half my wickets were taken bowled through the gate,' he told Pat Pocock in 1980. 'Nobody does that now.' He accepted limited-overs cricket as a fact of life, but was increasingly worried about the game losing its essential character. He showed no particular enthusiasm for coloured uniforms, floodlights or incessant advertisements. 'It's all a load of tommy rot,' he wrote. When someone expressed the opinion to Laker that he would have taken 'tons of wickets' in one-day cricket, he replied, 'Only fools get worked up about numbers.'

Comfortable with himself, he needed no outward validation of what he had accomplished. Tony Lock once said of him, 'You can criticise Jim for being uptight, but not for being greedy. He cared a lot less about figures than I did.'

Although Laker was a traditionalist on the game's laws, he wasn't above calling for changes in the way 'the old guard treat the public who pay for the whole thing in the first place'. He wanted comfortable seats and proper facilities at English cricket grounds, for instance. 'And there should be an undertaking that spectators will get their money refunded if there is no play, or half of it back if there's less than, say, two hours,' he wrote, a revolutionary concept at that time.

It's sometimes easy to forget just how different things were only 50 years ago. Professional cricketers still took the train to away matches, lodged in unassuming guest houses and lived on a diet of meat pies and fags. Most of them earned no more than a semi-skilled plumber for their day's work, a far cry from today's BMWs, agents and endorsements. The proper means of assessing an English first-class player was on the county circuit, which operated six days a week from late April to early September, while Tests started at 11 o'clock on a Thursday morning, not when sponsors told them to. All too many of cricket's fee-paying customers endured conditions that had changed little since Charles Dickens's day, although even that great chronicler of Victorian slum life might have been shocked by some of the outlying grounds' bathroom and catering facilities. It was in some of these areas, not the central balance between bat and ball, where Laker saw room for improvement when he wrote in 1972, 'Cricket is the most beautiful game in the world, an idea of the Gods. But it's run by a tiny elite of old duffers sitting in smoke-filled committee rooms who would have us believe that they and a few of their ilk have the right to enjoy the fruits of it all.' In his last years, Laker, a man of sound traditional views on many walks of English life, never tired in his campaign to help free cricket and cricketers from the petty restraints of the past.

One of Laker's governing beliefs about Britain in the 1970s was that all too many of his fellow citizens had lost their once-intuitive balance between the healthy and confident sense of self needed to live life fully, and their obligation to respect the sometimes opposing needs and aspirations of others: in short, that many Britons had abandoned such flagrantly old-fashioned concepts as self-restraint, delayed gratification and a proper degree of deference, and more specifically that this had encouraged a regrettable trend for society – as he saw it – to make life progressively easier for criminals and harder for law abiders and enforcers. This strange sensation of feeling himself to be 'the last sober person in a room full of drunks', as he sometimes put it, came to take tangible form when in early 1977 burglars broke through a downstairs window in Laker's home in Putney and helped themselves to most of his cherished memorabilia. There was a dense fog at the time, and the sweet-natured family Labrador, Toffee, did nothing in the night. Laker was philosophical, remarking that perhaps the thief or thieves had been 'Aussie cricket fans', but his wife Lilly admitted that the violation had understandably shaken them both. 'Jim's engraved England silver mugs, which he particularly treasured, were taken and that upset him most. Some other trophies, less valuable, were found on Wandsworth Common.'

In March 1977, the organisers of the Centenary Test celebrations in Melbourne decided that Laker and Lock made a natural pair, and put them up together in a local hotel room for the week. The match itself was interesting. There was Dennis Lillee's astonishing bowling effort – 6-26 in admittedly helpful conditions, which saw England collapse to 95 all out in response to Australia's first innings 138. And then Derek Randall's wonderfully idiosyncratic 174, to take the visitors within touching distance of an improbable victory on the final day, the entertainment continuing even after the batsman was out when he took the wrong turn and ended up in the royal box. The daily parade of old Ashes players around the ground was good; the sportsmanship of both sides, even Rod Marsh at one point calling Randall back after the umpire had given him out caught behind, a welcome bonus; the fact that the margin of victory – 45 runs in favour of Australia – was identical to the inaugural Test played 100 years earlier a definite addition to the proceedings. But in its own quiet way, nothing that week was quite as affecting as the sight of the two former Surrey and England team-mates strolling down to breakfast each morning before making their way in the sunshine along the nearby riverbank in order to spend the day sitting convivially side by side at the ground. Lock later said of the experience:

> We were very nearly sharing a bed, let alone a room, because they were only about a foot apart. Anyway, something clicked during the time we were together in Melbourne and at last we became friends. Perhaps I had matured, or Jim had relaxed, but everything ran so smoothly. I [found I] genuinely liked the old boy.

It's hard not to find that poignant.

By the spring of 1977 Laker had been a Test match commentator for six years, generally unremarkable ones for the national game as a whole, at least until the leaked announcement early that May of the Australian media tycoon Kerry Packer's World Series Cricket. Overnight, it was bedlam. 'Cricket "Circus" Threat to Test Matches' ran the comparatively subdued headline in *The Times*, while extra-bold, war-is-declared type and multiple exclamation marks typified the coverage elsewhere. Those first reports suggested that Packer was planning a tournament between Australia and the rest, that

England's current captain Tony Greig and his colleagues Derek Underwood, Alan Knott and John Snow had all signed up, and that the matches would be played in 'unconventional format'. That was putting it mildly.

While sympathetic to the idea that most professional cricketers the world over were ludicrously ill paid for their services, Laker couldn't abide 'the underhand way in which the established game has been stabbed in the back' – a measure of how far his views on cricket administration had moved to the right since his retirement, perhaps, but also reflecting his deeply ingrained moral code. 'Greig should never have been recruiting players [for Packer] while he was captain of England,' he wrote in the *Daily Express*. Laker subsequently agreed to represent the forces of tradition in a widely aired David Frost TV programme, which somehow failed to reveal that Frost himself was a friend and business associate of Packer. It was thought that the 'man in the stocking mask', as one newspaper dubbed the marauding Aussie, won a clear victory on points, particularly after a spectacularly counter-productive intervention on the establishment's behalf by an emotional Robin Marlar, late of Cambridge University and Sussex. As Laker saw it, 'Robin completely lost his rag and was quietly and clinically taken apart by Kerry. It was a disaster.'

For Laker, clearly, there were principles involved that transcended the rights or wrongs of Packer's basic business proposition. He never forgave Tony Greig, whom he thought had 'dishonoured the high office of the England team captain' as he put it a little fustily in the *Express*, and for a time also had to clutch hard at the remnants of his goodwill towards Richie Benaud, who became a top Packer aide. But he was also prepared to make a more personal stand against the sort of cricket epitomised by coloured kit, helmets, yellow (later white) balls, pert young cheerleaders clad in diaphanous blouses and gold lamé hotpants, and drop-in pitches grown in greenhouses. 'Packer made me a most lucrative offer,' Laker later revealed. 'In essence the terms for roughly an eight-week engagement in Australia were the same as a full three-year contract with the BBC. It took me less than 24 hours to thank him for his interest and decline.' Laker always allowed himself a quiet chuckle at the thought of it. 'Luckily, Fred Trueman, who had been waiting anxiously in the wings, accepted the offer with alacrity.'

As a commentator, Laker chose to cultivate a sort of wry detachment from the proceedings in front of him, and became known as much for his extended silences as for the cogent insights in between them. In time his gruff, slightly nasal 'Mornin', Richie' became a sort of national catchphrase. Much the same laconic qualities applied when it came to Laker's private speaking engagements. Far from being a fire-breathing faux-standup comedian, he seemed quiet and faintly embarrassed by the fuss being made over him. That's not to say he wasn't suitably opinionated when he thought the situation called for it. Laker was vocally outspoken, to put it no stronger, in his criticism of Ian Botham's tenure as captain of England, in which we should perhaps remember the great all-rounder boasted a record of no wins, eight draws and four losses. The two men never quite reconciled after that. Laker could, and did, often stand on his rights if he felt himself unduly slighted or put upon. At one function in Leeds, the keynote speaker sat with a frozen expression as a succession of local businessmen took to the floor to allegedly entertain the audience. It must have raised some of the same hackles for Laker as his previous ordeal at the hands of Peter Walker in Tewkesbury, because when eventually called upon, he rose slowly to his feet, gazed without evident enthusiasm around the room and said, 'I was contracted to speak on August 23. It is now August 24. It has been very nice to meet you all. Thank you and good night.'

There would be certain other indications that Laker, while significantly more relaxed about life than in the days of *Over to Me*, was no pushover when it came to asserting his own interests. Entering his 60s, there were still bursts of the old chippy style that had marked his playing career. He thought it strange, for instance, never to be officially invited into the Headingley committee room ('I *am* a bloody Yorkshireman, after all'), as though that in itself were further proof of his being adrift in a socially restrictive world. He rarely suffered fools gladly. His daughter Angela remembered cringing with embarrassment when once accompanying her father to a Sunday League game, where the young steward on duty in the car park at first failed to recognise them. 'Dad rolled down the window, brusquely called out *"Jim Laker"* and then drove on.'

Drawing on this sort of attitude, one well-known current sports writer chides Laker's 'frequent outbursts of liverish behaviour and repeated displays of gender-based superiority'. Yes, the message seems to be, the old boy could play cricket in his day. But he clearly was not an enlightened modern. Laker demanded respect. Perhaps it's simplest to say that he remained a reserved and intensely private man, perfectly affable on his own terms, but difficult to get to know. 'You made a big error if you ever presumed too much on Jim,' Tom Graveney once told me. In some ways Laker was the Peter Cook of cricket, a rare talent who spent the second half of his career living down the sheer audacity of the first, but always capable of flashes of his old sardonic self. He sometimes signed autographs, and sometimes he didn't.

This was more than mere middle-aged grumpiness on Laker's part, though there was doubtless some of that. Starting in early 1981, he complained continually of fatigue and headaches. In May he was struck down while attending the Surrey Old Players' dinner at The Oval and had to be rushed to hospital. The diagnosis was an aortic aneurism, and the subsequent life-saving operation proved a close call. The editor and journalist David Frith went to visit Laker while he convalesced at home in Putney, and was shocked by his appearance. 'Jim was a shrunken, grey figure. He had lost stones in weight. He showed me his scar, from collarbone down to lower abdomen, and I had to sit down. My legs simply went.' Perhaps the whole near-death experience concentrated Laker's mind. I was lucky enough to meet him later that summer, after he returned to the press box for the final two Tests of the stirring Australian series that became known as Botham's Ashes. Laker's excitement at the whole spectacle was well contained, although he admitted he'd allowed himself a small flutter on the outcome of the Oval Test. 'How much?' I asked him. 'Big money,' he replied. 'Ten bob.' At one point I offered the commonplace view that the series as a whole had been a great advertisement for cricket. 'Yes, but does it really matter?' Laker replied drily.

For the two Laker daughters, despite the occasional embarrassment, their father was a boon companion whom they remembered in various guises: as a wit and raconteur, a shy but generally friendly presence at school events, a stickler for correct dress and good manners, an untiring supporter of Chelsea Football Club. When in time grandchildren arrived, he seemed a spry fellow who joined in their games as best he could, whether playing hide and seek in the park or dressing up as a rather gaunt Santa Claus to distribute gifts on Christmas morning. He was probably a less colourful specimen than Charles Laker had been to his own family in the 1920s, if a significantly more solid one. Though never exactly rolling in cash, Laker did better than many of his generation of retired cricketers, adding lucrative freelance berths late in life as an adviser to the Gordon's Gin Wicketkeeper of the Month award ('the perfect sponsor', said his fellow pundit Godfrey Evans) and a regular columnist in *Wisden Cricket Monthly*. He still wrote the occasional book and succumbed to various interviews in which he always seemed confident and affable, if with little indication of any emotional hinterland. Perhaps he never quite forgot his mother's advice to him when he was ten years old to 'never tell my business'.

Tony Lock was less visible in the professional cricket world following his retirement, although he still continued to coach local youths when asked to do so, and once or twice when he wasn't, and kept himself busy on other fronts. His family was now proudly Australian, and he was a popular and highly visible figure around the north Perth suburbs, grabbing a walking stick to stride up to the shops and back most mornings, or pushing his lawnmower promiscuously around the neighbourhood each halfway dry afternoon. In between times he still liked to relax over his beloved cowboy yarns, and perhaps to take a brief midday nap in a nearby glass-fronted sunroom, which enabled onlookers to view him, like some Edwardian cricketing waxwork, sitting inside. He still came back whenever he could for the northern summer, and was on hand in August 1980 to represent an Old England team against Australia at The Oval, staying as Laker's houseguest for the occasion. Lock took 1-66 in ten overs of somewhat eccentric light-medium pace, and wasn't called upon to bat.

I happened to have been writing a slim book on the full-scale Centenary Test that followed at Lord's, and was lucky enough to interview Lock among several other past and present players that week. He was loud, indiscreet and fun, and on the whole I think pleased to be reminded of the old days, although I remember at one point he cordially invited me to bugger off when I slipped in a quick question about throwing. The storm passed, however, and when I turned off the tape recorder Lock said, 'Well bowled, mate,' and invited me to join him for a drink. We went to the pub immediately outside The Oval's front gate, which allowed me to watch Lock in action when, as happened roughly once every four minutes, some middle-aged fan appeared unbidden at his elbow and announced himself by saying, 'You won't remember me, Tony, but I was sitting at the Vauxhall End when you …' He signed a lot of autographs, posed for numerous photos, was stood several drinks. There was no false modesty about him. Lock knew exactly how good he'd been, and appeared to enjoy the fact that a stranger might care to approach him to say so again. I awoke the next morning with a serious hangover.

Later in the 1980s Lock was able to secure a summer coaching job at Mill Hill School in north London. After a long day spent in the nets there, followed by a pub dinner, he would catch the train south to spend the night with his cousin Nova Hearne at Sevenoaks in Kent. 'My husband would meet the train, often vainly,' she recalled. 'Tony had fallen asleep and carried on past his stop. Then we got another phone call from Hastings. "Meet me on the way back," he would say.'

By his mid-50s, Lock had managed to establish warm-weather bases in both England and Australia, an enviable combination in many ways. In addition to his paid work at Mill Hill and elsewhere, he still sought out promising young candidates for private coaching sessions, as often as not on a pro bono basis. This seemed to be a commendably public-spirited gesture on Lock's part, but it was to prove a ticking time bomb.

* * *

Laker slipped comfortably into relative old age. Although he never again enjoyed good health, he found plenty of writing work, at least some of it well paid, to supplement his BBC income. Starting in 1983, he also joined his fellow commentator Brian Johnston in a touring stage show called *That's Cricket* which mixed a little archive film footage with some gentle reminiscences and thoughts on the modern game in an atmosphere of the sort of exasperated love that often afflicts the sport's longest-serving observers. It sold out regional theatres each winter. Confirming his rehabilitation at Surrey, Laker also took over as chairman of the county's cricket committee. The mid-1980s were not, on the whole, golden days at The Oval. The first team generally underperformed in the County Championship, and some of the ground facilities would have appeared antique even in Laker's era. He was at least able to push through a few modest reforms, such as knocking the two separate dressing rooms – one for the senior players, and one for the rest – into one.

Laker still travelled the country for the BBC, but now paced himself between matches. The former Glamorgan and England captain Tony Lewis once asked him for any words of advice he might have for a new commentator, 'and instead of some technical stuff about microphone technique, Jim said, "Don't drive above 60mph on the motorway. And don't rush home. Find a little hotel to pull over for some rest. Your wife won't thank you if you wrap your car around a tree."'

It wasn't all gentle into that good night, however, and there was a fraught scene when Johnston's travelling show reached the Theatre Royal, York, at the height of the controversy about whether or not Geoff Boycott should be offered a renewed county contract. Laker thought he should. Fred Trueman, who was also on the panel that night, thought he shouldn't. Don Mosey describes what happened next:

Fred was late in arriving, and when he finally put in an appearance Brian Johnston was already on stage doing a warm-up to keep the audience from becoming too restive while Jim and I had a quiet drink in the Green Room. Suddenly, Fred roared in with all guns blazing. His first act was to launch a violent verbal attack upon Laker, who tried vainly to turn away his wrath with a soft answer. Fred was not to be appeased and as I stepped (literally) between them I had a quick glimpse from the wings of Brian's anguished expression as he stood centre stage trying to keep the audience happy while his three guests could be seen, out of the corner of his eye, very nearly locked in physical combat at stage left. Fred stormed off home immediately after the show.

Laker again became unwell in early 1986, and went in for what was thought to be a relatively minor operation that March. He survived the procedure but grew increasingly ill and contracted septicaemia after moving to a clinic near his home in south London. The end came with brutal suddenness. Laker died on the morning of 23 April. He was 64. It was St George's Day, and another England stalwart, Bill Edrich, succumbed to his injuries after falling backwards down a flight of stairs just a few hours later. Despite some imaginative treatment in the press, the two players had not been especially close. Edrich was one of those vocally unhappy at his depiction in *Over to Me* 26 years earlier. But it was a grievous double loss for the game. Around the world, players in almost all organised teams observed a minute's silence on 24 April.

Early death is often seen as a sort of martyrdom. Certainly Laker's was widely portrayed that way, particularly when it emerged that he might not have even needed his final, and ultimately fatal, surgery. In both his national and local obituaries, qualities were now found that had somehow previously failed to surface, and Laker himself might have been mordantly amused by some of the more fulsome tributes. E.W. Swanton perhaps spoke for many when he said, 'Jim's supreme skill as a cricketer is a legend that will last as long as the game is played.' At both Lord's and The Oval, the grounds where Laker's welcome had once been so equivocal, the flags flew at half mast in his honour. A memorial service that July packed Southwark Cathedral to the rafters. The departed was remembered fondly by Len Hutton and without insult by Freddie Brown. Peter May wrote a moving eulogy. The only sour note came when the BBC saw fit to send Laker's widow Lilly an *ex gratia* payment of £100, the equivalent of a day's fee for television commentary at the time, or, to put it another way, roughly 90p for each of the 111 Tests Laker had covered over the years. Lilly herself died only in 2021, at the age of 102.

Perhaps the most poignant comment of all was the one Tony Lock supplied for the 1987 edition of the Surrey yearbook. When the material first arrived at The Oval by post, the county officials noticed that it was somewhat rambling, and untroubled by any sordidly conventional notions of spelling or grammar. In fact there was no punctuation involved whatsoever. Lock had been noted as 'awkward' in written English while at school, and always struggled with his prose, which could be suggestive of a light fog moving over a dim landscape. Nonetheless, his edited yearbook remarks were in their way both eloquent and heartfelt, dwelling as they did on Laker the cricketing genius, not Laker the cantankerous egoist.

'The telephone rings constantly in my house,' Lock wrote, 'so it was not out of the ordinary when it did so one morning in the Australian winter. As I picked up the nearest receiver the call was from London and in the next two minutes my world was completely shattered. A gentleman from the BBC was informing me of the death of Jim Laker. The voice at the other end asked if I had a few words to add on this sad event. From memory, I said, "The world may have lost a great cricketer but I have lost a bloody good friend." The rest of the day was fairly hazy. The phone rang all the time; most of the time my wife answered.'

These sentiments were handsome on Lock's part, even if some of the specific phrasing may have betrayed the work of a second party.

'Naturally,' he continued, 'my thoughts went back a number of years to when I played opposite probably the greatest spin bowler I have ever seen. Jim used to wander in to bowl; he knew exactly where it was going to land, and the scoreboard would read "Caught Lock, bowled Laker". I had the greatest confidence in his ability, so I was able to stand very close in the knowledge I wouldn't get hit. If a catch was not held, "J.C." would stand there looking at me, one arm folded across his chest, cupping his chin in the other hand. Not a word passed his lips but I would know what he was thinking.'

While, again, a word or two of Lock's panegyric may have owed something to the Oval public relations team, there can be no doubt about the sincerity of its author's emotions. Shortly after the initial phone call from the BBC, Audrey Lock had come back from walking the dogs and found her husband sitting alone in front of an old England Test cricket video, shaking violently.

* * *

As Laker's posthumous legend grew, so did Lock's ambivalence on the subject. 'I still get letters,' he noted in 1989, 'calling me an utter bastard for having taken that one wicket at Old Trafford, spoiling Jim's perfect record. You'd think I'd vandalised the Mona Lisa or something.' After reading a brief appreciation Lock once sent in referring throughout to 'J.C.', an editor rang back and enquired puckishly if the initials stood for 'Jesus Christ' or 'James Charles', as in Laker. 'What's the difference?' Lock replied. To some, it seemed that the one bowler was already half forgotten, while the other one was now immortal, although Imran Khan rather bucked this trend when, in 1992, in the course of an article on cheating, he wrote, 'Jim Laker, England's greatest off-spinner, regularly fiddled with the ball.'

Lock himself still had his moments. He endorsed products, wrote ghosted articles and all but commuted between England

and Australia, complaining dryly of the hassles of airports and the general unpleasantness of being on planes 'with the gurgling toilets and rubber-chicken food'. But the truth is that for large stretches of the late 1980s and early 1990s he was a sort of cricketing celebrity without portfolio: someone you might invite to your club's annual dinner, perhaps to give a more defiant and combative tone to the usual speeches, but most of whose days were spent slumped in an easy chair nursing a drink and a cigarette, or snoring away the afternoon with a cowboy book splayed open across his chest. He could still be bitterly sardonic or brutally funny about the modern generation of cricketers, 'although I try to be kind', he once told me.

I remember Lock in this context fast asleep in a leather armchair in the downstairs restaurant of the Cricketers Club in London with a full glass of wine in his hand, cocked at a precarious angle. A waiter hovered nearby, absorbed in the fate of the tipping glass. Lock's capacity for food and drink, like his growing bulk, was impressive. But it never slowed him down. He rarely bothered about the other sort of spin, and instead gave it to you straight. Someone once said of Lock that he could be such a grump that he was grumpy about other grumps. But he was also an unswervingly loyal friend. While in Britain he often took the train to Pembroke in west Wales to help coach local schoolchildren. Lock's old pupil Julia White had since become president of the town's cricket association, and she remembers him as 'the most accommodating and kind man', in contrast to the sometimes explosive character she'd known in the 1950s.

'I never saw him out of temper,' White reported of these latter-day sessions. No one ever complained about Lock for any reason, and the general feeling in Pembroke was that they were wonderfully lucky to have him at their disposal. He placed a particular premium on fielding skills, and was something of a pioneer in insisting that a cricketer should be able to collect and return a ball as fluidly as his or her counterpart in professional baseball. One Pembroke schoolteacher wrote, 'We were all very impressed by the delightful rapport Tony had with the children, and recognised the sure hand of a very fine tutor. They responded so well that if they had been asked to walk on water they would have done so without hesitation.' Perhaps Lock was good with children because in many ways he was a child himself. He never pretended that a student had played well if they played badly. Nor did he ever complain if he considered they had done their best. A woman now in her forties told me that she'd been one of a group of 'giggly Welsh schoolgirls who took coaching from Tony, and he was strict but fair. You got given an ice cream if you did what he said, and ordered to run a lap around the field with your pads on if you didn't. There was never anything improper.' Lock was equally devoted to White's elderly mother – another echo, perhaps, of his own childhood experience – and sent a huge bouquet when she died, along with the note, 'In loving memory of my second Mum.'

Lock was in between summer coaching engagements when in late May 1989 he found time to attend a star-studded benefit dinner at the Grosvenor House Hotel in London in honour of the great Lancashire and England seamer Brian Statham. They were all there that night, from the dowager figure of E.W. Swanton, with 86-year-old Gubby Allen on his arm, up or down to a richly tinted Denis Compton and most of the other surviving members of the England team that won the Ashes at The Oval in 1953. I happened to then be writing a book about the side's irrepressible stumper Godfrey Evans, and went to the affair as his guest. Little did I know when I first signed on as his biographer that there would be a significant social component to the job. Evans then lived in somewhat makeshift circumstances in a friend's house in Northamptonshire, and as a result I often put him up for the night when he was in town. As a rule, this involved crawling around the casinos of Soho together, with Godfrey continually expressing the confidence, alas never quite fulfilled, that his 'system' at roulette would make us both millionaires.

One of the highlights of the Statham event was the opportunity it afforded to observe certain old cricketing partnerships, and sometimes also old feuds, extended into the cummerbund world of a glittering hotel dinner. Apart from Compton and Evans, there were former greats of the game who defined cricket as physical (Frank 'Typhoon' Tyson), graceful (Tom Graveney) and intense (Brian Close). Peter May, Alec Bedser and Trevor Bailey all sat less than a pitch length away, and in time Fred Trueman got up to do a revue that turned 'arse' (no ladies were present that night) into the longest one-syllable drawl in comedic history, and went on from there to get a bit bawdy. You could see how he might once have fallen foul of the austere Len Hutton. Hutton himself was at our table. He asked me for a cigarette just as we were sitting down to eat, a query followed by 'Then I'll smoke one of my own,' and I remember him dragging away through much of the meal.

One way or another, it was heady company for a fitfully employed, freelance sports writer to be keeping. Evans himself was on my left, and on my right was a now nearly spherical Tony Lock. The latter had made his initial approach to our table with long, erratic steps, swerving from one direction to another without apparent purpose. You felt a bit apprehensive as you watched him bang past the backs of other diners, as if a physical altercation of some sort might break out as a result, inappropriate here in the Grosvenor House ballroom. When Lock finally reached his destination he slapped me, surprisingly hard, on the back and then collapsed into his chair. There wasn't the least suggestion that he'd overdone the Bacchic rites, just that he was in one of his sunny moods. Never known as a clotheshorse, he was dressed in an impressively ancient dinner jacket with comically wide lapels, a pair of once-white socks, and slip-on grey shoes polished to an unnatural lustre. A faint but discernible tang of stale cigarette hovered around him as he sat down. He was loquacious, unapologetically rude about some of the 'MCC twats' sitting nearby, and still very funny.

Of course, like most of us Lock had two sides to him, possibly more. Listening to his old war stories, often shading off into a long list of unresolved grievances, could sometimes be the reverse of pleasurable, a bit like taking medicine with no assurance it would do you any good. But at other times he was riotously good company. At one stage a retired England batsman who had somehow gone on to a job in the media stood up to address the room. With a certain inevitability, his speech turned to the current breed of Test cricketers and how they were so sadly lacking in any of the basic skills of the game. By the time he reached the end of his remarks he was really letting them have it with an old sweat's assumed wisdom, and there was more than a touch of the Monty Python sketch about the four well-dressed Yorkshiremen sitting around remembering when they had lived in a paper bag on a rubbish tip, or worked 25 hours a day down at the mill with a farthing a year to show for it.

Absorbing this routine from his seat in the shadows, Lock waited patiently for the speaker to finally conclude his remarks before delivering his own verdict. He showed a born comedian's timing, first sitting still, a thin smile slowly playing on his lips, for several seconds. 'He was a good player,' Lock allowed at length, gesturing to the top table. He gave it another moment, then added, 'And he's a fuck of a lot better now since he's retired.' No doubt the comment might have been construed as inappropriate, or offensive, had one of today's culture police overheard it. But everyone at the table was guffawing. Later in the evening Lock again made it clear to me that he had only mixed feelings when it came to the media as a whole, but that by the same token, 'You're not the biggest bastard of the bunch,' intoxicatingly high praise coming from that quarter,

I thought, and which encouraged me to believe I might one day write his biography. In many ways he would have been the logical successor to Evans. For the rest of the meal Lock sat quietly in his seat rolling crumbs of bread into balls or occasionally making paper planes. It's possible he may have rested his eyes for a moment or two during some of the later speeches, but then so did many others in the course of a protracted evening. At the end of it all I got another slap on the back, a warm handshake and a promise to stay in touch. 'Be lucky,' Lock told me. I never saw him again.

From this point on, real tragedy befell Lock and his family.

In early 1991, a 20-year-old unnamed Australian woman contacted the Perth police after having seen a television phone-in show inviting sexual abuse victims to come forward with their stories. Four years earlier, she said, she had gone by appointment to Lock's home for a private coaching session. Following that, he'd taken her back inside the house, sat down next to her on the sofa, put his arm affectionately around her shoulder, and then promptly started to rub either her genitals or his own, depending on which account you read. It was obviously a serious accusation, although the subsequent judicial proceedings unfolded with excruciating slowness. Lock was eventually arrested in February 1993, and went on trial that November on a charge of indecently assaulting a minor.

Lock told the court that he had indeed sat down next to the teenaged girl, but that what had followed was no more than a regrettable accident. 'We were side by side … The next thing I knew her hand was on my shorts,' he said. 'I was a little startled. I don't think it was done intentionally.' Lock added that he had then left the room because he was embarrassed but came back and gave the girl a light kiss to ease the tension, which he said was offered in the spirit of 'an uncle', with no sexual intent. The jury found him not guilty by a 10-2 majority after three hours' deliberation. Lock later related the shock of his arrest in an interview with Australia's *Sunday Times*. 'I was photographed, given a number, fingerprinted and chucked in a locked cell. It was humiliating and very, very frightening.'

Lock was re-arrested the day after his acquittal for a second offence said to have taken place against an under-age girl 13 years earlier. There were preliminary hearings of the case in March and June 1994. Dozens of English cricketers began to get letters that same summer appealing for funds to help finance their former colleague's defence. Many of these same players suddenly remembered that they had pressing expenses just then, and thus sadly couldn't help, although one or two others, Tom Graveney and John Murray prominent among them, loyally sent a cheque.

Meanwhile, there were further humiliating stories in the Australian press, and at some stage that summer of 1994 it was learnt that Lock had been diagnosed with inoperable cancer. In August the family moved to a smaller house in order to be closer to one of their adult sons. In September, Audrey Lock, Tony's staunchly loyal wife of 42 years, suffered a stroke and died. It was another devastating blow among the series of misfortunes that characterised her widower's final years. The curtain was now rapidly falling. Once the most gregarious of cricketers, Lock increasingly became a hostage in his small suburban Perth home, incapacitated by a terrifying agoraphobia.

In December 1994 a jury failed to reach a verdict in Lock's second sexual assault case, and the matter went back to the Western Australia state prosecutor's office. Six weeks later, the authorities announced that they were dropping all the charges, though they were at pains to point out that this fell some way short of a full exoneration of the accused. The decision showed purely 'a degree of goodwill and mercy', it was reported, presumably the result of Lock's illness as much as any other factor. By then the cancer had spread through his body; all the cricketing memorabilia had been sold, the new house refinanced to help pay the mounting legal and medical bills. A touch of the old feistiness returned when Lock told the press, 'I will never forget what I've been through. At least I can hold my head a bit higher when I walk down the street. My reputation has been destroyed but I'm lucky that I've got friends who don't give a stuff, and they're the only ones who matter.'

Still, this was a lot of grief for even a stoic like Lock, and by all accounts it showed. He changed horribly in his last few months. Lock's round, heavily lined features came to suggest more of the monk than the jester, while friends in Perth found that he no longer answered his doorbell. 'The house would be locked up and he would be sitting there watching television, scared to go out in case someone recognised him,' his son Richard recalled. Towards the end, Lock gave a final interview in which he said bitterly that he would be remembered only for the sex charges and not for cricket. On reading this I immediately wrote to him, promising he would be proven wrong. I like to think that he got and perhaps even enjoyed this tiny gesture, which was no more than the truth, but I'll never know. Even at the best of times, Lock hardly seemed to grasp what letters were for. If he wanted to tell you something he did so the only way he knew how – loud, clear and very upfront.

Tony Lock died on 30 March 1995. He was 65, just a year older than Jim Laker had been at the time of his death. An hour or two after the end, a group of close friends went to the hospice in Perth to pay their final respects. They found Lock's body laid out on a bed, immaculately dressed in white flannels and a striped sweater, a cricket ball gripped in his left hand with the fingers expertly positioned for the really unplayable delivery. There was a thin but definite smile on his lips, they later reported.

Source Notes

THIS BRIEF section shows at least the formal interviews, published works, and/or archive material used in the preparation of the book. Although I don't claim any intimate familiarity with either man, I was lucky enough first as the holder of a somewhat spurious press pass, and later as a friend and biographer of Godfrey Evans and others, to have met both Jim Laker and Tony Lock on many social occasions. I put on record here my profound if properly critical admiration of both these great cricketers. I should also particularly acknowledge the pioneering research of the late Alan Hill, whose books on Laker and Lock are duly listed in the bibliography. I've more than once quoted from these works, as credited, either verbatim or slightly edited for sense.

A primary source for the early part of the book was Middlesex and England's Peter Parfitt, who kindly shared his experience of escorting Laker to his family gravesite. My late friends Godfrey Evans and Tom Graveney both spoke to me at some length, variously on and off the record, on the subject of the 1956 English home season. I should also particularly thank Jon Surtees, head of media at Surrey CCC, in this same context, and of course Micky Stewart, who came into Surrey's championship-winning side in 1954 and who answered all my questions on his colleagues with unfailing patience and courtesy. I can also recommend

Anthony Asquith's often overlooked 1953 film *The Final Test*, not only for its strangely compelling storyline (written by Terence Rattigan), but also the unintentional comedy of some of its cricketing cast members' performances. The General Register Office provided details of vital but strangely often incorrectly given details such as the dates and circumstances of Laker's and Lock's births and marriages. The quote from Laker in Chapter 2 beginning 'She told us – my sister ...' can be found in Alan Hill's book, *Jim Laker*, as cited in the bibliography. The quote in the same chapter by Fred Robinson beginning 'Very positive ...' is from Don Mosey's *Laker: Portrait of a Legend*, also as noted in the bibliography. The line attributed to Lock's father insisting, 'He rushed up to me and excitedly said ...' appears in Alan Hill's *Tony Lock: Aggressive Master of Spin*, also as cited. The description of Errol Holmes recalling him as a 'beautiful player [who] made all hearts beat ...' appears in that wonderful if also sometimes mildly overwrought book of cricket reminiscences *Sing all a Green Willow* (London: Epworth Press 1967) by the late Ronald Mason.

I'm indebted for much of the information covering the years 1946–56 to the late Godfrey Evans and Tom Graveney, as well as to my much-missed friend John Murray of Middlesex and England. Richie Benaud once kindly put his recollections of the 1956 season at my disposal, and in 1989 I was also lucky enough, through Evans, to have come to interview Keith Miller on the subject. I should also particularly again thank Jon Surtees and his colleagues at The Oval, as well as Sir Oliver Popplewell, Neil Robinson of the MCC, Nigel Hancock of the Cricket Society, and those great players the late Ted Dexter, Neil Harvey, Jim Parks, Pat Pocock, Micky Stewart, Garry Sobers, Raman Subba Row and the late Fred Titmus. I consulted both *Wisden Cricketers' Almanack* and the CricketArchive website throughout.

The direct quotes appearing in these pages of the book remarking 'I wasn't conscious of it at the time …'; '[Laker] hadn't stopped competing, though …'; 'I had begun to despair of receiving it …'; 'The first time I handled a ball in a Test match …'; 'The umpire at square leg, W.F. Price …'; 'My leap for joy measured the ecstasy …'; 'Several of our [team] came up to me and said …'; and 'I thought Wardle was caught in the slips by Peter May …' all appear in Tony Lock's thoroughly enjoyable if necessarily partial book *For Surrey and England*, as cited in the bibliography. Similarly, the lines beginning 'Be a sport and toss one up …'; 'If the selectors want to seek out the young players …'; and 'As a [bowler] he was as smooth as they come …' all appear in Jim Laker's notorious suicide note of a book, produced in the first flush of his retirement, *Over to Me*, as cited in the bibliography. The line beginning '[The] Leeds Test stayed with [Laker] for a long time …' appears in Richie Benaud, *Willow Patterns* (London: Hodder & Stoughton, 1969); the lines starting 'He exults and suffers …' and 'Many great spin bowlers have found themselves …' both appear in the Neville Cardus anthology *Cardus in the Covers* (London: Souvenir Press, 1978). E.W. Swanton's account of the offended party in the Barbados hotel complaining 'rather in the manner of Bertie Wooster's Aunt Agatha …' appears in his book *Sort of a Cricket Person*, as cited in the bibliography; and the quote opening '[Laker] was a very fine bowler, but he was a funny bloke …' appears in Brian Scovell's equally fine *Jim Laker: 19-90*, also as cited in the bibliography. I'm especially grateful to Kevin Powell, who kindly supplied me with Oxted CC's centenary brochure, with its various accounts of Tony Lock's exploits in the area.

For details of the period 1956–61 I'm grateful to the late Richie Benaud, the late Ted Dexter, Peter Parfitt, Jim Parks, Micky Stewart, Raman Subba Row, Roy Swetman, the late Fred Titmus and Roger Tolchard, as well as to Jon Surtees at Surrey CCC, and to the Surrey History Centre. Again, I consulted the pages of both *Wisden* and the CricketArchive service throughout, as well as the likes of the *Cricketer International*, the *Daily Express*, *Daily Mail*, *Daily Mirror* and *The Times*. I'm grateful for the help of the UK National Archives and the British Newspaper Library.

The quotes beginning '[Tayfield] took more liberties ...'; 'Oakman had borrowed a car to go out for the evening ...'; 'A stupor overtook [Bailey] ...'; 'I took my wife and two daughters to South Africa ...', 'The pathetic little pattern continued ...', 'Our defeat by Kent ...'; 'May was no man-manager ...'; 'The tour was badly managed ...'; 'May walked into the dressing room ...'; and 'Bert Lock was under orders ...', the last of them slightly adapted for sense, all appear in Laker's still semi-iconic memoir *Over to Me*. Similarly, the lines beginning 'It's a funny thing, but if Bob ...'; 'Whether the disappointment of being ...'; and 'Magnificently as Jim bowled ...' all appear in Tony Lock's *For Surrey and England*, as noted in the bibliography. The lines starting 'He was a hero to me, a loving father ...'; 'Do you realise that all 11 players ...'; 'I [was] asked thousands of times what went through my mind ...'; and 'I was sitting alongside some of the other young players ...' all appear in Brian Scovell's peerless *Jim Laker: 19-90*, as cited. Some small confusion surrounds the account in the same book concerning Peter May's 1959 wedding to Virginia Gilligan. While Scovell writes, 'Jim did not have an invitation,' the surviving Pathé News footage of the event suggests that Laker was present. Perhaps it was one of those occasions where there was one audience for the church ceremony, and another, larger one on hand for the reception. The lines beginning 'When [the] fourth wicket fell Tony pushed me to one side ...'; 'Lock could be quite amusing ...'; and 'He used all sorts of styles until he hit on the right one ...' all appear in Alan Hill's *Tony Lock: Aggressive Master of Spin*, as cited. The line remarking that Harold Macmillan was 'very unhappy with the way the matter was handled ...' appears in Macmillan's memoir *Riding the Storm* (London: Macmillan, 1971); and Jim Laker's line noting, 'Lock was a bit upset after [Old Trafford] ...' appears in Bill Frindall's *The Wisden Book of Cricket Records* (London: Headline, 1993).

For advice or source material in the final chapters of the book I'm also indebted to Dennis Amiss, Mike Atherton, the late Ted Dexter, Keith Fletcher, Stephen Hall of the Western Australia Cricket Association, Robin Hobbs, Richard Holdridge of Leicestershire CCC, Robin Marlar, my late friend John Murray, Jim Parks, Peter Perchard, Pat Pocock, Micky Stewart, Roy Swetman, Roger Tolchard and the late and irreplaceable John Woodcock.

The quotes beginning 'Dad liked nothing better than going down to work ...'; 'I estimate that there were 5,000 people ...'; '[Lock] didn't suffer fools gladly ...'; 'My husband would meet the train, often vainly ...'; 'We were very impressed by the delightful rapport Tony had with the children ...'; and 'The house would be locked up and he would be sitting there ...' all appear in *Tony Lock: Aggressive Master of Spin*, as cited. The quotes beginning 'It's difficult even to say that ...'; 'Richards started on his way to a brilliant ...'; and '[Laker] was a shrunken, grey figure ...' all appear in *Laker: Portrait of a Legend*, a superlative book in its way, if one occasionally labouring under the weight of its author's tone of indignation at the then-prevailing British class system. The lines attributed to Trevor Bailey beginning 'It was hard to accept the criticism ...'; and Peter Walker's account beginning 'It came at the start of one of my earliest appearances ...' are both included in *Jim Laker: 19-90*, as cited. The line beginning 'Defiantly rolling up his sleeve ...' appears in R.A. Roberts's *The Fight for the Ashes* (London: George Harrap, 1961); the line from Ted Dexter recalling '[there] came a lull in the speed of falling wickets ...' is from Dexter's book

Ted Dexter Declares (London: Stanley Paul, 1966), for which I'm indebted to my late father Sefton Sandford, a great cricket man; and the quote beginning 'One of my fondest memories is to have fielded at leg slip ...' appears in Richie Benaud's *Willow Patterns*, as cited.

Statistical Index

1

JIM LAKER, season-by-season record in first-class cricket

Batting and fielding:

	M	I	NO	Runs	HS	Average	100	50	Ct
1946	3	3	1	3	3	1.50	-	-	1
1947	18	26	4	408	60	18.54	-	1	13
1947/48	8	12	2	212	55	21.20	-	1	4
1948	29	44	10	828	99	24.35	-	3	16
1949	28	39	7	548	100	17.12	1	-	25
1950	30	42	6	589	53	16.36	-	1	22
1950/51	10	10	1	171	61	19.00	-	1	5
1951	28	38	6	624	89	19.50	-	4	22
1951/52	4	4	0	77	35	19.25	-	-	3
1952	30	34	5	310	26	10.68	-	-	15
1953	31	34	3	502	81	16.19	-	1	25
1953/54	7	9	1	123	33	15.38	-	-	4
1954	29	33	9	607	113	25.29	1	1	29
1955	30	38	6	706	78*	22.06	-	4	26
1956	25	34	5	320	43*	11.03	-	-	8
1956/57	14	16	6	79	17	7.90	-	-	3
1957	28	28	11	210	44	12.35	-	-	9

1958	28	29	6	325	59	14.13	-	1	11
1958/59	10	13	3	107	22*	10.70	-	-	1
1959	24	30	7	301	28	13.08	-	-	15
1962	12	11	2	43	13	4.77	-	-	5
1963	10	12	5	95	24*	13.57	-	-	4
1963/64	2	1	1	0	0*	-	-	-	1
1964	8	6	1	110	28	22.00	-	-	2
1964/65	4	2	0	6	5	3.00	-	-	1
Total	**450**	**548**	**108**	**7304**	**113**	**16.60**	**2**	**18**	**270**

Bowling:

	Overs	Mdns	Runs	Wkts	Avge	5WI	10WM	BB
1946	60	12	169	8	21.12	-	-	3-43
1947	575.5	135	1420	79	17.97	5	-	8-69
1947/48	388.5	117	973	36	27.02	3	-	7-103
1948	1058.4	251	2903	104	27.91	4	-	8-55
1949	1192.1	419	2422	122	19.85	8	1	8-42
1950	1399.5	522	2544	166	15.32	12	5	8-2
1950/51	315.2	131	579	36	16.08	3	-	6-23
1951	1301.3	400	2681	149	17.99	13	5	7-36
1951/52	228.1	88	379	24	15.79	3	1	5-44
1952	1071	342	2219	125	17.75	9	1	7-57
1953	1155.5	382	2366	135	17.52	7	1	6-25
1953/54	333.5	113	756	22	34.36	-	-	4-47
1954	966.2	315	2048	135	15.17	13	5	8-51
1955	1093.1	362	2382	133	17.90	9	3	7-95
1956	959.3	364	1906	132	14.43	8	3	10-53
1956/57*	387.7	122	875	50	17.50	2	-	6-47
1957	1016.5	393	1921	126	15.24	5	-	7-16
1958	882.5	330	1651	116	14.23	7	2	8-46
1958/59*	282.1	63	655	38	17.23	3	1	5-31
1959	797.2	246	1920	78	24.61	5	2	7-38
1962	390.5	96	962	51	18.86	5	1	7-73
1963	374	128	828	43	19.25	2	1	7-89
1963/64	72	13	221	5	44.20	-	-	2-50

1964	226	55	577	17	33.94	-	-	4-41
1964/65	133.4	23	434	14	31.00	1	-	5-54
Total**	**16663.3**	**5421**	**35791**	**1944**	**18.41**	**127**	**32**	**10-53**

* 8-ball overs

** Overall total includes both 8-ball and 6-ball overs

Twelve or more wickets taken in a match:

19-90	England v Australia	Old Trafford	1956
15-97	Surrey v MCC	Lord's	1954
13-159	Essex v Kent	Dover	1962
12-78	Surrey v Sussex	Hove	1958
12-86	Surrey v Gloucestershire	Bristol	1950
12-98	Surrey v Kent	The Oval	1949
12-130	Surrey v Australians	The Oval	1956
12-144	Surrey v Worcestershire	The Oval	1951

Eight or more wickets in an innings:

10-53	England v Australia	Old Trafford	1956
10-88	Surrey v Australians	The Oval	1956
9-37	England v Australia	Old Trafford	1956
8-2	England v The Rest	Bradford	1950
8-42	Surrey v Warwickshire	The Oval	1949
8-45	Surrey v Gloucestershire	Bristol	1950
8-46	Surrey v Sussex	Hove	1958
8-51	Surrey v MCC	Lord's	1954
8-55	Surrey v Gloucestershire	The Oval	1948
8-57	Surrey v Middlesex	The Oval	1950
8-69	Surrey v Hampshire	Portsmouth	1947

Ten wickets in an innings twice in one season:

10-88 and 10-53 in 1956

The only instance in the history of first-class cricket

Fifty or more wickets in a month:

June 1950 Innings: 16 Wickets: 55 Average: 13.80 Best bowling: 8-45

May 1951 Innings: 16 Wickets: 60 Average: 13.53 Best bowling: 7-36

How Laker's victims were out:

Caught	1065	54.78%
Bowled	557	28.65%
Lbw	246	12.65%
Stumped	72	3.70%
Hit wicket	4	0.21%
Total	1944	100%

Most fielders involved in Laker's dismissals:

124	G.A.R. Lock
110	A.J. McIntyre (77 ct, 33 st)
107	W.S. Surridge
68	J.C. Laker
64	M.J. Stewart
43	A.V. Bedser
32	E.A. Bedser
30	P.B.H. May

2

TONY LOCK, season-by-season record in first-class cricket

Batting and fielding:

	M	I	NO	Runs	HS	Average	50	Ct
1946	1	1	1	1	1*	-	-	1
1947	2	2	0	8	8	4.00	-	1
1948	2	3	2	20	14*	20.00	-	2
1949	25	33	14	212	29	11.15	-	28
1950	26	34	7	223	23	8.25	-	33
1951	32	38	17	192	31	9.14	-	33
1952	32	27	15	170	24*	14.16	-	54
1953	19	22	7	274	40	18.26	-	36
1953/54	9	12	2	105	40*	10.50	-	6
1954	32	35	7	353	46	12.60	-	42
1955	33	41	9	669	55	20.90	2	48
1955/56	11	15	2	237	62*	18.23	1	9
1956	26	33	6	338	43	12.51	-	44
1956/57	14	18	4	229	39	16.35	-	11
1957	31	32	6	464	46	17.84	-	63
1958	29	31	2	610	66	21.03	5	46
1958/59	15	18	1	191	44	11.23	-	9
1959	28	38	4	521	64*	15.32	1	34
1959/60	2	4	0	75	40	18.75	-	6
1960	34	41	6	474	60	13.54	1	37
1961	31	46	9	621	67*	16.78	1	48
1961/62	15	17	5	182	49	15.16	-	20
1962	32	36	2	563	70	16.55	3	33
1962/63	10	18	3	264	48	17.60	-	14
1963	28	36	5	656	60	21.16	5	19
1963/64	5	9	1	194	53	24.25	1	5
1964/65	8	13	2	208	41	18.90	-	8
1965	8	8	0	64	40	8.00	-	8

1965/66	10	13	3	215	44	21.50	-	17
1966	29	43	6	658	56	17.78	3	38
1966/67	8	13	2	136	66	12.36	1	9
1967	28	33	5	603	81*	21.53	2	33
1967/68	12	17	2	242	89	16.13	1	11
1968/69	10	11	0	153	37	13.90	-	13
1969/70	7	9	2	116	39	16.57	-	4
1970/71	10	12	2	101	24*	10.10	-	7
Total	**654**	**812**	**161**	**10342**	**89**	**15.88**	**27**	**830**

Lock failed to score a century in first-class cricket. His career total of 830 catches (sometimes given as 831) is the third-highest of any first-class cricketer, after Frank Woolley (1,018) and W.G. Grace (873); he played roughly 200 fewer matches than either of the men ahead of him in the list.

Bowling:

	Overs	Mdns	Runs	Wkts	Avge	5WI	10WM	BB
1946	10	2	24	0	-	-	-	-
1947	56	15	128	4	32.00	-	-	2-52
1948	64	12	168	11	15.27	2	-	6-43
1949	754.5	287	1672	67	24.95	-	-	4-27
1950	919.2	371	1762	74	23.81	3	-	6-40
1951	1155.4	448	2237	105	21.30	5	-	6-32
1952	1109.4	416	2237	131	17.07	6	1	6-15
1953	732.2	284	1590	100	15.90	8	2	8-26
1953/54	490.1	158	1178	28	42.07	1	-	5-57
1954	1027.1	412	2000	125	16.00	7	2	8-36
1955	1418.4	497	3109	216	14.39	18	6	8-82
1955/56	557	296	869	81	10.72	10	4	8-17
1956	1058.2	437	1932	155	12.46	15	5	10-54
1956/57*	352.7	120	833	56	14.87	4	2	6-14
1957	1,194.1	449	2550	212	12.02	21	9	7-47
1958	1014.4	382	2055	170	12.08	14	3	8-99

1958/59**	502	129	1328	57	23.29	4	1	6-29
1959	972.5	287	2374	111	21.38	8	1	7-66
1959/60	93.3	31	210	15	14.00	2	1	6-76
1960	1183.4	352	2976	139	21.41	10	2	9-77
1961	1266.1	363	3618	127	28.48	8	-	6-54
1961/62	695.3	287	1405	59	23.81	2	-	6-65
1962	1115.1	390	2840	108	26.29	7	1	6-32
1962/63*	321.5	55	1088	39	27.89	1	-	7-53
1963	874.2	302	2149	88	24.42	3	-	6-39
1963/64*	110.6	31	344	8	43.00	-	-	4-49
1964/65*	273.2	85	718	25	28.72	1	-	5-90
1965	324.1	113	665	35	19.00	3	-	5-8
1965/66*	406.6	84	1133	44	25.75	3	-	5-61
1966	954.1	328	2132	109	19.55	9	2	8-85
1966/67*	398.4	105	1086	51	21.29	3	1	6-85
1967	1154.1	431	2319	128	18.11	10	5	7-54
1967/68**	358.6	78	999	51	19.58	4	-	5-36
1968/69*	385.7	66	1293	53	24.39	3	1	7-61
1969/70*	256.2	43	723	27	26.77	1	-	5-53
1970/71*	323	62	965	35	27.57	-	-	4-22
Total**	**23885.3**	**8208**	**54709**	**2844**	**19.23**	**196**	**50**	**10-54**

* 8-ball overs

** Includes both 8-ball and 6-ball overs

Among other feats, Lock managed to have precisely the same number of runs scored off his bowling in the 1951 and 1952 seasons. Only seven players have taken more wickets in the history of first-class cricket. Just for purposes of comparison, Lock's figures are shown here for each phase of his three distinct bowling styles:

Phase by phase:

	Runs	Wkts	Avge	5WI	10WM	BB
1946–1951	5991	261	22.95	10	-	6-32
1952–1958/59	19681	1331	14.78	100	35	10-54
1959–1970/71	29037	1252	23.19	86	15	9-77

Eight or more wickets in an innings:

10-54	Surrey v Kent	Blackheath	1956
9-77	Surrey v Oxford University	Guildford	1960
8-17	MCC v East Pakistan	Chittagong	1955/56
8-26	Surrey v Hampshire	Bournemouth	1953
8-36	Surrey v Glamorgan	The Oval	1954
8-81	Surrey v Nottinghamshire	Trent Bridge	1956
8-82	Surrey v Lancashire	Old Trafford	1955
8-85	Leicestershire v Warwickshire	Leicester	1966
8-99	Surrey v Kent	Blackheath	1958

Fifty wickets in a month:

	Runs	*Wkts*	*Avge*	*5WI*	*10WM*	*BB*
May 1955	587	67	8.76	6	3	6-25
August 1955	790	73	10.82	8	3	8-82
July 1958	620	56	11.07	6	3	8-99

No first-class bowler has exceeded Lock's monthly total of 73 wickets recorded in August 1955.

How Lock's victims were out:

Caught	1786	62.8%
Bowled	579	20.4%
Lbw	342	12%
Stumped	131	4.6%
Hit wicket	6	0.2%
Total	2,844	100%

Most fielders involved in Lock's dismissals:

202	G.A.R. Lock
162 (122 ct, 40 st)	A.J. McIntyre
130	M.J. Stewart
107	K.F. Barrington
97 (75 ct, 22 st)	R. Swetman
79	W.S. Surridge
66	P.B.H. May

Bibliography

Allen, D.R. (ed.), *Arlott on Cricket* (London: Collins, 1984)

Bannister, Alex, *Cricket Cauldron* (London: Stanley Paul, 1954)

Barrington, Ken, *Playing it Straight* (London: Stanley Paul, 1968)

Blofeld, Henry, *The Packer Affair* (London: Collins, 1978)

Cowdrey, Colin, *M.C.C.* (London: Hodder & Stoughton, 1976)

Evans, Godfrey, *The Gloves are Off* (London: Hodder & Stoughton, 1960)

Foot, David, *Beyond Bat and Ball* (London: Good Books, 1993)

Frindall, Bill, *The Wisden Book of Cricket Records* (London: Headline, 1993)

Hill, Alan, *Jim Laker: A Biography* (London: Deutsch, 1998)

Hill, Alan, *Tony Lock: Aggressive Master of Spin* (Stroud: The History Press, 2008)

Howat, Gerald, *Len Hutton* (London: Heinemann, 1988)

Laker, Jim, *A Spell from Laker* (London: Hamlyn, 1979)

Laker, Jim, *Over to Me* (London: Frederick Muller, 1960)

Laker, Jim, *Spinning Round the World* (London: Muller, 1957)

Lock, Tony, *For Surrey and England* (London: Hodder & Stoughton, 1957)

Mosey, Don, *Laker: Portrait of a Legend* (London: Queen Anne Press, 1989)

Pocock, Pat, *Percy* (London: Frost Publications, 1987)

Sandford, Christopher, *John Murray: Keeper of Style* (Worthing: Pitch Publishing, 2019)

Scovell, Brian, *Jim Laker: 19-90* (Stroud: Tempus, 2006)

Swanton, E.W., *Sort of a Cricket Person* (London: Collins, 1972)

Titmus, Fred, *Talk of the Double* (London: Stanley Paul, 1964)

Trueman, Fred, *Fast Fury* (London: Stanley Paul, 1961)

Index

101; 1952 107; 1953 291; 1956
151, 225; 1962 238; 1963 244;
Ashes won in 1953; Errol
Holmes regime 71; *Over to
Me* 227, 229, 247; Surrey Old
Players dinner 282
Knott, Alan: 280

Ladies' Night at the Turkish Baths
(theatrical show): 165
Lahore Gymkhana: 151
Laker, Jim (1922-86): childhood,
47-54; army experience, 55-
59; joins Surrey CCC, 68; Test
match debut, 76; tormented
by 1948 Australians, 81-83;
record figures in 1950 Test
Trial, 91-93; overlooked for
tour of Australia, 95-97;
marriage to Lilly Gottleib,
101; in 1953 Ashes-winning
side, 120-124; Old Trafford
1956, 169-184; altercation
with Peter May, 200-205;
with MCC in Australia, 208-
216; retires, 222; *Over to Me,*
224-229; on astrology, 252-
253; BBC commentator, 266;
death, 287
Laker, Angela: 101, 282
Laker, Doreen: 67
Laker, Fiona: 101
Laker, Lilly (Mrs. Jim Laker, née
Gottleib): 20, 44, 106, 177-178,
182, 205, 278, 288
Laker, Margaret: 93
Lara, Brian: 182
Larwood, Harold: 102
Leach, Jack: 18, 25
Leicestershire County Cricket
Club: 17, 31, 132, 138, 141,

144, 249, 250-252, 254, 255,
258-259, 272
Lester, Ted: 146
Lewis, David: 223-224
Lewis, Tony: 286
Leyland, Maurice: 52
Lillee, Dennis: 268-269, 278
Lindwall, Ray: 79, 121, 160, 162,
163, 173
Loader, Peter: 18, 28, 107, 116,
150, 194, 203, 218, 231
Lock, Audrey (Mrs. Tony Lock,
née Sage): 289, 295
Lock, Bert: 34, 87-88, 110, 221
Lock, Bryan: 61
Lock, Tony (1929-95):
childhood, 60-65; joins Surrey
CCC, 66; awarded county
cap, 94; new bowling action,
98-102; marries Audrey Sage,
108; Test match debut, 109;
called for throwing, 110-
113; with MCC in West
Indies, 126-136; Idrees Beg
affair, 153-155; destroys New
Zealand in 1958 series, 198;
remodels bowling action, 216-
218; joins Western Australia,
242; joins Leicestershire, 249;
England comeback, 262-265;
Laker tribute 288; sex-abuse
allegations, 294-296; death 296
Lock, Richard: 257
London Evening Standard: 167
Long, Arnold: 200
Lucozade (advertising): 16

Maddocks, Len: 173, 180
Mankad, Vinoo: 109
Marlar, Robin: 280
Marsh, Rod: 279

Price, Fred: 111, 118, 142
Price, W.F.: 112
Priestley, J.B.: 36

Quick, Arnold: 239

Randall, Derek: 278-279
Rattigan, Terence: 115
Richards, Viv: 273-274
Richardson, Peter: 176, 179
Rix, Brian: 247
Roberts, Ron: 234
Robinson, Fred: 52-53
Rosenwater, Irving: 176
Ross, Alan: 228
Ross, Gordon: 147
Rothman's tobacco: 42
Row, Raman Subba: 125-126
Royal Army Ordnance Corps (RAOC): 54
Ryneveld, Clive: 190

Sage, Audrey (Mrs. Tony Lock): 67, 108
Salt School for Boys: 51
Saltaire club: 92
Sandham, Andrew: 66, 68
Shackleton, Derek: 28, 207
Sheahan, Paul: 261
Shepherd, Barry: 242-243
Sheppard, Rev. David: 108, 139, 176, 185, 177, 218
Shirreff, Alan: 85
Shropshire: 75
Smales, Ken: 19
Smith, Don: 104
Smith, Mike: 253
Snow, John: 280
Sobers, Garry: 28, 135, 245
Sparling, John: 200
SS *Iberia*: 208, 214

St. Barnabas Church: 51
Stackpole, Keith: 261
Statham, Brian: 136, 176, 226, 291
Stewart, Micky: 88, 102, 137, 144, 197, 204, 231-232, 250-251
Stollmeyer, Jeffrey: 76
Sunday Mail: 216
Sunday Times: 273, 295
Surrey County Cricket Club: 1946 31; 1950s 33; 1956 17-18, 42; 1957 tour 195-196; 'all-rounders' 141; Alf Gover 67; Andrew Sandham 66, 68; Arthur McIntyre 54, 139; Australia visit 211, 214; Bert Lock 34-35, 61; Cambridge 143; charity matches 252; Commander Bob Babb 202; County Championship 113, 116, 150, 184, 199; Dennis Cox 16; Eric Bedser 92; Errol Holmes 20, 71; Jack Hobbs 65; Jack Parker 101; Julia White 147; Ken Barrington 26; Laker 14, 74-75, 183, 223, 238, 247, 256; Lock 9, 41, 72, 219, 241, 245, 248; Lord Tedder 15; Major Nigel Harvie Bennett 69; Michael Barton 87; Micky Stewart 88, 102, 137, 232; Monty Garland-Wells 70; Old Players' dinner 282; *Over to Me* 225; Peter May 29; Trent Bridge 117; v Australia 1956 13, 15, 38, 40; v Cambridge University 218; v Derbyshire at Chesterfield 105; v India 1952 107, 109, 111; v Kent at Blackheath 204;

About the Author

Christopher Sandford is a regular contributor to newspapers and magazines on both sides of the Atlantic. He has written numerous biographies of music, film and sports stars, as well as *Union Jack*, a best-selling account of President John F. Kennedy's special relationship with Great Britain, described by *National Review* as 'political history of a high order – the Kennedy book to beat'. Christopher's reminiscence of his childhood hero, the Middlesex and England stumper John Murray, *Keeper of Style*, was published by Pitch Publishing in 2019. His book *The Final Innings*, praised by the *Daily Mail* as 'a comprehensive account of the 1939 domestic and international season, played against the backdrop of the impending war', was named the Cricket Society and MCC Book of the Year 2020.

Christopher was born and raised in England, and currently lives in Seattle.

(Author photo © *Nicholas Sandford*)

Also available at all good book stores

9781785317330

9781785317224

9781785318412

9781785316395

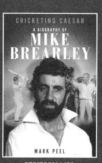

9781785316623

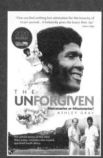

9781785315329

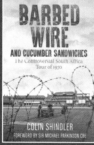

9781785316340

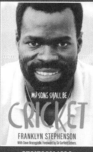

9781785316920

9781785316302